a guide to prayer

Opening To God

a guide to prayer

Opening To God

Thomas H. Green, S.J.

Ave Maria Press
Notre Dame, Indiana 46556

First printing, September, 1977
Eighth printing, July, 1987
145,000 copies in print

Imprimi potest:
    Joaquin G. Bernas, S.J.
    Provincial of the Province of the Philippines
    February 2, 1977

Nihil Obstat:
    Rt. Rev. Msgr. Benjamin L. Marino, P.A.
    Vicar General - Chancellor

Imprimatur:
    ✠Jaime Cardinal L. Sin, D.D.
    Archbishop of Manila
    January 24, 1977

Library of Congress Catalog Card Number: 77-83197
International Standard Book Number: 0-87793-135-6 (Cloth)
                                     0-87793-136-4 (Paperback)
Cover photo: Candida Photos, Inc.
Design and typography: Cae Esworthy

Printed and bound in the United States of America.

Contents

Preface 10

Introduction: One Bread at Many Tables 12

PART ONE

The What and Why of Prayer

Chapter 1   What Prayer Is 26

Chapter 2   The "Irrelevance" of Prayer 36

Chapter 3   The Relevance of Prayer: Discernment   44

PART TWO

The How of Prayer

Chapter 4   Are There Techniques of Prayer? 56

Chapter 5   The Active Purification of the Soul 68

Chapter 6   The Ways of Prayer of Beginners 84

Epilogue: Prayer Beyond the Beginnings 102

Preface

This book has been "germinating" for several years. The encouragement to write it came from many friends in the Philippines and elsewhere—sisters, priests, seminarians and laity—who urged me to put in writing what I have been sharing with them on prayer in retreats, in lectures, in my course on "Apostolic Prayer," and in private direction. The opportunity to meet their request came when I was granted a sabbatical leave by the Provincial of the Jesuits in the Philippines, Rev. Benigno A. Mayo, S.J., and the authorities of the Loyola School of Theology of the Ateneo de Manila University.

During the months spent in the actual composition of the book, I have been greatly helped by discussions about its content with my mother and other friends. Two people have given it an especially close reading, and have made a number of suggestions to improve it, both in content and in clarity of expression: Sister Mary Ellen Doyle, of the Sisters of Charity of Nazareth, Kentucky, and my own sister, Marie Green James. To complete the family involvement in the project, my niece, Miss Peggy Green, carried through the thankless task of deciphering my handwriting and typing the manuscript. Sister Sheila, Sister Francis Mary, and the St. Joseph Sisters of Sacred Heart Cathedral Convent have generously handled the initial reproduction of the text, and Sister John Miriam Jones, S.C., Assistant Provost of the University of Notre Dame, has helped in exploring the possibilities of publication. Mr. Eugene Geissler, Book Editor of Ave Maria Press, has been a wise and understanding guide for my first venture into the mysterious world of book publishing.

One man on whom I counted to test the Spirit in these pages was Father Jim McCann, S.J., the latest of the three great directors whom the Lord has given me. Unfortunately for me, he died in Manila just a week before my return to the Philippines, so I never had the chance to share this adventure in grace with him. Until eternity, I shall have to be satisfied with the knowledge that the mark of his influence is in every chapter which follows.

It has been my hope that the Lord would use this book to say whatever *he* wanted to say. Thus, if there is any good in the book it is due, first of all, to the God and Father of our Lord Jesus, for he is, after all, the "Lord of the dance"; and then to all those, on various continents and islands, who have been praying for the project and who have shared the experience of their inner life with me. I owe a special debt to the men of San Jose Seminary. They have made life as a child of the third culture a real adventure in grace for me. It is really their book—their experience is the proof of whatever is true in these pages—and to them, and to Jim McCann who brought me to them and taught me to love them, I gratefully dedicate it.

Manila, Philippines
July 31, 1977
Feast of St. Ignatius Loyola

Introduction:
One Bread at Many Tables

In recent times, sociologists have sought to explain some of the phenomena of our shrinking world in terms of a "third culture." The concept is different from, although not entirely unrelated to, the much more common idea of the Third World. When two cultures meet, from whatever world they come, we are told that a third culture is formed at the point of intersection. For example, the British colonial administrator, who spent many years in India, was changed by his experience. While not really becoming Indian, he was also no longer wholly British. And the Indian civil servant with whom he worked was similarly changed, for better or worse, by his experience at the meeting of two worlds. The Englishman who returned home after many years in India would not find himself really at home in his native land. Nor would he be totally at home in a completely Indian milieu. He is a child of a new world, formed from the interaction of two living cultures, as is the black student of talent who is transplanted from the streets of Harlem to the gracious campus of an Ivy League university.

He may never feel really at home in the white world of the Ivy League, but he also discovers that, psychologically, he cannot go home to Harlem again. He, too, is a child of the intersection of two worlds.

I am not competent to pass judgment on the sociological merits of the third-culture concept. I mention it, however, because it has been of great help to me, personally, in understanding my own situation, and in seeing the meaning and place of prayer in the Christian life. I am a child of a third-culture myself, born and raised in the United States and called to live out my life as a missionary in the Philippines. Who am I really? To cling to my "Americanism" in an alien culture would be a certain formula for frustration and ineffectiveness. To seek to become wholly Filipino would mean reverting to the womb and living over again my whole history—an impossible task. The attempt would guarantee a nervous breakdown. Who am I then? Am I rootless, or am I rooted in two soils at once?

In this day and age, when the missionary can no longer even try to transplant a "little piece of America" to alien soil, these questions can provoke a real identity crisis. But it is also possible, thank God, that they be productive, although not without pain, of a real personal deepening and enrichment. The child of the third culture has a unique perspective. He can, if he has the eyes, begin to discern the constant and fundamental human values which underlie all concrete cultural embodiments of these values. He can discover his real roots as a human being. And he can wonder at, and be enriched by, the very diversity of expression of these roots.

This brings us to the topic of this book, for I have discovered that one of these constant and fundamental human values—and indeed the most important—is prayer. I have had occasion to move back and forth between my two worlds. It never ceases to amaze me that I hear the same questions about prayer in a convent in the isolated

13

province of Antique by the Sulu Sea and in a convent at the Cathedral in Rochester, New York. The seminarians of San Jose in Manila and the seminarians of St. Bernard's in Rochester are confronted by the same problem of integrating prayer and service in the following of Christ. God reveals himself in essentially the same way to a lady dentist in Quezon City and a philosophy teacher in Columbus, Ohio, to a parish priest in Hornell and in Cavite.

This book, in fact, is born of that cross-cultural experience. Working as a director of souls in Antique and Rochester, in Columbus, Ohio, and Quezon City (and in Sydney and Singapore and Kuala Lumpur), I have found that the principal concern people share with me is their life of prayer. This has been a great challenge to me, for it has forced me to reflect constantly on the way God works in my life and in the lives of those I direct. It has driven me back, again and again, to the Church's masters of prayer, and to my own experience as a pray-er these past 25 years. And it has made me realize that there are certain common patterns of the interior life which transcend time and space —which are as valid in 1977 as in 1577, and in the Philippines as in the United States. This might have seemed self-evident 15 years ago, but it is by no means as obvious today in the light of the tremendous ferment in the Church after Vatican II. Tranquil assumptions, in prayer as in every other area of Christian life, have had to be subjected to searching reexamination.

Not Everyone Alike

The interior life, or the life of prayer, is a very mysterious reality. In one sense it just happens—to some people, apparently, and not to others—and there seems to be very little we can say to explain the mystery. Whether by temperament or family background or whatever, some people are "religious" and many more are not. When I was a boy, I had a great-aunt who had been educated by the sisters in Canada. She was a sincere believer according to her own lights, but she would never consider herself religious. In fact, she used to recall that, in school, the sisters urged the girls to say three Hail Marys every day to pray for a religious vocation. And she never said the Hail Marys, because she was afraid she might get the vocation! If she were alive today, and were to read my book, she would be proud of me for having written it—but she would be convinced it was not for her. God, I am sure, played a very real part in her life; but there were limits to her involvement with him. Piety was for sisters, and for a few lay people. It was not for her.

What would have surprised my aunt is that not a few sisters probably felt as she did. They were committed to a life-style that was externally more pious. Yet, deep down, they had come to the conclusion that a real personal encounter with the Lord was not for them. More than once a good sister, long in the religious life, has told me that she was not called to be a pray-er. She never got anywhere in prayer, and she could only envy those around her who seemed to be on a first-name basis with the Lord. Reluctantly she (or rather they, since I have heard the story many times) had come to the conclusion that prayer was not for her. Whatever real prayer might be—whatever people around them who appeared caught up in the Lord might be experiencing—it was not part of their lives. They had no hope it ever would be, at least this side of the grave. If the Church be divided into queen bees who pray and worker bees who labor, their lot seemed clearly to be with the workers.

Desire to Pray Crucial

These sisters are in a somewhat different situation from my great-aunt: in a sense, she decided she didn't *want* to be religious; they would like to be, but it seems impossible to them. There are many lay people who would feel the same way. They would like to know the Lord better, but the demands of their daily life and constant pressures of life in the world seem to make real growth in prayer impossible for them. Such people, whether religious or laity, are definitely among those for whom I write this book. The *desire* to pray is itself a clear sign of the Lord's presence. We cannot reach out to him unless he first draws us. Since he is Lord, since he cares more for us than we do for ourselves, he would never plant this desire in us merely to frustrate us. He would never lead us to seek something which was impossible.

How would this book be of help to such people— i.e., to people who would like to pray but who feel it is impossible for them, either because of their temperament or because of the circumstances of their lives? At first glance, the description of the way God works in prayer may seem too demanding for them. But certain points in the chapters that follow should be carefully noted.

In the first place, as Chapter 3 stresses, good prayer should not be divorced from daily life. To pray is *not* to withdraw from our daily concerns into some ethereal world. The religious person, in the true sense, is not someone who is out of touch with reality. Rather, good prayer means bringing our real concerns and responsibilities before the Lord and learning to hear what *he* has to say about them. What is not good—and this is the major point of Chapter 2 —is to look upon prayer as a way to manipulate God, to *use* him to accomplish our own desires.

God Speaks in Many Ways

This brings us to another important point. If only we have the ears to hear, God is speaking to us in all the events of our lives and not merely in times of formal prayer. Busy people will often say that their work is their prayer—a tricky slogan but one that contains an important grain of truth. It is true that everything that happens, everything that we do, is a revelation of God to us. But *not every revelation by God is a genuine encounter for us.*

How often have we had the experience of speaking to someone else and not being heard? We are speaking, revealing ourselves, but the other person is either not listening or is misunderstanding us. In Chapter 1, I stress that the art of listening is at the heart of genuine prayer. As we learn to listen with attention and sensitivity, all the events of our lives become encounters with the Lord, become prayer. That is why St. Ignatius Loyola, along with other great apostolic pray-ers, sees times of formal, systematic prayer as much more important to beginners than to those who have already learned to be sensitive to the way God speaks. Ignatius speaks of the mature apostle as a contemplative in action, someone who can "seek God in all things." It is in this sense that everything—work and play and rest—becomes truly prayer for the *mature* pray-er.

To reach this level of sensitivity, however, takes time and effort. This is where "my work is my prayer" can be a misleading slogan and a smoke screen to conceal the lack of any real depth in our lives. Chapter 3 makes clear that discernment is an art, and like any art it is only learned by experience. An "introduction to prayer" is really a guide to the experience which can teach us this art. The techniques of coming to quiet (in Chapter 4), of positively disposing our spirits to hear the Spirit (in Chapter 5), and of taking those initial steps in "mental prayer" which I call meditation and contemplation in Chapter 6, are not intended as mechanical steps to guarantee successful prayer. They are not an abstract theory of prayer. Rather they are the distillation of the experiences of praying Christians over the centuries as reflected through the prism of my own experience as a pray-er and a spiritual director. They are good only insofar as they help interested readers to a greater sensitivity to the Lord speaking in the daily events, ordinary and not-so-ordinary, of their lives.

Book to Be Lived

It should be noted, however, that this places a special burden on the reader. Many books can be read for the vicarious experience or the information they provide us—and then can be set aside. They can divert us, distract us, provide a break from our responsibilities, without making any further demands on us. But an introduction to prayer is not like that. To read it properly takes years, because it must be lived, experienced. Each time it is reread it will say something new to us—because we read it from a new experiential base. This is what I myself have discovered with the basic guides of my own interior life, like Teresa of Avila's *Way of Perfection* and Leonard Boase's *The Prayer of Faith*.

I can't help wondering, as I write them, what my great-aunt would think of these lines. Hopefully she would be enlightened to see that pious or prayerful do not have to have the otherworldly connotations she gave to them. But would she really want to read this book? Would she want to get that involved in it—to take it as a guide to her own exploration of a world that might make too many demands on her? I don't know. If I could talk to her about it now, though, I would not soft-pedal the commitment such a book requires. I would, however, try to tell her that prayerful people are *real* people—down-to-earth and truly involved and very human. They pay a price, not in order to be divorced from reality but in order to live life fully. I would count on her sharp Irish wit to puncture my balloon if my piety was pompous or condescending or unreal!

Those Who Pray Spontaneously

Among my readers there will also be some who already find prayer an important part of their lives. They would not be "turned off" by prayer—either out of disinterest or out of frustration. But they might feel that prayer is a very simple

18

thing for them, that it is something spontaneous and natural and not in need of any elaborate explanations or justification. Tevye, in *Fiddler on the Roof,* would appear, at first sight, to be such a man. He speaks spontaneously and unaffectedly to a God who is as real to him as his own wife, and with whom he is more at home than he is with his liberated daughters.

Tevye, while an unusual figure, is not unique. One of the stories which made a great impression on me in my youth was about Jimmy, the laborer. Jimmy was a simple man, of little formal education. Each day, when returning from work, he stopped in the church and sat in the back for several minutes. The parish priest noticed the regularity of Jimmy's visits, and his fervor. He wondered just what a simple man like Jimmy did during these visits. One day he asked him what happened. Jimmy replied: "Nothing much, Father. I just say 'Jesus, it's Jimmy.' And he says 'Jimmy, it's Jesus.' And we're happy to be together."

What could be simpler or more spontaneous than Jimmy's encounter with the Lord? What could a book on prayer do for Jimmy except complicate a very real and deep, spontaneous relationship? The answer, of course, is that Jimmy's relationship to God *is* very deep and nothing should be done to complicate it or confuse it. No director, and no manual, can tell us how we *must* grow. Prayer is experienced and is utterly personal. There is no single method of prayer and no *one* way to encounter God. If Jimmy has found the Lord in his simplicity, then his way of arriving there is the right way for him.

This is a point which needs to be stressed. Four centuries ago, St. John of the Cross, one of the great spiritual directors of all time, wrote that the three great enemies of interior growth are the devil, oneself—*and the spiritual director!*[1] While he discusses the danger from the devil and

---

[1]*The Living Flame of Love,* Stanza III, par. 29-63.

from oneself in about two paragraphs each, he spends some 30 paragraphs on the danger from the spiritual director. Why? His point is, very simply, that most directors over-direct. They try to mold their directees according to their own experience or their own theories of prayer. For John, and for every good spiritual director, the director's role is not to mold souls according to some preconceived pattern, but to help them to interpret *their own* experience. The good director helps people to be free to follow the Lord in whatever way *he* chooses to lead them. We will discuss this point further in Chapter 3, when we speak of discernment—but note, for the moment, that "director" is not really a very happy title for the spiritual director. He would more aptly be called a "codiscerner."

To return to Jimmy and our question about the value of this book for him: it is clear from what we have said that nothing should be done to complicate Jimmy's relationship with the Lord. Yet, I think our Jimmy story may be misleading in its simplicity. Spiritual life, like all life, is growth and change. Jimmy has a history. He arrived at where he is now via a long process of joy and suffering, of doubt, perhaps, and testing. We don't know his history, but the story derives its depth of meaning from our own experience, our own history. Jimmy is a striking figure precisely because we know how rare and difficult such simple faith is for anyone who has really lived life with his eyes open. Jimmy may not need this book at the present point in his life with God. But Jimmy's story is told—and was told when I first heard it—not to canonize him but to move the hearer to desire to arrive where Jimmy is.

How does one, beginning where most of us begin a life of prayer—preoccupied, self-centered, and yet desirous of something better—come to such a real and simple experiential faith? To this question the book does try to provide an answer. Our hypothetical Jimmy might not need such an answer. But the apostles did, as is clear from their request, when Jesus was at prayer, that he teach them to pray (Lk 11:1). He had already given them numerous instructions on prayer and had taught them by his own example, but they still felt they did not really know how to pray. They needed help, and so do we.

Always "On the Way"

There is another sense in which our story about Jimmy needs amplification. We said that spiritual life, like all life, involves growth and change. Jimmy has a history. He has come from somewhere—and *he is going somewhere*. Whatever his present experience of God may be, he still must grow. In this life we are always "on the way." St. Paul says: "Now we are seeing a dim reflection in a mirror; but then (in eternity) we shall be seeing face to face. The knowledge that I have now is imperfect; but then I shall know as fully as I am known" (I Cor 13:12). No matter how deep our experience of God is, we are always just beginning to know the Lord. As Job, called the most godly man on the face of the earth (Job 1:8), says at the end of his testing, "I had heard of you by the hearing of the ear, but only now does my eye see you" (Job 42:5). Even though he was the godliest of the sons of men, he was really only beginning to know the Lord.

Tevye, who in a sense is a modern Job, illustrates my point well. *Fiddler on the Roof* begins with Tevye on easy and intimate terms with the Lord. But the play itself is an allegory of the purification of Tevye which John of the Cross calls the dark night of the senses. His world collapses. His final flight from the ancestral home in Anatenka is a symbol of the erosion of the traditional values which had made his life meaningful and his faith secure. To continue to encounter God as his world collapses will require much more of Tevye than a simplistic "whistling in the dark" kind of faith. Even the proficient pray-er of simple depth must grow, and at times that growth will entail a "shaking of the foundations." At times like that, I would hope this book would offer sounder guidance than Job received from his "friends."

Time of Transition

I was ordained a priest on the same day that Paul VI was elected pope. This has been a significant coincidence for me because it symbolized to me that I am truly a child of transition. My own religious formation, thoroughly traditional in the early years of the seminary, was profoundly influenced by the new winds which the great Pope John XXIII, as the instrument of the Spirit, sent blowing through the Church. The early years of my priesthood reflected, in a small way, the heroic struggle of Pope Paul VI to be open to all that is genuine in *aggiornamento* while, at the same time, remaining firmly rooted in faith. The changes consequent upon Vatican II—the renewed stress on community, both in liturgy and in the living of the Christian life, the stress on finding Christ in others and on the social dimension of the Gospel—did not produce a personal crisis in me. In fact, they appealed to me as liberating and enriching, as a much-needed expression of the personal commitment to the Lord which had come to define my vocation for me.

These changes have, however, had a significant impact on my work as a director of souls. Many pray-ers of my generation, as well as older generations, either questioned the relevance of their own formation and their own view of prayer and spiritual direction, or they clung to the old and rejected the new—or they were confused and troubled by the conflict between old and new. For a younger generation the problem was somewhat different. Very often they had not learned to pray as we had. Their approach was much more free-form, unstructured. They saw prayer as too personal to be governed by the methods on which an older generation relied. They came to maturity with a strong sense of social concern, and were impatient with and intolerant of any "me and Jesus" spirituality. They saw the latter as too egocentric, too self-indulgent to be tolerated as the world burned around them.

In my work as a director, I have had to deal with both young and old (and those in between) on both sides of the world. My directees have been a representative mix of ages and temperaments. They have been laity and religious and parish priests. But they are *not* a cross section of the general population. They had one concern in common: they cared enough about learning to pray, or continuing to grow in prayer, to seek direction and to share with me their inner lives. It is important to note this, because it is for them that this book is written. Whether priests or laity or religious, they want to learn to pray.

One final word is in order, concerning the use of books on prayer. Such a book is much more like a cookbook than like a novel or a treatise on economics. We read it not in order to be informed or vicariously moved, but in order to be guided in our action. No normal person, I presume, simply reads a cookbook from cover to cover for the enjoyment of reading it. While this book has, I hope, more unity and continuity than the average cookbook, it too is meant to be lived, acted upon, and not just read. Some parts of this book, or any book on prayer, may not speak to the reader's needs here and now. They can be skipped over lightly. Other parts will touch upon and illuminate points which do speak to one's present experience. They should be read and reread, and tested in the living of what they say.

Thus, the purpose of this book is to *describe* the life of prayer, at least in its initial stages, for those who truly want to learn to pray. It thus attempts to be not an attempt to convince the doubter of the value of prayer (necessary and valuable as such a book might be today), nor a suggested technique or techniques for praying (as I shall say later, I don't believe there are any such), but what might be called today a *phenomenology* of prayer—i.e., a *description* of the way the Lord actually seems to work, and the type of response he seems to desire, in the lives of men and women to whom he chooses to reveal himself. It would thus be a "justification" or "defense" of prayer only in the sense that what is described might move someone, under grace, to seek to experience for himself the same encounter in his own life. It is true that in the first part of the book I do discuss the question of the relevance and irrelevance of prayer. But this is done not in a way designed to convince the skeptic, but rather to help the convinced beginner to understand better the need he or she already feels to learn to pray. It is "faith in search of understanding," *fides quaerens intellectum.*

I believe, in fact, that experience is the only proof for such realities as prayer and love. The wife cannot really prove to someone else that her husband loves her. Every bit of evidence she presents can be explained in some other way ("He treats you tenderly because it is cheaper than having to hire a housekeeper!"). But she *knows, by experience,* that he loves her. Similarly, St. John says that he and Andrew first followed the Lord by the lakeshore at the bidding of John the Baptist.

> And Jesus turned, and saw them following, and said to them, "What do you seek?" And they said to him, "Rabbi" (which means Teacher), "where are you staying?" He said to them, "Come and see." They came and saw where he was staying; and they stayed with him that day, for it was about four o'clock in the afternoon. (Jn 1:38-39)

John rarely mentions the time of day in his Gospel, but this was the moment when he fell in love. If you asked John to prove that Jesus is Lord, I believe John would say: "The only proof is this. If you go to the shore of a certain lake at four in the afternoon, you may see what I saw. If you do, you will know that Jesus is Lord." The only proof is experience.

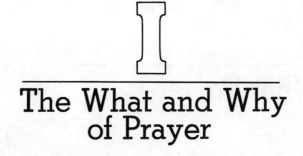

I

The What and Why
of Prayer

1

What Prayer Is

For the past several years, I have been a spiritual director in a major seminary. The spiritual director's job is a unique one for which there seems to be no real training except experience. He is a curious mix: an *alter ego*, or other self, sharing with young people what is most precious and most private to them—their own inner selves; he is something of a guru, from whom they hope to learn their secret mantra; he is a strong shoulder in their troubled times and a sounding board for their hopes and plans. In all this, it seems to me, the spiritual director is above all a listener. The hardest thing he has to learn is truly to listen, not passively but creatively and responsively.

The importance, and difficulty, of listening were brought home forcefully to me on one occasion. A fine seminarian was beginning a directed retreat. He was somewhat quiet, and I, in my usual style, wanted to put him at ease and draw him out. When we met in the evening to discuss how the first day had gone, I began to ask him about his experience. He cut me short by saying: "Before we start, I'd like to ask one favor." "What is that?" I asked. He said: "Whenever you start talking, I get nervous and forget what I wanted to say. So please don't say anything until I have finished sharing what I want to share." For the next several days I successfully (heroically!) held my tongue—and since then I have found that, for me, talker that I am, learning to listen well has demanded much personal discipline.

As I reflect on those years of learning to listen, I realize that the very effort to do so has taught me more about prayer than any other aspect of my priestly ministry —both because the art of listening seems to me to be at the very heart of prayer, and because prayer itself has been the central topic which the seminarians have wanted to talk about. There are many problems which arise: family, studies, vocation, celibacy, community. But the continually recurring theme in our conversations is prayer. The basic question is: Just what is prayer? We can't really talk about how to do it unless we have some definite idea of what it is.

Those of us who are old enough to have been raised on the Baltimore Catechism (and its counterparts) learned early in life to define prayer as a lifting of the mind and heart to God. This was an easy definition to memorize— clear and brief. It was a good definition in that it taught us that (1) God is far beyond our ordinary experience; (2) prayer entails effort on our part; and (3) prayer involves both the mind and the heart—the understanding and the feelings and will—of man. If we explore these three elements of the catechism definition a little further, perhaps we can come to a clearer picture of just what prayer should be.

The last point—the place of the heart in prayer— is an important one, and one that has not always been so clear. For many of the desert fathers and theologians of the early Church, perhaps largely under the influence of Greek philosophy, prayer was primarily a matter of the understanding, of knowledge. As such it was very much like

27

theology, which sought to place reason at the service of faith—to use reason to understand and clarify the divine revelation. The theologian and the pray-er differed not so much in what they did—both were knowers—as in the means they used to achieve knowledge. The theologian employed his *natural* faculties of reason and reflection, while the pray-er, in this early tradition, employed esoteric or secret techniques which were supposed to lead to a privileged, supernatural, "mystical" way of knowing God and understanding ultimate reality.

This view of prayer and spirituality was condemned by the Church as heretical very early in her history. Its major defect, however, was not its stress on the understanding to the relative neglect of the heart.[1] The really fatal flaw in these early theories of prayer pertained more to the second of the three points we noted above, namely that prayer entails effort on our part. It was condemned because of its *excessive* reliance on man's own efforts. In the partisan terminology of the times, it was found to be "Pelagian" or "semi-Pelagian," i.e., to follow the theologian Pelagius in overestimating man's ability to encounter God by his own efforts and to neglect the absolute primacy of God's grace. There is an infinite chasm between God and man; man, no matter how hard he tries, cannot come to God—cannot

---

[1]Almost a thousand years later St. Thomas Aquinas, one of the greatest pray-ers and greatest theologians in the history of the Church, would still be very much in the intellectualist tradition (i.e., emphasizing man's understanding in prayer). And 300 years later still Martin Luther would react against a predominantly intellectualist Catholic view of faith. It is true that a one-sided, exclusive stress on the understanding would be rare after the fifth century. But, despite the Franciscan emphasis on the will and on love, the primacy of man's intellect or understanding had a long history; and it is probably no exaggeration to say that the Catholic tradition of prayer is much indebted to Luther and the great Protestant thinkers who followed him—as much as to any human agency—for the emphasis on the heart in recent centuries. Luther, in turn, felt greatly indebted to the spiritual theology of St. Bernard of Clairvaux.

leap across infinity.[2] He cannot even, as the semi-Pelagians maintained, take the first step in coming to God. God must come to man. He alone can leap the infinite gulf between creator and creature; this is what he did in the Incarnation of Jesus and what he does in the life of every pray-er who truly encounters him.

Although it is easy enough to label this idea semi-Pelagian, and thus to relegate it to the dustbin of history, I am afraid the real situation is not as simple as that. As I look at my own years of learning to pray, it seems clear that there was a good bit of the semi-Pelagian in me, too. The structures within which I was formed as a religious tended to reinforce this stress on a "pulling-myself-up-by-my-bootstraps" kind of spirituality. The format of our novitiate times of prayer (about which I will have some positive things to say later) was rigidly prescribed. Point books provided structured meditations; some 60 of us novices meditated in one room; the one acceptable posture was kneeling. If someone was not kneeling during prayer, he could expect a summons from the director of novices and an inquiry whether he was ill. I quaked through a few of these encounters myself; at the time, while I dreaded them, I came to see them as developing manliness and self-discipline. Later I came to resent the regimentation they implied. Later still, when I myself began to direct souls, I realized that these practices were all part of a widespread spirit of an age:[3] asceticism, self-denial, killing one's own

---

[2]This was the first of the three elements we noted in the catechism definition of prayer.

[3]The pendulum has swung very far to the other side in just 20 years, and the catchwords have now become "self-expression," "personal fulfillment," "doing my own thing." Since this extreme is even more harmful to a solid spirituality, we shall have to discuss, in Chapter 5, the positive value of asceticism in any genuine interior life. What we seek, throughout the book, is a balance between God's work and man's—a dialogue between grace and personal initiative.

will and desires were, in a sense, at the very core of spirituality. It was as if Jesus' mysterious saying "Since John the Baptist came, up to this present time, the kingdom of heaven has been subjected to violence and the violent are taking it by storm" (Mt 11:12) had been appropriated, alone and out of context, as the basis for a whole spirituality.

The fruit of the semi-Pelagian controversy has been to make us realize that our own effort is utterly secondary to the work of God in our encounter with him. Yet I have felt for some time that this is still a defect in the catechism definition of prayer with which we began this chapter. The idea of *raising* our minds and hearts to God still seems to imply that prayer is largely a matter of our own efforts—that God is simply there, while we, in prayer, find ways and means to pull ourselves up to him. Such a view would obviously be semi-Pelagian, and hence unacceptable to the Christian.

Since Christians have recently shown much interest in Yoga and Zen and their derivatives, it is worth noting in this context that such a view (i.e., that prayer is totally, or largely, a matter of our own efforts) does find considerable support in the great Oriental religions such as Hinduism and Buddhism. In those Oriental traditions which do not know a personal God, prayer depends totally on the effort of the pray-er—even if that effort is, paradoxically enough for the Westerner, wholly devoted to emptying the mind, to coming to quiet, to passivity. It is important to note, however, that even in the mainstream Oriental traditions— and particularly in the classical literature of Hinduism— there are affirmations of the personality of God and intimations of a doctrine of grace. In *The Bhagavad Gita,* "the Blessed One" says of his true disciples:

> To them, constantly disciplined,
>   Revering Me with love,

I give that discipline of mind,
     Whereby they go unto Me.[4]

There has been some dispute within Hinduism about the literal meaning of texts like these.[5] But for us Christians, there can be no doubt: God is a person (in fact, three Persons!), and prayer is a personal encounter with him. More than that, it is an encounter which depends almost entirely on his grace, since he is God.

This is not the place to attempt to explain to the puzzled Christian what exactly lies at the end of the road of prayer for the Hindu or Buddhist contemplative. My point is simply that Christian prayer is grounded in a very specific conception of God: a personal God who encounters his creatures in love. To return to the catechism definition, the idea of prayer as a raising of our minds and hearts to God seems to me to overstress our own effort and activity in prayer. For some time, I have been suggesting that a better approach would be to define prayer as an *opening* of the mind and heart to God. This seems better because the idea of opening stresses receptivity, responsiveness to another. To open to another is to act, but it is to act in such a way that the other remains the dominant partner.

Perhaps the clearest example of openness is the art of listening, which we discussed at the beginning of this chapter. Listening is indeed a real art, which some people never learn. We all have experienced people who cannot or do not listen. They hear but do not understand; their bodily ears pick up sound, but their hearts are not attentive to its meaning. You can talk *to* them, but you can scarcely talk *with* them. Yahweh uses this image of hearing and yet not hearing to express his frustration with Israel: "Hear this, O

---

[4]*The Bhagavad Gita,* translated by Franklin Edgerton, Chapter X, stanza 10 (p. 51). Harvard University paperback, 1972.

[5]See, for example, K. M. Sen, *Hinduism* (Pelican paperbacks, 1970), pp. 20, 74, 91.

31

foolish and senseless people, who have eyes, but see not, who have ears, but hear not" (Jer 5:21); and Jesus uses it to the same effect when speaking of his own "hearers" after the multiplication of the loaves: "Why do you discuss the fact that you have no bread? Do you not yet perceive or understand? Are your hearts hardened? Having eyes do you not see, and having ears do you not hear? And do you not remember?" (Mk 8:17-18).

Hearing or listening is a good metaphor for prayer. The good pray-er is above all a good listener. Prayer is dialogue; it is a personal encounter in love. When we communicate with someone we care about, we speak and we listen. But even our speaking is responsive: What we say depends upon what the other person has said to us. Otherwise we don't have real dialogue, but rather two monologues running along side by side.

I believe that our remarks have carried us a good way toward understanding what prayer is. In the past we have catalogued prayer under four headings: *a*doration, *c*ontrition, *t*hanksgiving and *s*upplication (or petition)—easy to remember because the initial letters spell "acts." This is helpful in that it makes clear that there is much more to prayer than merely asking for things (supplication). But we have seen that we need to go deeper than "acts" of our own to get to the real meaning of prayer. Prayer is essentially a dialogic encounter between God and man; and since God is Lord, he alone can initiate the encounter. This is the important implication of the first element of our catechism definition. Hence what man does or says in prayer will depend on what God does or says first. Here, above all, it is true that "You have not chosen me; I have chosen you" (Jn 15:16). God's choice, his call, is fundamental and all-important.

At the same time, prayer is a dialogue, an encounter between two persons. What man does or says is an integral part of prayer, since even God cannot speak *with* us unless we also speak. Even God cannot dialogue with a man who is interiorly deaf and mute. This was the second element of value in our catechism definition: Prayer does entail effort on the part of man, even though it is always God who reaches across infinity to us, and even though man's effort is itself impossible without the sustaining grace of God.

Moreover, as the third element of the catechism definition made clear, man's response involves both his head and his heart. The understanding plays an important role in prayer, since man cannot love what he does not know. His love is proportioned to his knowledge. At the same time, prayer is not mere reasoning or speculation about God. As Teresa of Avila says in the *Interior Castle,* "The important thing (in prayer) is not to think much but to love much."[6] The goal of prayer is the encounter with God in love. And love, as Teresa goes on to say "consists, not in the extent of our happiness, but in the firmness of our determination to try to please God in everything." Thus prayer involves the heart and will of man, even more fundamentally than his understanding.

It was St. Augustine, one of the greatest intellects the Church has produced, who said "Our hearts are restless until they rest in thee."[7] For the learned man fulfillment may lie in the mind's coming to rest, but for the pray-er, the lover, it is the heart that matters most.

In this connection, it is important to note that *spontaneity* is of the very essence of prayer, as it is of all dialogue. Augustine's "heart" is a spontaneous organ, responding to the sacrament of the present moment. Its responses cannot be programmed, because we cannot know in advance the word which God will speak to us at any given moment. When we were novices we were encouraged

---

[6]The Fourth Mansions, Chapter One (volume II, p. 233 in the translation by E. Allison Peers of *The Complete Works of St. Teresa of Jesus,* Sheed & Ward, 1946).

[7]*Confessions* of St. Augustine, Book I, Chapter 1, trans. Frank Sheed (Sheed & Ward, 1943) p. 3.

to plan our conversations for recreation—presumably so that the topics discussed would be fruitful and uplifting. The result, of course, was some very stilted conversations—and some very funny, though frustrating, encounters where each participant labored mightily to steer the talk to his own planned area. Since then I have heard the same thing at social events and cocktail parties, with the same ludicrous results. In the novitiate the intention was good, but the loss in spontaneity was disastrous. The same thing will be true in a programmed approach to prayer.

To the beginner, there is still a puzzle and a mystery in listening to God. (To the proficient pray-er it is no longer a puzzle, but it will always be a mystery.) Since we never encounter God in the same way we encounter another human being, how do we know when God talks? How do we interpret what he "says" when he does not speak as men speak? How can I respond meaningfully to someone whose coming is always veiled in the mystery of faith? In short, how do I know I am not just talking to myself when I pray? The central purpose of this book is to help to answer these questions—not in a way that will eliminate the mystery of faith, but in a way that will encourage the beginner to begin and to continue to discover God speaking in his or her own life.

We have based our explanation of what prayer is on the human experience of dialogue and listening. I think we will see, in the chapters that follow, that our ordinary human experience of love and dialogue—whether between husband and wife, between director and directee, or between friend and friend—can help us a great deal to discover and interpret our experience of prayer as a personal encounter in love between God and man.

2

The "Irrelevance" of Prayer

In the second part of the book, I will attempt to describe in fuller detail the way God normally works in the initial stages of the personal encounter with man which we call prayer. But first it might be helpful to consider certain questions which are often posed today, and which could be a block to the (prospective) beginner. One question, which we will discuss in this chapter, has to do with the "irrelevance" of prayer for the ordinary person: is not prayer, at least as we have described it, a luxury which the average layman, and even the average active priest or religious (active in the sense of being professionally committed to serving their fellowmen and preaching the gospel in the marketplace) can ill afford? Are we not talking about something exotic and unreal in a world where social justice, human rights, and even the basic demands of family and job, require of most people more energy than they have? These are real questions today. I have been asked them by seminarians in Manila, who felt that responding to the needs of the poor in the slums near the seminary was far more pressing, and far more Christian, than spending time wrapped up in their own private prayer life. The same questions have been put to me by parents of young families, who could not even find the time and quiet space to talk to one another, to say nothing of finding time and space for prayer.

This last difficulty suggests that we would do well to explore the analogy of human love in seeking an answer to our question about the relevance of prayer. A husband and wife who don't have time for each other may be heading for serious trouble, whatever their reasons for this lack of time. Similarly, a couple who sought to justify their intimacy solely in terms of its usefulness in raising the children could be heading for difficult times. Imagine the relationship between a husband and wife who truly love each other.[1] They live for each other day by day. There are good days and bad days, but both are part of a relationship which deepens with the years and gives meaning to both their lives. There are moments of intimacy when they are able to experience and to express all that they mean to each other.

Suppose that it is such a moment of deeper intimacy. They are filled with the joy of their love for each other. Suddenly a troubling thought comes to the wife, and she is moved to voice it out. "What," she asks her husband, "is the *relevance* of our love for each other?" What a queer question that would be at such a time! He would be puzzled, surprised, irritated perhaps. The mood of their loving encounter would be broken.

Why? Because love is *not* relevant—timely, opportune, pertinent, useful. Once lovers begin to ask these questions their love has become an object to be examined and not an experience to be lived. And love objectified is love distorted —the very thought of it makes uncomfortable those who have known love.

---

[1]Caryl Houselander and Rosemary Haughton, two of the best "spiritual writers" of our time, have both explored some of the implications of this analogy. See Houselander's *This War Is the Passion* and Haughton's *The Transformation of Man*.

It is the same way with the love of God. If we try to analyze it like a watch or a scientific problem, we destroy it or distort it. If we try to determine its relevance, to justify it by showing that it is useful, it slips through our fingers. Love is a splendidly useless passion—whether it be the love of man or the love of God. Love is the thing, *par excellence*, which, in the happy phrase of Wittgenstein, cannot be said but can only be shown. The experience itself is the only proof, the only justification. That, perhaps, is why proofs for God's existence always seem unsatisfactory: for the unbeliever, they don't prove (only experience can); and for the believer they fall far short of the reality of his experience.

Since we have described prayer as a love relationship with God, the pray-er faces the same problem as the wife. Prayer is not to be used but to be lived. Either the experience of God in prayer is its own justification or no justification is possible. For the beginner this can pose a special problem, at least if he comes to prayer not because he experiences God drawing him, but because he or she (for example, as a seminarian or as a novice in a congregation of sisters) is told that he or she should pray. It would seem difficult, from what we have said, to provide an argument why a beginner—who has not experienced prayer—should try to pray. Judging from my experience, this is true. Often beginners are drawn to pray because they have had some previous experience of the joy of knowing God. But it is increasingly common today that young men and women enter the seminary or the novitiate not because they desire to know God but because they desire to serve their fellowman. The Church, thank God, seems to many a good channel for their desire to serve—but the personal knowledge of Christ on which the Church's mission is grounded (see I Jn 1:1-4) is vague and unreal to them. They are quite at home with talk about "finding Christ in others" as long as no one raises the question just *who* Christ is for them. Concern about knowing God, encountering Christ, praying, seems an unnecessary, and even sinful, self-indulgence in a disjointed and fragmented world. Granted the point of our analogy to human love's irrelevance, what right do we have to waste time on the irrelevant in this day and age?

Is this true? Is prayer a luxury, exotic and unreal in today's pressurized and shrinking world? The question has a special urgency in the third world today, with its wide gulf between rich and poor and its relative lack of a middle class. The average Christian worker earns very little (in the range of $1.00 to $2.00 a day), has a large family (often six to eight children), and works six days a week. And the average apostle—priest, sister, brother or lay apostle—is overwhelmed by the demands of bringing a measure of social justice and development to such a desperate situation. What time or energy would such a worker, or such an apostle, have for a personal encounter with God?

The situation is by no means as desperate in the developed world. But the problem is there. Parkinson's law holds true, that the work (and problems) expand to fill the time available. Even the Rockefellers probably feel that they have trouble making ends meet, and most people in a developed society feel far less secure than the Rockefellers. Consumerism, which has been the wellspring of development, must continually create new needs in order to survive. The media create the needs (and they become all too real to those who feel them) and credit cards postpone the day of reckoning. Again, in such a climate, what time or energy would the average worker, or the average apostle (who breathes the air of consumerism every bit as much as his brethren), have for a personal encounter with God?

These questions can be answered in several ways. Perhaps the first thing that we must recall is that *God* is the initiator of the encounter which we call prayer. Jesus says, "You have not chosen me; I have chosen you" (Jn 15:16). St. Paul, in his Epistle to the Romans (8:14-34), gives magnificent expression to the fact that it is the Spirit of God who works in us—not only to justify us but also to teach us how to speak to God; that, in fact, "we do not know how to pray as we ought; but the Spirit himself makes intercession for us with groanings which cannot be expressed in speech. And he who searches hearts knows what the Spirit means, for the Spirit intercedes for the saints as God himself wills" (Rom 8:26-27).

Thus the encounter with the Lord is primarily his work, and since "the Spirit breathes where he wills" (Jn 3:8), the experience of prayer can occur in what, for us, are most unpromising situations and to most unlikely persons. God is the Lord; "The Spirit is not bound" by events, by social situations—a freedom which Jesus exercised magnificently in appearing first to Mary Magdalene, "from whom he had cast out seven demons" (Mk 16:9), on the morning of the Resurrection. What the late Bishop Ian Ramsey has called "disclosure situations," events of our concrete experience which suddenly become revelations of the presence and love of God, can occur most unexpectedly: on a bus, while watching TV, in ordinary conversation. I have had the experience of vainly seeking God throughout a fruitless hour of prayer, only to suddenly hear his voice or feel his presence in the sunset or in the passing word of a friend, or even while preparing a class lecture on a topic quite unrelated to prayer.

But, one may ask, does this really answer our question of relevance? Are we not simply saying that God is a law unto himself and our worldly concerns are really of no value? This would be to say, in effect, that our question of relevance is itself irrelevant. Such an interpretation has, indeed, had a long and vigorous history in the Church, in both Protestant and Catholic traditions. I hope to show shortly that it is mistaken, at least in being too one-sided; but we must acknowledge that it has a solid grounding in scripture. From the beginning of Israel's history as the people of God, Yahweh insisted that he was different from the gods of the Gentiles: He could not be manipulated by men; he was not simply a human being with all the foibles of men, like the Homeric and Canaanite gods. He was the totally other, so far beyond the comprehension of men that they could not even name him (Ex 3:13ff). In the book of Job, the answer to the problem of suffering is that God's providence is to be trusted, not explained. And Jesus makes abundantly clear that, in the New Covenant, too, the ways of God are not the ways of men. This is clear, for example, in his response to the complaint of Judas about the waste of the precious ointment (Jn 12:3-8). Similarly, one of the best descriptions I have found for the primary task of the pray-er is "learning to waste time gracefully."

What, then, can we say about the relevance of prayer —or, for that matter, of religion? Given the biblical picture of God's otherness (his transcendence)—given that "his ways are not our ways"—it would seem that it is misleading, at best, to speak of prayer as relevant. In an important sense, I believe this is true. If by revelant we mean a useful means to accomplish ends which we determine for ourselves, then, I believe, it is a serious distortion of prayer (and religion) to treat it as relevant. That is the flaw in much of what we actually call prayer. Jesus teaches us to say, "Thy will be done." If we are honest with ourselves, we know that most of the time what we really say is, "My will be thine, O Lord." That is, we make up our minds what is really best —a job, health, security, love—and then we beg the Lord to bring about what we want. Prayer as a means to accomplish our ends is indeed a very limited relevance; God, being God, simply cannot be manipulated to our ends.

To summarize what we have been saying in this chapter, there is an important sense in which prayer is, and must be irrelevant. If by relevant we mean useful as a means to accomplish our ends, then prayer is no more relevant than is human love. "Fall in love, get married, have a friend, because it will make you a more useful member of society."

Such advice sounds queer—and even indecent, to one who has known by experience the meaning of love and friendship. Adolescents do indeed seek friends to bolster their own self-image, to reassure themselves that they are OK. But as they become adults they quickly realize the difference between real friendship and being used. They resent it when others are friendly only when and because they want something. They feel guilty if they catch themselves behaving the same way.

The same thing is true in our relationship to God. The death of God theologians of the 1960's criticized conventional religion for worshiping a "god of the gaps," a god who was merely a need-fulfiller and problem-solver. Their point was that most people simply use God as a last resort when their own resources fail them. He is a *deus ex machina,* as he was for the classical dramatists, who is trotted out only to resolve situations (saving a country, healing sickness, passing an exam) which have become humanly impossible to resolve. In our terms, most people try to make God and prayer relevant in the wrong sense; they want to know how prayer can be useful to them in living their lives.

In opposition to this view we have said that: 1) love and friendship are not means but ends, and hence prayer, which is our love-relationship to God, cannot be relevant in the sense that we simply use it, whether to change the world or to achieve peace of heart; and 2) prayer is unique among human relationships in that it is a relationship to God, who is the unutterably Holy One and hence always remains the master of the encounter, who cannot be used or manipulated by man. In this sense it is correct to say that prayer is supremely irrelevant.

There is, however, another sense in which prayer is supremely relevant. If we think of relevance as measured, not in terms of our own social or personal goals, but rather in terms of God's creative work in the world, then the focus of our question is altered. Now it is no longer a question whether prayer can be shown to be revelant to those goals which we set for ourselves and for society. Rather the question is whether prayer can be shown to be relevant to our search for God's designs for us and the world. Can we know without prayer what is the will of God for us? If not, can prayer enable us to discern his will and to follow it? These are the questions to which we now turn.

The Relevance of Prayer: Discernment

In what sense can prayer be said to be supremely relevant to the life of man in the world? To answer concretely, let us suppose that a father of a family or a young religious is truly committed to "doing God's will" in his or her life—that he or she is convinced that God is the Lord of history, that he cares about his people and involves himself in their destiny.[1] In that case, the question arises: How do I discover God's will for his people, for me? Very often in the past, committed Catholics have answered this question for themselves by an appeal to authority. I know God's will for me by listening to those through whom God speaks: the pope, the bishop, the parish priest, civil authorities, parents. To discover God's will for me I simply have to listen to them.

---

[1]Recall that this is the reader for whom this book is written. To make faith reasonable to the unbeliever is a very important part of the Church's mission, but this task would require a separate, and a very different, book from the present one.

There is truth here. God has chosen to speak through men, a wondrous truth which finds its grounding and its climactic expression in the Incarnation of the Son of God. Jesus himself affirmed the fact that God speaks to men through other men, even in the critical situation where the authoritative mouthpieces of God are unworthy of their calling. In St. Matthew's Gospel (Mt 23:1-3), Jesus begins a scathing denunciation of the scribes and Pharisees by saying to the crowds and to his disciples: "The scribes and the Pharisees sit on Moses' seat (i.e., have inherited the authority of Moses to lead God's chosen people); so practice and observe whatever they tell you, but not what they do; for they preach but do not practice."

That God should have spoken through the mouth of a jackass (Num 23) is wondrous enough; that he should choose to speak through the mouths of evil men[2] is more remarkable still. There is, in fact, probably no greater test of the faith of the believer. Such faith would, I suspect, be impossible for the reflective believer unless he were a man of prayer.

Granted this faith, however, and granted the necessity of prayer to sustain it, what are we to say of discovering God's will in our lives? Is it simply a question of listening to those, be they good or bad, through whom the Lord chooses to speak authoritatively? No, it is not as simple as that—and for two reasons. In the first place, the spokesman of God can only learn what he is to say by listening to God, by prayer. God *can* lead by blind guides, can speak through mouths that do not themselves comprehend what they are saying (see Jn 11:49-51 and 18:14). But such people also do great harm and will have much to answer for when their day of judgment comes.

Moreover, even *sincere* leaders—civil and religious, priests, sisters and laymen—fail in their "prophetic" (i.e.,

---

[2]If this seems too harsh a description, read the rest of Chapter 23 of Matthew to see what Jesus thought of certain scribes and Pharisees of his time.

speaking in the name of Yahweh) role if they are not men and women who listen to the Lord and are guided by him in their guidance of men. To seek to lead others by my own best lights is a commendable human act; but it is .not prophetic, not priestly. The Epistle to the Hebrews puts it forcefully: "For every high priest chosen from among men is appointed to act on behalf of men in relation to God . . . And one does not take the honor upon himself, but he is called by God, just as Aaron was" (Heb 5:1,4). Much of the Old Testament is dominated by the conflict between the true and the false prophets (see, for example, I Kings, Isaiah, Jeremiah), and the point of the contrast between the two is clear: The true prophets listen to God and speak to men the word they hear from him; the false prophets do not.

This is the first reason why authority alone will not suffice to discover God's will: those in authority do not learn his will by some magical grace of office but by listening to him, by encountering him in prayer. There is also a second reason, which pertains not to authority as such but to what it means to be Christian. Most Christians are called to be mature, responsible adults. Their maturity and responsibility are not left at the Church door. Precisely as Christians they must discover God's will in their lives. Authority can help them (for example, by providing authentic guidelines on matters such as abortion, worship, social justice). But authority can never spell out *in detail* how an individual Christian should live his or her life.[3] Thank God such a use of authority is impossible; if it were possible, it would keep Christians in a state of perpetual preadolescence.

The average Christian is not called to this kind of perpetual childhood, but rather to be a mature man or

---

[3]St. Thomas Aquinas is very clear on this, in his discussion of the more general and the more specific principles of the natural law. See *Summa Theologiae* I-II, question 94, article 4.

woman in Christ. St. Paul was a strong personality and spoke with authority, and yet he continually exhorts his converts to realize the maturity to which they are called (see especially I Cor 14:20 and Eph 4:13-15). In the concrete, for Paul, this meant being able to recognize and follow the good spirit and to reject the evil spirit in the actual life-situations of the Christian in the world. Divinely constituted authority can provide authentic general guidelines for Christian action. A good spiritual director can help to interpret the way these guidelines apply to the concrete life-situation of an individual Christian. But the challenge remains for the Christian himself; he must make, and take personal responsibility for, the specific faith-decisions which determine the direction of his life. If these are truly to be *faith*-decisions, then the average Christian must also be able to recognize the Lord's will for him. He must open his mind and heart to God and be able to hear and understand the Lord's word. He must, in short, be a man of prayer.

Thus we have seen that prayer is truly relevant, both for the apostle *and* for the ordinary Christian, insofar as it is in prayer that we hear God and discover his will for us in the specific circumstances of our life. This link between prayer and action has been known in the Christian tradition as discernment.

Discernment is, in popular terms, an art and not a science—that is, it is learned only by doing. Like any artist, the person skilled in discernment finds it difficult to formulate rules to teach another person how to discern well. A skilled bicycle rider would find it hard to explain how he balances his weight on two small tires. When he began to ride, he was probably very unsteady and continually losing his balance. How did he master the bicycle? He could not say, except to tell us that "practice makes perfect." In fact, if he did try, while cycling, to analyze for himself how he manages the balancing act, he would probably get entangled in the wheels and fall off. Similarly, an experienced doctor would probably find it difficult to explain to an intern the reasoning process that led him to a successful diagnosis. A good insurance agent could not put into simple logical form the knowledge acquired through many years of experience in his profession.

Since discernment is the art of interpreting God's word to us and his will for us, the experience required is an experience of God—of his likes and dislikes, his desires for us and for the world. Perhaps the best analogy is, again, the experience of human love. When two people love each other, each becomes expert at interpreting the moods, the wishes, the hopes and fears of the other. A small example: I can remember, when my father was still living, going into a store to shop with my mother. We wanted to buy a necktie for Father's Day. The counter before us was filled with neckties, and yet my mother looked through them quickly and "instinctively" said: "No, he wouldn't like that one," . . . "Not that one either," . . . "Nor this," . . . "Ah, yes! This is the one he would like!" And she really meant: "*He* would like this"; not, "This is the one I like . . . The one *I* want him to like." How did she know? (She was right; he did like it!) Only by years and years of living together and sharing day by day.

Similarly, in our relationship with God the signs or touchstones of mature love are instinctive judgments about what would please him, instinctive sensitivity to the quiet word or small gesture which anyone except a lover would overlook. How does one come to such a union of hearts and wills? Only by years of fidelity and experience and reflection. Young lovers don't possess it. Beginners in prayer don't possess it, either. There is no shortcut to acquiring it.

We can, however, give some guidelines for the beginner. Let us begin from the question which all of us who pray ask ourselves at one time or another: When I pray, how do I know that it is God I am talking to and not just myself? I have been asked this question many times, by lay people and religious alike. One dedicated diocesan priest was particularly concerned about it; his work was demanding and challenging, and he did not want to be deluded into wasting precious time just talking to himself.

Normally, pray-ers do not have visions or hear mystical voices. We try to come to quiet—to get some distance from the noise and distractions of our busy lives—and to reflect on what the Lord wants of us. Certain ideas come to us: "I should try to be more attentive to my husband." "Perhaps I should be living a poorer life—after all, Jesus did not have a place to lay his head." "My coming to the novitiate was a mistake; God wants me to serve him in the lay state." The Lord normally does speak to us in this way—through our own ideas. But how do we know they are from God and not just from ourselves? How do we know they truly convey his will for us?

The question cannot be answered quickly and simply. This is why, in important matters, a good spiritual director is essential, especially for beginners. The role of the director is to be a codiscerner, to help us to interpret what God is saying to us in the concrete events of our lives. He or she should be someone experienced in the ways of God, *simpatico,* to whom we can be open and in whom we have confidence—someone, in short, whom we believe to be attuned to God and attuned to us.

Since a good director, however, is a *co*discerner, his or her task is not to tell us what to do but to help us to make our own sound judgments about God's word to us. A good director forms mature people, able to stand on their own spiritual feet. A book for beginners in prayer would not be the place for a full discussion of the what and how of discernment. But perhaps we can suggest a few basic rules which, in my experience, can be very useful even to the beginner.

(1) The basic touchstone of all good discernment is the *scripture.* For the Christian, God has revealed himself "by a Son, whom he appointed the heir of all things, through whom also he created the world" (Heb 1:2). Jesus

49

himself is the revelation of the Father to men. In his life we find the pattern of our lives as Christians, followers of Christ. Paul exhorted his followers to "be imitators of me, as I am of Christ" (I Cor 11:1). In his letter to the Galatians (2:20), he gives glorious expression to the mystical identification (and not merely imitation) with Jesus which is the essence of being Christian: "I have been crucified with Christ; it is no longer I who live, but Christ who lives in me; and the life I now live in the flesh I live by faith in the Son of God, who loved me and gave himself for me."

For the early Church, this sense of identification with Christ was very strong. As time passed, however, and more and more came to believe in Jesus who had never known him in the flesh, it became increasingly important to put in writing who Jesus was and what he stood for. For Peter and James and John, the memory of Jesus remained strong as long as they lived. For those who believed in him because of their preaching, but who had never walked the roads of Palestine with him, something more was needed. The original ending of St. John's Gospel makes clear that this was the *raison d'etre* of the scriptures, the reason why they were written. The final incident of John's Gospel[4] is the encounter between Jesus and "doubting Thomas," and Jesus' very last words are: "Blessed are those who have not seen and yet believe." *We* are the ones who have not seen and yet believe, and John concludes by explaining that it is for us that the Gospel has been written: "Now Jesus did many other signs in the presence of the disciples, which are not written in this book; but these are written that you may believe that Jesus is the Christ, the Son of God, and that believing you may have life in his name" (Jn 20:30-31).

---

[4]Chapter 21 was added later, although an original draft of much of it may well have been written by John. See verse 24 for evidence that it was added later and verse 23 for the reason why it was added. Contrary to the expectations of the early Church, John had died. His death seemed to belie a prediction which they thought Jesus had made to Peter.

Thus we come to know Jesus through the scriptures. To know God's will is basically to test our inspirations against the scriptures in which God is revealed to us through his Son. For this reason also, as we will explain more fully in Part II, the scriptures form the one essential "prayer book" for the meditation of the beginner.

(2) A second basic rule of discernment for the beginner is the following: for those who are sincerely seeking to serve and love God, he always works in *peace,* and usually *slowly.*[5] Why in peace? Because, as St. Ignatius explains it, the soul seeking to serve God is basically attuned to him and, while there may be things in such a soul that God wants changed, he does not want to create turmoil, to call into question the basic orientation—what we would call today the fundamental option—of the soul.

This rule, so simply stated, can be enormously helpful to the beginner. Let us take an example which is quite common in a country like the Philippines, where many families are poor. A seminarian comes to me with a dilemma: he wants to continue for the priesthood and yet his family is in financial need. Should he leave or should he stay? What really is God's will for him? Frequently I find it very helpful to ask him: "How do you feel about it when you are most at peace?—When you are at prayer and quiet (not emotional) and most open to whatever the Lord wants?" Very often he will reply: "At such times I always feel God is asking me to persevere and he will take care of my family. It is only when I am reflecting on it myself outside of prayer that doubts arise and I feel maybe God wants me to leave." In such a case I can say confidently to

---

[5] The idea that God works in peace is basic to the tradition of discernment. See, for example, St. Ignatius' *Spiritual Exercises,* "Rules for the Discernment of Spirits," rules 1, 2, and 5 of the first week, and rules 1 and 7 of the second week; pages 141-143 and 147-148 of the translation by Louis J. Puhl, S.J. (The Newman Press, 1960).

the seminarian that God's will for him is to persevere[6] and that he should not doubt this unless and until he feels God is speaking differently, precisely at those times when he is most at peace.

I said that God works not only in peace but *usually slowly*. This certainly is the pattern of Jesus' formation of the apostles, and it seems to be the lesson of the history of the Church. I am convinced that there are no shortcuts to holiness, despite the fact that men and women are always looking for a shortcut. The seed that springs up quickly does so because the ground is shallow and the nourishment is all going into the stalk and leaf instead of into the roots —and such plants quickly die, as Jesus says (Mk 4:5-6). Cursillos don't really aim to change men definitively over-night. Charismatic prayer does not effect instantaneous sanctity.[7] God chooses to work slowly, and we must have great patience, with him and with ourselves, on the road to holiness.

The one clear example of a sudden transformation might seem to be St. Paul, whose life was changed in an instant when he was stricken by a light from heaven as he journeyed to Damascus (Acts 9:1-8). But Paul himself tells us (Gal 1:16-20; Acts 22:9-16) that it took some time, including, apparently, a long retreat in Arabia's desert, for him to learn the Lord's will for him. In fact, Paul's full transformation from Saul to Paul took much longer still, as Romans, Chapter 7, makes painfully clear.

(3) A final rule for the beginner is this: Real growth

---

[6]The situation could be reversed, e.g., when prayerfully at peace, the seminarian feels he has no vocation, and doubts about his leaving arise only outside of prayer (when he begins to think about parting from all his seminarian friends). In this case, the sign would suggest at least the probability of a lay vocation.

[7]This is not to belittle the cursillo or the charismatic renewal, or similar movements. It is just a warning that we should not expect of them what they cannot give. Properly understood, the cursillo and the charismatic community underscore the need for gradual growth.

in knowledge of God and sensitivity to his will normally require a good spiritual director. We discussed this point briefly above in explaining the role of a director as a co-discerner. But it is important to make it a guiding principle of attunement to God that we must be open to hear him through his human instruments. Paul had to go to Ananias to learn God's message to him. Why did the Lord not tell Paul directly? He could do so, and in the lives of some few saints he apparently has done so. But in general the sacramental principle works in our lives: God works through human instruments, in forgiving, in consecrating—and in revealing his will. As St. Ignatius says, in the 13th rule for discernment of the First Week, the devil loves secrecy. Like a false lover, he will try to persuade the soul to keep its doubts and trials secret—because "no one will really understand," or because "I have to learn to stand on my own feet." How many times I have seen, in my own life and in the lives of those I direct, the wondrous way the Lord blesses openness! Anxiety is dispelled and peace descends and the road ahead becomes clearer because we have listened in faith to God speaking through another person.

It has been said that he who guides himself has a fool for a guide. This is not entirely true, since, as we have stressed earlier, the goal of good direction is the formation of mature and responsible Christians, who can properly discern the Lord's word to them. But it is undoubtedly true that he who listens *only* to himself has a fool for a hearer. As a matter of fact, such a person does not listen only to himself, but also, albeit unwittingly, to the evil spirit.

In this first part of the book, we have considered the "who" and the "what" of prayer. We have defined prayer as a personal encounter with God in love. We have explored the paradox that prayer is both irrelevant and supremely relevant to our daily lives and concerns. We have also noted some important basic guidelines for determining that we are truly hearing God. With this solid foundation we can safely and confidently proceed to a consideration of the "how" of prayer. We can ask about techniques of prayer, fully aware that the initiative is God's, and that most of the work must be done by him.

The How of Prayer

Are There Techniques of Prayer?

The past 15 years have been a time of unusual ferment in the Church, with radical change suddenly overtaking many stable institutions and practices. Formation in prayer has not been exempt from this ferment. For generations, beginners in prayer had been nurtured on point books and other aids to meditation. Seminarians learned to pray by gathering in the seminary chapel for a daily reading of a meditation, with appropriate pauses for them to reflect personally on what they had heard. Even the colloquies, or personal conversations with the Lord, which were supposed to conclude the time of prayer were often read aloud to the group or spelled out in a book. Mental prayer, as it was called, had a well-defined structure: preparatory acts, the reading of the text, personal reflection and the concluding colloquy. Learning to pray meant becoming familiar with this structure and letting it become second nature in one's life. The patterns which could sustain one for the next 50 years of active life were thus acquired.

Then, in the mid-1960's, things suddenly changed. The whole structured, point-book approach to prayer seemed much too rigid and impersonal in a spirit-led world. The fresh air which the great Pope John XXIII let into the Church seemed to topple the structures that had stood for so long. Prayer should be personal, spontaneous, unique to the moment. How could the Spirit of God be bound by the repetitive, mechanical structures of prayer which man devised? Who, after all, could *teach* another person how to pray, or pass judgment on the genuineness of the other's encounter with the Lord?

Many people involved in formation lost their self-confidence and virtually abandoned their formative role at this time. Given the drastic changes taking place, how could any man or woman (especially a child of Vatican I) presume to teach another how to encounter God? Father Henri Nouwen, in a classic chapter of *Intimacy* entitled "Depression in the Seminary," has discussed the overall effects, psychological and spiritual, of this collapse of confidence. It led to a situation in which leaders were unable or unwilling to lead, and in which followers gradually discovered that they were wandering alone in darkness. With respect to formation in prayer, it meant that no formation came to be considered the best formation—or at least the only one possible.

If this seems exaggerated, I well remember a situation which dramatizes the sudden and drastic shift in formation. As a graduate student at the University of Notre Dame in the late 1960's, I was an unofficial chaplain to the women religious in graduate studies. For most of the sisters, graduate studies were (like ordination for a Jesuit) the reward of a life well spent; they had already seen the darker side of 30. Thus our discussions often centered on the defects in our formation, and particularly the overly structured, mechanical approach to prayer from which we seemed to be struggling to free ourselves.

One sister, just out of the novitiate, was much younger than most. She was an active participant in our discussions, but it was only in private conversation with her one day that I realized how dated our hang-ups seemed to her. She said she could appreciate the difficulties the others were expressing, but she didn't think they realized how much things had already changed. They were concerned about a lack of freedom of spirit; her problem—and, she felt, that of her peers —was that nobody had given them any definite guidance on how to pray. They were subjected to a sink-or-swim approach to prayer: Throw the baby in the water and it will either learn to swim (to pray) or it will drown. What she felt was most lacking was any guidance in learning to swim in the sea of the Lord.

I was startled at the time, but in the years since I have shared this experience with many people of post-Vatican II vintage and have become convinced how accurately she represented their feelings. The sink-or-swim approach can perhaps, with grace, produce a few genuine pray-ers at an early age—but only at the cost of many tragic drownings!

Our story does not, of course, end there. Soon enough the rejection of classical method in prayer led to a search for new and better methods and techniques: a fascination with the Orient in its pure forms of yoga and Zen as well as its commercialized hybrids like transcendental meditation; a gradual institutionalizing of the structures of charismatic prayer; a search for gurus from whom one could acquire the key to unlock the inner realm. The implication was, in other words, that it was not method itself which was bad—but the *old* methods which were defective. There has been a return to method without a return to the traditional methods, among those who seek to encounter the Lord today.

It is in this context that we must ask about techniques of prayer. To ask whether there are such would have seemed peculiarly wrong-headed 15 years ago—of course there are! And 10 years ago the answer for many, spoken with equal conviction, would have been, "Of course not!" Now, perhaps, we are not so sure. We want techniques, but we fear the rigidity of established techniques. Deep down, perhaps, what we really want is a surefire technique, which is quick and painless and does not involve the labor and uncertainty of the past. If so, we are seeking for a shortcut to holiness, and we have already said that there is no such thing. In this sense there are no foolproof techniques of prayer.

Let us, however, not dismiss the whole question of technique or method so quickly. Our uncertainty today is healthy and reflects a genuine problem in prayer. How can we learn unless some man teaches us? (cf. Rom 10:14). And yet, how can we be taught without thereby "binding the Spirit" (cf. 2 Tim 2:9) and imposing our ways on God?

The last question raises a fundamental point, so let us begin from there. Since the Spirit is free to "breathe where he wills" (Jn 3:8) and to speak as and when he chooses, there clearly cannot be any techniques for making him speak. We cannot turn God on and off like a water faucet or an electric light. For this there are no techniques. So radical is our dependence on the good pleasure of the Lord that we cannot even *desire* to pray unless God draws us.[1] Even the beginnings are sheer gift. Hence no techniques of "meditation," be they yogic or transcendental or Ignatian, can ever guarantee an encounter with the Lord.

Granting this very important point, let us return to the first question above: How can we learn to pray unless some man teaches us? It might seem from the above paragraph that human teaching is of very little relevance here, that God speaks to whomever he wishes and whenever he chooses—and that is all we can say. To assert this, however,

---

[1]This is a very consoling and important point in these times of dryness known as the "dark night" or the "prayer of faith": even the desire to pray is a clear sign of God's presence, for without him we could not desire him.

is to overlook the apostolic and sacramental nature of the Church: God has chosen to work through men, and to embody his gift of grace in visible, structured signs. With respect to prayer he has willed that we learn through the teaching of other men and women. When I was young, I decided one day to read about John of the Cross. I was eager to learn to pray, and it seemed best to sit at the feet of an acknowledged master. But the more I read, the more troubled I became; it seemed that, if John was right, my whole intellectual and apostolic life as a Jesuit was wrong. Fortunately, before I ran off to be a hermit I spoke to my spiritual director. What he said wounded my pride, but it was just what I needed to hear: "Maybe you are not yet mature enough to read John properly and to understand him. Maybe you will just have to wait awhile before you can profit from his teaching." The advice was painful to accept, but I followed it—and have since repeated it to others more than once! But, to be more precise, just what is it that a good spiritual guide can teach us? In what sense are there communicable techniques and methods of prayer?

I believe there are two senses in which we *can* speak legitimately of techniques of prayer. In the first place, we can speak of techniques for coming to quiet, for bringing ourselves to that stillness in which the voice of God can be heard. Secondly, we can speak of techniques for positively disposing ourselves to encounter the Lord. For the Christian, of course, neither is possible—nothing good is possible —without the grace of God. But each of them does represent a way that we can and must cooperate with grace in opening ourselves to the advent of the Lord in our lives.

St. John of the Cross, with St. Teresa of Avila the Church's preeminent doctor of prayer, began his treatment of the topic with that purification of the soul which must precede transforming encounter with God. He distinguishes between the active and the passive purification which takes place: the active being what *we* can do to dispose ourselves for God and the passive being what *God* does to dispose us.[2] For John, the passive purification—what God does to purify us—is far more important, but he is by no means a quietist or passivist; for him, what we contribute, while secondary, is essential to growth. We cannot simply sit back and leave all to God. In prayer, for Teresa as for John, God helps those who do what they can to help themselves.

Suppose that I want to listen to a radio or TV program. I must get away from or block out other competing noises— this is coming to quiet—and I must turn on and tune in the radio or TV—this is positively disposing myself to hear. Neither will produce the sound if the station is not broad- casting, but both are necessary if I am to hear whatever is being broadcast. Let us now examine how each part of our radio analogy applies to techniques of prayer.

God, obviously, is the broadcaster, and our hearts and minds are the receiving sets. How do we go about getting away from or blocking out other competing noises? How, that is, do we come to quiet? The first point we can make is that coming to quiet is *essential* to prayer. That our analogy to radio or TV is applicable to prayer is clear from a famous passage in the First Book of Kings (19:11-13). The prophet Elijah has aroused the enmity of the evil queen, Jezebel. She threatens to kill him because of his prophesying. Frightened and discouraged, he goes "a day's journey into the wilder- ness" and lies down to die. But the angel of the Lord feeds him and leads him to Mt. Horeb to speak to the Lord. We are told that he stood upon the mountain waiting,

---

[2]See especially *The Ascent of Mount Carmel,* Book I, Chapter 13; pp. 152-153 of the translation by E. Allison Peers (Doubleday- Image paperback, 1958). John treats of the active purification in his first great work, *The Ascent of Mount Carmel,* and the passive purification in the second, *The Dark Night of the Soul.* Both are commentaries on the same poem—a classic of the Spanish language which begins "On a dark night, kindled in love with yearnings . . ."

> And behold, the Lord passed by, and a great and
> strong wind rent the mountains, and broke in
> pieces the rocks before the Lord, but the Lord
> was not in the wind; and after the wind an earth-
> quake, but the Lord was not in the earthquake;
> and after the earthquake a fire, but the Lord was
> not in the fire; and after the fire a still, small voice.

And the still, small voice was the voice of the Lord. Elijah
heard the Lord's healing word to him, but only when he was
able to hear that "still, small voice." God speaks in silences,
and only those who are quiet of heart can hear what he says.

It is in coming to quiet that the techniques of yoga
and Zen can be of help to the pray-er. They are essentially
ancient methods for withdrawing from the distractions of
ordinary life, and for coming to what the Buddha would call
"The still center of the turning world."[3] Over the centuries
yoga and Zen developed highly formalized traditions and
rubrics, but at heart they seem to have been experiential—
attempts by holy men of the East to share with their disciples
methods which they had found helpful in coming to quiet.[4]
They are not an end in themselves, nor are they a magical
means to anything. But they are means which many have

---

[3]The phrase is used by a prominent contemporary Buddhist
writer, Christmas Humphreys, in describing the ultimate contemplative goal of the Noble Eightfold Path of Buddhism (Christmas
Humphreys, *Buddhism,* Pelican paperback, 1969, p. 117). T. S.
Eliot uses a similar phrase ("the light is still/ at the still point of
the turning world") in *Four Quartets* ("Burnt Norton," IV), and
William Johnston, S.J., derives from Eliot the title of his "Reflections on Zen and Christian Mysticism": *The Still Point,* Perennial Library paperback (Harper and Row), 1970. For a fuller
description of the Buddhist experience of this "still center," see
Humphreys, *Concentration and Meditation,* Pelican paperback,
1973, pp. 158-161.

[4]This is not to say that this is *all* that yoga and Zen are intended
to be. The fact that Christian prayer is an encounter with a personal
God, whereas Hindu and Buddhist prayers generally are not seen as
such, would give a very different coloring to yoga and Zen, as
practiced by a Christian and as practiced by a Hindu or Buddhist.

found helpful in achieving a genuine quiet of heart. As such they can be as useful to the Christian as to the Buddhist.

They are not, however, the only means to this end. In fact, when I discovered yoga myself, and attempted to practice some of its basic exercises, I realized that I had already learned, or worked out for myself, similar techniques. The preparatory acts in the old schema of meditation had a similar purpose when properly understood and practiced. One was told to take some moments to recall the scriptural theme of the day's prayer; to recall who God is and who I am, and what a wondrous thing it is that God should speak to me (the analogy of coming into the presence of a human king was often used); to "place oneself in the presence of God" in reverence and in humility. These steps, adapted to the circumstances of the individual pray-er, still form a very effective means for coming to attentive quiet.

Similarly, people often ask me whether walking is proper during prayer. St. Ignatius mentions various postures as helpful in prayer—sitting, kneeling, standing, lying prone or supine—but, significantly, does not mention walking. I believe the reason is because walking, or quietly strolling about, can be a very helpful means for coming to quiet and achieving attentive peace, but would be a distraction once we are at peace in the presence of the Lord. Notice how two friends strolling together often stop and face each other when they come to a point of deep sharing. Their strolling, as it were, creates the mood of encounter. Good classical music can also be a very effective instrument in this coming to quiet and achieving an attentive and concentrated spirit.

I suspect this also was the origin of ejaculations as a form of prayer. Like the Jesus prayer of orthodoxy or the mantra of Hinduism, the ejaculation was a short prayer form repeated over and over again. This repetition of the same formula, slowly and quietly, can be a great help in stilling the distracted spirit. But the subsequent stress on indulgences for saying ejaculations may have obscured the real value of these short prayers. If we become preoccupied with supernatural bookkeeping, then the *number* of such prayers said occupies our attention, rather than their value in bringing us to quiet before the Lord.

Even the repetitive structure of the rosary seems to be valuable to prayer in the same way. Used in such a manner, the *specific* content of the rosary prayers or ejaculations or the Jesus prayer would not be so important; rather they would be seen primarily as a help to achieving a prayerful spirit and a tranquil and attentive heart.

I have also found the divine office, or Prayer of Christians, helpful in achieving the same end. Often people ask me how to give more meaning to the office; they seem to find the familiar structure and repetitive phrasing a source of boredom or monotony, rather than a help to devotion. If, however, the office is seen primarily as a way of coming to quiet before the Lord—of being *reminded* of his love and providence at certain pivotal moments of the day, rather than as a source of *new* ideas about God and his place in our lives—then perhaps the repetition of familiar phrases can be seen in a new and more fruitful light.

The means I have suggested—ejaculations, the rosary, and especially the divine office—are already properly prayer since they entail a coming to quiet before, or in the presence of God.[5] Other simple practices, while not explicitly prayer in the same sense, can also help to bring us to quiet and open us to God. For example, psychologists suggest that we concentrate on our own bodies—first, let us say, on our right foot, gradually "thinking" our big toe into a relaxed state, and then our other toes in turn, then our instep, our ankle, our calf, our thigh, and so on until our

---

[5]St. Teresa calls this use of vocal prayers to come to quiet in the Lord's presence the prayer of recollection. She has some very helpful comments on it in *The Way of Perfection,* Chapter 29.

whole body is relaxed. I have tried this with various groups, and have been happily surprised at how helpful it can be. One interesting side benefit is that it often reveals to us where our real tension or disquiet is. People have said, "I am all relaxed, except for my mouth"—or ". . . except for a place on my forehead between my eyes." This says much about the source of our anxiety; once we realize it, we can begin to work in a concentrated, but peaceful, way on overcoming it.

Another exercise which I have discovered for myself, and have found very helpful, is the following: to get outside in a place where a panoramic view of nature confronts me, and where I can let my eyes wander over the entire scene (for example, a hillside overlooking a woods). I find it good just to let my gaze wander over the scene, without any concern for time and without any attempt to force concentration. Gradually one part of the woods catches my attention, and then one tree, and eventually one branch on the tree. My scattered thoughts come to focus on a single experience, and then dive deeper and deeper into that one reality (the universe in a blade of grass). Oftentimes the result is that my attention is absorbed by some small flower or leaf at my feet which I had not even noticed before—and I am at peace!

We have been discussing various techniques for coming to attentive quiet before the Lord. Not all of them are prayer proper—i.e., a personal encounter with God in love —but they are a normal prerequisite for prayer. The effort to come to quiet can often be the principal effort of the beginner. Today, especially, we live in a scattered and distracted world; it can be a major achievement just to come to peace. At the same time, it is important to realize that, for the Christian at least, this is only the preliminary step. As we grow and mature in prayer, we will be able to come to quiet more quickly and more easily. In fact, if we are faithful to prayer, we will find a natural drawing to quiet as the state where we are most at home. This takes time, and the beginner may have to exert long effort to mature in this way—but it is important to remember that it is only the beginning. The effort to come to quiet is not in itself prayer. The time will come when the gazer must close his eyes, when the background music must be turned off, when the stroller must sit still and the pray-er of ejaculations must keep silent—the time, that is, to "be still, and know that I am God" (Ps 46:10).

5

The Active Purification
of the Soul

In the last chapter we raised the question whether
there are techniques of prayer, and we saw that there
cannot be, in the sense of techniques for guaranteeing an
encounter with the Lord. He is Lord, and his coming to us
is sheer gift. We said, however, that we can speak of techniques with respect to prayer in two senses: techniques for
coming to quiet, which we discussed in the preceding
chapter, and techniques for positively disposing ourselves
to encounter God. The two are not entirely distinct, and
they do overlap; but the difference I have in mind is clearer
if we recall the radio or TV analogy. We may not hear the
radio because there is too much noise around us—and in
this case we need to get the noisemakers to quiet down, or
else get away ourselves to a quiet place. On the other hand,
we may not hear the radio because it is not working
properly, or because it is not turned on or not tuned in.
In this case, it will not help us to be quiet, unless we also
fix the radio, turn it on, tune it in. It is this latter repairing
and tuning that we are concerned about when we ask, in

this chapter, whether there are techniques for positively disposing ourselves to encounter God.

The radio analogy is a good one. Just as a broken radio set cannot pick up the broadcast, so too a broken soul cannot hear God. Sinful man must first be healed, "repaired," purified, before the voice of the Lord can truly penetrate his spirit. This is clear from the scripture and from the whole tradition of the Church. In a beautiful but ironic exchange with the scribes and Pharisees, Jesus says: "Those who are well have no need of a physician, but those who are sick," and he immediately goes on to apply this to himself: "I came not to call the righteous but sinners" (Mk 2:17, and the parallel verses in Matthew and Luke). The passage is ironic because Jesus really means that *all* of us are sick and he came for all. All of us have been poisoned by original sin. But the divine physician can only heal us if we are willing to acknowledge our illness and to seek healing.[1]

This need to be purified is difficult for men to accept in every age. Especially today, people want a religion of joy and fellowship and camaraderie—no hell, no pain, no penance. But the gospel knows nothing of such a painless faith. The grain of wheat must die before bringing forth a rich harvest. The hundredfold can be possessed only by those who leave everything to follow Jesus. In Baptism, the old man must be crucified, that he may rise to a new life in Christ.[2] It is not a popular way today, and it never has been, but it is the only way.

This is even clearer if we consider two of the works on prayer which the Church has recognized as perennial classics: *The Spiritual Exercises* of St. Ignatius Loyola and the *Ascent of Mount Carmel* of St. John of the Cross. Both Ignatius and John of the Cross were contemplatives of a

---

[1]See Jn 9:39-41, where Jesus, having healed the blind man, develops the same idea in terms of the metaphor of blindness.
[2]Jn 12:24; Lk 18:29-30; Rom 6:6.

high order, who drew on their own deep experience of the ways of God in writing about the interior life. It is striking, therefore, to see how strongly both of them stress the long process of purification which precedes true union with God.

At the very beginning of the *Spiritual Exercises,* St. Ignatius places this title: "Spiritual Exercises, which have as their purpose the conquest of self and the regulation of one's life in such a way that no decision is made under the influence of any inordinate attachment."[3] The language is striking—the very purpose of the Exercises is the conquest of self and the freeing of ourselves from any inordinate attachment which might color our decisions and distort our vision of the divine will. An eminently practical purpose, worthy of a practical man, but far from the contemplative grandeur we might expect. The reason, I think, is that these are exercises, things *we* can do to dispose ourselves for God. The contemplative experience is God's pure gift; the spiritual exercises which we undertake are, Ignatius says, ways "of preparing and disposing the soul to rid itself of all inordinate attachments, and, after their removal, of seeking and finding the will of God in the disposition of our life."[4] What Ignatius calls exercises are what we have called techniques for positively disposing ourselves to encounter God.

John of the Cross was a younger contemporary of Ignatius (he was born in 1542, while Ignatius died in 1556) who received his early education under Ignatius' Jesuits at Medina del Campo in Spain. John, however, was drawn to the contemplative life, and soon after his ordination in 1567 he joined with St. Teresa of Avila in the discalced Carmelite reform. At the time they met, John was 25 and Teresa was 52. Despite the disparity in their ages, and despite the fact that they were of remarkably different temperaments, John and Teresa became one of the greatest teams in the history

---

[3] Page 11, par. 21, in the translation by Louis J. Puhl, S.J.
[4] Page 1, par. 1, in the Puhl translation.

of spirituality. Both are doctors of the Church today, recommended to Christians precisely as masters of prayer.

It is striking, then, that John of the Cross, whose name has become virtually synonymous with Christian mysticism, should present a doctrine on the foundations of prayer very similar to that of Ignatius.[5] It is, in fact, from John that we have taken the title of this chapter: "The Active Purification of the Soul." We explained above (pages 60-61) that John distinguishes between the active and the passive purification of the soul. Active refers to what we must do to dispose ourselves to encounter God, whereas passive refers to what God does to purify us. The latter, for John, is much more important and is the subject matter of the *Dark Night of the Soul*. There are, in fact, two dark nights which John describes, that of the senses which "is common and comes to many (and) they are the beginners" and that of the soul or spirit, which "is the portion of very few (namely), those who are already practiced and proficient."[6] Although John here refers to those who experience the dark night of the senses of beginners, they are not really beginners in prayer. In Book I, Chapter I, in fact, John says this passive dark night begins when God begins to lead souls beyond the state of beginners; he says there that beginners are "those that meditate on the spiritual road,"[7] those who are engaged in the active purification of the soul described in the *Ascent of Mount Carmel*.

It is in this latter sense that we can properly speak of beginners in prayer. For reasons that will be clearer in the next chapter, they are those who meditate, whose prayer may properly be termed meditation. Meditation is, in fact,

---

[5]The same could be said, with equal validity, of the teaching of St. Teresa of Avila. See especially her *Way of Perfection*, which she wrote when her nuns asked her to teach them how to pray. See also the first three Mansions of the *Interior Castle*.

[6]Book I, Chapter VIII of the *Dark Night of the Soul*; p. 61 in the excellent translation of E. Allison Peers (Doubleday-Image, 1959).

[7]Page 37 in the Peers translation.

the way such beginners, during their time of prayer proper, may positively dispose themselves to encounter God. This, however, is not all that beginners can or must do to prepare themselves to meet the Lord. In addition to meditative prayer—which, as we will see in the next chapter, is a way of coming to know who *God* is and what he stands for— we need techniques to bring us to a deeper and more honest knowledge of ourselves, and to enable us, with the help of grace, to purify in ourselves whatever makes us unworthy of standing in God's presence. Let us consider these techniques now.

The basic principle of purification is that knowledge of self and knowledge of God go hand in hand. We cannot come to a deep knowledge of God without, at the same time, coming to a profound realization of who we ourselves really are.[8] This is painful. One of the most obvious results of sin in our lives is that we find it very difficult to face honestly who and what we really are. Adam, as soon as he had eaten the apple, began to make excuses for his action. The people of Israel, when confronted by the prophets with hard truths about themselves, invariably reacted by trying to silence the prophets. The same pattern is evident in the reaction of the scribes and Pharisees to John the Baptist, and then to Jesus, in the Gospels. When Jesus stripped away their masks and revealed what was really going on in their hearts, they could not face the truth themselves or stand to be revealed before others as they really were. Rather, they acted defensively and sought to destroy Jesus, "just as they had attacked the Baptist" (Lk 7:31-34). St. John puts it powerfully in his Gospel, in his comment on Jesus' dialogue with Nicodemus:

> And this is the judgement, that the light has come
> into the world, and men loved darkness rather

---

[8]St. Teresa has an excellent discussion of the continuing need of self-knowledge, no matter how advanced our state of prayer. See *The Interior Castle,* First Mansions, Chapter two.

than light, because their deeds were evil. For everyone who does evil hates the light, and does not come to the light, lest his deeds should be exposed (3:19-20).

This is true, not just of the scribes and Pharisees, but of all of us. Think how children react when accused of wrongdoing—or even when they lose a game. Their first instinct is to save face, to deny the wrong or to find excuses for the loss. It is the mark of a truly mature person to be able and willing to be seen as he really is—and how few mature people there are, even among adults! Most of us wear masks. We are concerned about how we *appear* to others; and we even attempt to fool ourselves about ourselves. We find it very hard to face the truth about who we really are—this is why psychiatrists and psychologists never lack for clients. Their role is to help people strip off the masks and to face and accept themselves as they really are.

Psychiatrists deal with abnormal situations, i.e., situations in which the failure to face reality has led to serious difficulties in functioning as a human being. As we said, however, not only abnormal people tend to wear masks. We all do. All the masters of Christian spirituality—beginning with the Lord Jesus himself—have stressed the need to strip away these masks if ever we are to encounter God. Self-knowledge (with self-acceptance) and knowledge of God go hand in hand. It is a painful process to come to see ourselves truly, but "the truth will make you free" (Jn 8:32).

For John of the Cross, man's desires are the root of his lack of freedom. The active purification (what we ourselves do) consists in recognizing and uprooting these desires. In fact, John's stress on freeing ourselves from all desire (the *nada,* or stress that everything human and natural is nothing) is what has made him appear austere and almost inhuman to most Christian pray-ers. Very few read him and many who do are frightened away. But we must keep in mind that by desires John means those purely natural desires of man which, however good or indifferent they may be in themselves, have not been tamed by the overmastering Spirit of God's love. Moreover, we must keep in mind the purpose of John's doctrine of *nada* or nothingness. He is very much attuned to the modern philosophy of freedom; freedom *from* something is worthless unless it is freedom *for* something else. If we seek to uproot all merely natural desires, it is only in order that we may be truly free to love. In fact, we can only love truly when we are free of pride, ambition, lust, and other self-centered desires natural to sinful man. "When I'm not near the girl I love, I love the girl I'm near" is a clever and witty line from a modern song, but what it describes is not love at all. True love makes a man indifferent to all competing desires. The man who truly loves his wife, and has grown to maturity in that love (a rare enough phenomenon, admittedly), is free from the desire for other women. The same is true of the person who has come to a mature love of the Lord.

This singleness of heart was beautifully and forcefully brought home to me one day. A woman who was very happily married was sharing with me the wonder of a love that had grown over many years between her and her husband. She said: "You know, the strange thing is that I can always tell, at a party, when he has had enough to drink and it is time to go home. From across the room, he will always begin winking *at me!*" She said it with pride, and she knew how fortunate she was. Their relationship was such, even after many years together, that he only had eyes for her. His heart was single, and all competing desires were not annihilated, but swallowed up in the one great love of his life. For this man, as I happen to know, the love of God was equally real and total. Love of God and love of wife were not competing desires; rather, one was the path to the other. As Rosemary Haughton has said so beautifully, the married person comes to the love of God *through* the love of a spouse, while the celibate comes to the love of men

74

through the love of God.[9] The problem is not too many loves, but the fact that our loves are in conflict, are eccentric, not centered and integrated. This is the root problem for every pray-er, whether married or celibate. We can have many loves in our lives, but only one center, one sun around which all our loves are satellites.

Coming to this freedom to love is, for most of us, a long and gradual process, and one that requires a great deal of help—grace—from the Lord. Perhaps John of the Cross (a great poet, a Spaniard, a 16th-century man) does not make clear enough for contemporary man the gradualness and the grace required. But his basic point is as valid today as in his own time—to be free *for* God, one must be free *from* all conflicting natural desires. Jesus said it long ago: "No man can serve two masters; for either he will hate the one and love the other, or he will be devoted to the one and despise the other. You cannot serve God and mammon (i.e., money)" (Mt 6:24; Lk 16:13). In Matthew's Gospel, this passage is followed by Jesus' beautiful command to be free from all worry and anxiety, like the birds of the air, like the lilies of the field. This is precisely the point John of the Cross is making—to be free to love is to be free from all desire, all anxiety.

St. Ignatius Loyola, a practical, methodical man of decision and action, sees his Exercises as intended to free us from any inordinate attachment, from any desire which blocks love and loving service. The means he proposes are meditative prayer on the life of the Lord Jesus, who is always our model of total freedom to love; the practice of penance; and the examination of conscience. We will speak more fully of meditative prayer in the next chapter. Let us now consider the ancillary means of penance and the examination of conscience.

Penance is not fashionable today. The Eucharistic fast

---

[9]"Marriage and Virginity: Two Ways to One End," in *The Gospel, Where It Hits Us,* pp. 1-20.

has practically disappeared. Penitential practices in semi-naries and convents—such as the discipline, the hairshirt, the penance table at dinner—have become the stuff of legend, with which older religious awe (or regale) younger religious about the good (or bad) old days. In the time of Teresa and John and Ignatius, and for long thereafter, pen-ance played a very prominent part in spirituality. It was often practiced to excess, and much of the change today is good. But all the saints have recognized that there is no genuine holiness, no solid spirituality, without penance. Ignatius, who was a child of his times and originally practiced much more severe penance than we would consider reasonable today, gives remarkably balanced guidelines for the proper use of penance.[10]

Ignatius is speaking of voluntary penance, that is, penance freely undertaken. The first thing to stress is that such penance is never an end in itself; God does not enjoy our suffering in itself, nor may we undertake it for its own sake. No. Penance is always a means to an end, and it must be chosen as any good means is chosen—insofar as it helps to achieve the end in view. Ignatius says the legitimate reasons for doing penance are: to make satisfaction for our sins; to help overcome our selfish inclinations (what John of the Cross calls our desires); and as a form of prayer, "to obtain some grace or gift that one earnestly desires." Since penance is a means, we should always be clear what our purpose is in doing it, and should choose that penance which is best suited to accomplish our purpose.

Penance as a means of making satisfaction for our sins, while not very fashionable today, is clear enough to anyone who has loved and has hurt the one loved. We *need* to make amends, to show by some visible sign our sorrow for wounding love. It is far from true that "love means never having to say you're sorry." Such a love, for fallible

---

[10] *The Spiritual Exercises,* #82-89 (pp. 37-39 in the Puhl transla-tion).

human beings, would be not love but selfishness and superficiality. We see here the real difference between Peter and Judas. Both denied the Lord. Both failed, one might say, equally seriously. Both were filled with remorse. But Judas *could not say he was sorry,* could not face the Lord and seek forgiveness. There is no contrast in scripture so dramatic as that between Judas' going out alone and hanging himself and Peter's leaping from the boat and racing to shore to encounter again the Lord he had betrayed just a short time before (Jn 21).[11] It is no accident that Jesus, after breakfast, leads Peter away from the group and, by means of the triple questioning, celebrates with Peter the Church's first liturgy of reconciliation. The triple denial and now the triple affirmation of Peter's love—the symbolism of the parallel was not lost on Peter, nor on the early Church. Men's love, frail and fallible as it is, *does* mean having to say—by word and by action—that you are sorry for wounding love.

Penance as a means to overcome our selfish inclinations or desires has a long history, even among the pagan Stoics, and is based on sound psychological insight. It is the *agere contra* of ascetical tradition—act against the natural inclinations which you wish to correct. If the sapling is bent to the east, pull to the west to straighten its growth. If you tend to overindulge in food or drink, cut down consumption even to less than is legitimate; in this way, the will is strengthened and the unruly instincts are brought under control. Here again penance is clearly a means and must be proportionate to the end sought. I well recall speaking with a good sister, who felt the need of more penance in her life and asked what I would suggest. "How about cutting down somewhat on food?" I proposed. "But," she replied, "I hate to eat anyway." Clearly for her that was not a helpful penance! I suggested some penance in the area of reading,

---

[11]See also Lk 22:61-62, where Luke recounts that Peter immediately repented when the Lord turned and looked at him.

and this time hit the mark. "I love to read," she said. "In fact, I devour the newspaper first thing in the morning." So I suggested, not that she stop reading the paper (which was necessary to her work), but that she wait until later in the morning to read it. This would not interfere with her apostolic effectiveness, but it would be a very good training of the will and mastering of desire. She happily followed the suggestion, and found it of great profit.

Penance as a form of prayer is somewhat more unusual. We don't often think of penance in this way.[12] But I think Ignatius' view of penance as a form of prayer is deeply incarnational. Man is not an angel, he is an embodied spirit. His most spiritual acts need to be incarnated, enfleshed, sacramentalized. In this sense, his acts of bodily penance are an embodiment, a visible expression of his inner attitudes. They should be done for God, and not to impress men (see Mt 6:16-18; 9:14-25); but they are an important human form of prayer. I have found, in fact, that at times when my spirit finds prayer hardest, my body, by its acts, can often say what my heart cannot. The Lord truly hears and blesses such penitential prayer.[13]

The other means which Ignatius proposes for disposing ourselves to encounter God, for freeing ourselves of inordinate attachments, is the examination of conscience. This is, in fact, the very first topic of *The Spiritual Exercises*.[14] It

---

[12]In Mark 9:29, an ancient tradition has Jesus reply to the disciples' discouragement at their inability to drive out an unclean spirit by saying: "This kind can only be driven out by prayer *and fasting.*" Other ancient manuscripts omit "and fasting," and many scripture scholars today believe it is a later addition to the text. But the idea of fasting (penance) as a form of prayer has solid scriptural grounding. See Acts 13:3 and 14:23; and also Isaiah 58 and Matthew 25:31-46, where the prevailing idea of fasting is purified and subordinated to fraternal love.

[13]Ignatius says, in the rules for discernment of spirits (#319: rule 6 of the first week), that doing some penance can be a very effective way to counter desolation in prayer. It must always, however, be seen as a means, and used insofar as it helps (see #89).

[14]Numbers 24-43; pp. 15-23 in Puhl's translation.

is a topic which he always advises the director to include in a retreat, no matter how poorly educated or how ill-disposed the retreatant.[15] Moreover, Ignatius is reported to have said that he would rather have his disciples miss their meditation than miss their examen—a surprising preference in the light of the fact that the examen is widely neglected today. What, then, is this technique which Ignatius valued so highly?

Again, it is not new to him, nor is it uniquely Christian. Even the great pagan Stoics saw value in such a practice. If we wish to overcome our faults, it is a great help to focus our attention upon them—to be aware of how and when we fail, and to note any progress we make in diminishing the frequency of failure. This leads to what Ignatius calls a general examination of conscience, a practice which the Church has incorporated into Compline or Night Prayer in the divine office. For the Christian, of course, the examination of conscience is not merely a sound psychological technique. It is also a channel of grace, both in the sense that we ask God to help us to see ourselves, our sinfulness, as he sees us, and also in the sense that it is a call for his healing power to work in our lives. Thus the stress is not merely, or even primarily, on our own efforts to overcome our failings. The work of healing is the Lord's and the examen is an opening of our hearts to his healing touch.

Another sound psychological principle of growth is divide and conquer. When we resolve to live a good life, we soon realize that our failings are many. In fact, the devil uses this realization to discourage beginners. We want instant holiness, and normally all genuine growth is slow, gradual and painstaking. We become frustrated as we realize how slow our progress is. In fact, as we grow we begin to discover failings in ourselves—pride, envy, timidity, laziness —which we were not even aware of before. How many

---

[15]See the Introductory Observations (for the director), #18-19 (pp. 7-9 in Puhl).

times I have begun a directed retreat with someone who, while good, sees the problems in his life as due to others' and not to his own faults. He is convinced he has been misjudged, persecuted, overlooked. Yet he gives himself generously to the retreat, and as the days pass he is overwhelmed by the realization that his faith has been weak indeed, and that he has been so preoccupied with other people's attitudes that he has drifted far from the fervor of his first love. John's strong words to the churches (Rev 2:4-5; 2:16; 3:1-3; 3:15-16) are heard spoken to him. He begins to see the great love of the Lord for him and the many hypocrisies in his own response of love. The danger now is the temptation of Judas. Confronted with our own many infidelities, we may be paralyzed and unable to act.

How can we avoid discouragement? By stressing faith, humility, patience with ourselves, and by realizing the profound truth that, even in our own interior lives, it is far better to light one small candle than to sit cursing the darkness. This is the idea of the divide and conquer principle—single out our failings and work on them one by one. Don't expect to change everything at once, but work and pray to change one thing at a time, beginning with those failings which most impede our growth. This is what Ignatius calls the particular examination of conscience, which he also recommends as a daily practice, especially for beginners. It is a review of how I have done during the day in the one specific area where my failures seem most to block the genuine encounter with God which I seek. The focusing on this area is a sound natural help to growth—having to face myself honestly once or twice a day will gradually make me conscious of my failings at the very time I am inclined to commit them. It is also a channel of grace in the same sense as the general examen; I expose to the Lord the precise area of my greatest weakness, and ask that his saving power be brought to bear especially there.

Both the particular and the general examen are time-tested techniques for what John calls the active purification of the soul, for positively disposing ourselves to encounter God. Perhaps now we can see why Ignatius would rather have beginners miss their meditation than their examen. He is convinced, of course, that both are necessary. But a prayer life without the healthy and humbling self-knowledge which the examen brings is very likely to be shallow and romantic and eventually harmful. It can lead to that false mysticism —a self-centered, "hearts and flowers" type of spirituality which forgets that the grain of wheat must die before bearing fruit—which has always been a danger in the history of the Church.

True knowledge of God always goes hand in hand with a painful self-knowledge. John of the Cross expresses it beautifully by means of the famous metaphor of the log of wood being transformed into fire.[16] As the wood burns, it becomes blackened, it cracks and steams, and all the knotholes and flaws are exposed. If the log could speak it would cry out: "My seeking to become fire was a mistake! I am now worse than when I started—black, ugly and flawed. I was better off before." The log is the soul and the fire is God. And the truth, of course, is that the log is not worse off than it was before. All the ugliness and defects were present before but they were concealed. The only way the log can become fire is to be revealed honestly and openly as what it is in itself. The process is painful but, contrary to appearances, it is the mark of real growth in union with God. That is why good souls who are making real progress often feel they are regressing and getting further from God.

I have not discussed the mechanics, the specific methods which might be employed in the particular and the general examen. There are various effective structures for the examen in different spiritual traditions. Moreover, several good articles have been written recently on the ques-

---

[16]*The Living Flame of Love,* Book I, #16 (in the first redaction; #19 in the second redaction).

tion.[17] There is, however, one further question which we should discuss. It is sometimes said that this approach to the interior life is too negative and too introspective. Are we not focusing too much on ourselves, and ultimately encouraging scrupulosity?

The question is a valid one. From my experience as a director in contemplative communities, I am convinced that the great danger of the contemplative life is confusing prayer with introspection. The contemplative comes to find God and is in danger of finding himself or herself instead. Self-analysis, and even self-knowledge, is not the goal of the interior life for a Christian; knowledge and love of God are the goal. If our focus is on digging deeper and deeper into ourselves, we will end in scrupulosity and not in genuine holiness. Yet, as we have stressed in this chapter, genuine self-knowledge is a necessary means to and concomitant of a true encounter with God in love.

A classic distinction from moral theology can help us strike the proper balance here: a sensitive conscience is a mark of holiness; a scrupulous conscience is a mark of sickness. The scrupulous conscience sees sin where there is no sin, constantly fears that it has not been forgiven past failings, goes over and over again the same ground of self-analysis. This is productive of anxiety and destructive of

---

[17]Especially helpful is "Consciousness Examen" by George Aschenbrenner, S.J. (*Review for Religious*, volume 31, #1, January, 1972, pp. 14 ff.) He presents the examen positively, as a time to review God's blessings and gifts to us, as well as our failings; to see the latter in the light of God's goodness and our response, and not merely in relation to law. The same approach is very helpful in the sacrament of Penance, which is the means, *par excellence*, to the active purification of the soul about which we have been speaking. Despite the fact that the sacrament of Penance has fallen on bad days recently, I personally believe that it is essential to any genuine growth in holiness in the Church. It must, of course, be approached in the spirit of this chapter—as a *means* to liberation and growth— and not as a mere laundry list of sins. (See Edward Farrell, *Prayer Is a Hunger*, Chapter Four, "Penance: Return of the Heart"; pp. 40 ff., Dimension Books, 1972.)

peace. As we saw in Chapter 3 (page 51), God always works *in peace* with those who are seeking to serve him.

The sensitive conscience, on the contrary, is one that becomes progressively more aware of smaller, *but genuine,* failings. This is a real sign of growth. The closer we come to the Light, the darker our own darkness appears by contrast. The prostitute who is actively plying her trade is unlikely to be bothered by, or even to notice, smaller failings like a tendency to gossip or a neglect of daily prayer. If, however, she gives up prostitution and seeks to reform her life, she is very likely to become conscious of many smaller faults which she has never adverted to before. This is not introspection or scrupulosity, although the devil will probably try to persuade her that it is. It is a sign of a growing sensitivity of conscience, a growing awareness of who she truly is, and if she perseveres peacefully, it will lead to a genuine knowledge of God.

What we seek, then, in the active purification of the soul, is a true knowledge of ourselves and a deeper sensitivity of conscience. It is by no means the whole of Christian spirituality, but it is an essential foundation for prayer. The other foundation is laid in our prayer life itself. It is to the laying of this second foundation that we now turn in our continuing exploration of the early stages of the road to God.

6

The Ways of Prayer
of Beginners

Thus far in this book, we have discussed what prayer is, how it may be said to be relevant, and irrelevant, to the life of man in the world, and what role is played by techniques—both of coming to quiet and of purification—in disposing the soul to encounter God. One major question remains: What does the beginner do when he actually comes to pray? If experiential knowledge and love of God are, as we have said they are, the goal of a life of prayer, where does one go, what does one do, to encounter the Lord?

In a sense, as we have seen, he doesn't go anywhere or do anything. The Lord comes to him unexpectedly and at a time not of man's choosing, as he came to Peter in a fishing boat, Matthew in a tax-collector's booth, Zaccheus in a tree, Paul on a journey. Man is, as C. S. Lewis expressed it beautifully in the title of his autobiography, "surprised by joy." There are no rules to govern such an event.

Still, we must do something. The first surprise encounter with the Lord is never a final, completely transforming revelation. As T. S. Eliot has put it, it is a drawing, a calling to explore, to inquire, to search. Such a call demands a response from man. The call may come dramatically as it did with Paul or it may come so imperceptibly that we cannot even say when it happened, as in the case of a person who has absorbed the faith right from childhood with the very air he breathed. However it happens, the time comes when we sense the Lord's call to know him, to become his friends. As I noted in the Introduction, this book is written for all those who, in one way or another, have heard this call, and now find themselves asking: What is our response?

In Chapters 4 and 5 we have discussed two of the essential preconditions of any authentic response to God's drawing: coming to attentive quiet, and cleansing our lives of anything which would block or hinder our capacity to return love for love. But how do we actually respond to the word the Lord speaks to us? What do we say or do in prayer? The answer to this question is the topic of the present chapter.

We can begin with an analogy to the deepest form of human love, the marital love of a man and a woman for each other. Such a love takes many years to mature. We sometimes speak of love at first sight, but in the strictest sense there is no such thing. There can be attraction at first sight—a boy and a girl can sense something in each other which draws them together and makes them sense that this relationship promises to be different from any other they have experienced. But real love demands knowledge; we cannot love what we do not know. And so the boy finds himself wanting to know all about the girl to whom he is drawn. If the girl responds, they spend endless hours in sharing with each other—their past, their hopes, their fears, their frustrations. They may even spend an evening alone together, and then, after the boy takes the girl

home and returns to his own home, spend another hour
on the telephone sharing what has happened in the half-
hour since they parted. It is exasperating to their fathers,
who pay the telephone bills, and appears silly to any on-
lookers who are not themselves suffering from the same
disease. But it is not as foolish as it appears. We can only
love what we know, and the boy and girl during courtship
are seeking that mutual knowledge which alone grounds
genuine love.

The same need is present in our prayer life, our love
relationship with God. Genuine love of God also demands
a time of courtship. Here, too, we can only love one whom
we know. There is of course an important difference: God
has known us before we were formed in our mother's
womb (Jer 1:5). He knows our inmost being, better than
we know ourselves. He "searches all hearts, and understands every plan and thought" (I Ch 28:9). But, while he
knows us fully, we do not know him. And before we can
fully respond to his love freely poured out in us, we must
come to know him.

Thus the first stage of a genuine interior life is
learning to know the Lord. We saw in Chapter 5 that
both Ignatius and John of the Cross refer to the prayer
of beginners as meditation.[1] Meditation means precisely
this—taking time to learn who this God is whom we are
drawn to love, what he stands for, what he values, what
it would mean to be his friend. We can learn this from a
consideration of creation, since nature, other persons and
we ourselves are all signposts which point to their Maker,
reflections which reveal the Artist who shaped them. Thus,
every human being can come to know the Lord.[2] For the
Christian, however, the primary revelation of the Father

---

[1]Chapter 5, pp. 65 and 69. Teresa of Avila also discusses meditation in Chapters 12 and 13 of her *Autobiography*, and in Chapter 19
of the *Way of Perfection*. See also Boase, *The Prayer of Faith*,
Chapter 5.

[2]See Rom 1:19-20.

is Jesus Christ. Hence the scriptures, which were written
that we, who have not known Jesus in the flesh, may believe in him, are the privileged way for Christians to come
to know God in and through Jesus Christ.[3]

Meditation, then, is the use of our understanding to
discover who God is—to learn to know him more fully in
order that we may love him more deeply and follow him
more faithfully. The principal sourcebook of Christian
meditation is the scripture, in which God reveals himself
to us. We may say that meditation is not properly prayer
in the sense we have defined it (a personal encounter with
God in love)—but, because love depends on knowledge,
meditation on the scripture is an essential first step to
genuine prayer. Thus it is the principal activity of beginners when they come to pray.

It is important to note that this "meditation" on the
scripture may start long before we begin a formal life of
prayer. In a good Christian home, the values of the Gospel
and the person of Jesus Christ will be communicated in the
very air the child breathes. In the Sunday liturgy—particularly in the new liturgy with its reading of the scripture
over a three-year cycle, and its stress on the homily as an
exposition of the scripture readings—that knowledge of
God which grounds genuine love can be communicated
gradually and very effectively. A good Christian schooling
contributes much to the same end. Hence the "beginner"
to whom this book is addressed may not really be a beginner. St. Augustine expressed this beautifully long ago, at
the beginning of his *Confessions*. He confronts the mystery
of knowledge and love, of the priority of knowing God over
seeking ("imploring") him, and he concludes: "My faith,
Lord, cries to Thee, the faith that Thou hast given me, that
Thou hast inbreathed in me, through the humanity of Thy
Son and by the ministry of Thy preacher."[4]

---

[3]See Chapter 3, pages 49-51.
[4]*Confessions*, I, 1 (trans. Frank Sheed, 1943), p. 3.

For some people, this diffuse sort of meditation may well suffice to ground a mature life of prayer. But in my experience, both as a pray-er and as a director of others, those who begin to be serious about a life of prayer normally need a deeper grounding in the knowledge of the Lord of Love, a more systematic searching of the scriptures, such as the meditation which occupies Augustine himself throughout much of the *Confessions.* For some who come to pray there has been very little of Christian formation. And for others, that which has been "inbreathed" into us during our formative years often needs to be made properly our own, and integrated into that coherent knowledge of the Lord of Love which Vatican I calls "the connection of these mysteries (of faith) with one another and with man's ultimate end."[5] Gradually, as we meditate, the bits and pieces of our knowledge of scripture and of the Lord become one seamless whole and our love takes on a sharper focus.

Meditation books have traditionally recommended a structure of prayer for beginners. While details may vary, it essentially involves three stages: the remote preparation, the immediate preparation and the actual meditation itself. Let us assume that we choose to make our meditation in the morning. This is often the best time, before our minds are filled with the concerns and distractions of the day. In this case, the remote preparation—reading over the scripture passage we are going to pray about, and consulting one of the commentaries to clarify the context and the basic message of the passage which we have chosen—would take place the evening before. This remote preparation, along with our daily spiritual reading, plays a very important role

---

[5]The First Vatican Council, Dogmatic Constitution *Dei Filius* on the Catholic Faith, Chapter IV. Quoted in *The Christian Faith in the Doctrinal Documents of the Catholic Church,* eds. J. Neuner, S.J., and J. Dupuis, S.J., volume I, p. 48.

in opening and sensitizing our minds to the things of God.[6] Without this remote preparation, we will not be doing what we can to open ourselves to God. We will be coming to prayer too casually, taking God for granted. And it is unlikely that we will hear his word in this way.

The immediate preparation for prayer is what we do when we are ready to begin to pray. St. Ignatius recommends that we stand back from the place where we are going to pray, and take a moment to recall the passage or theme we are to pray about, and then recall what a wondrous thing it is that we seek to do. I have found a short prayer like the following very helpful: "Lord, I realize that you are truly present and anxious to teach me to pray. You care more for me than I care for myself. Help me to realize the wonder of your speaking to me, and to respond as generously as possible." The purpose of this short prayer is that I may come before the Lord reverently and attentively, as his holiness demands.

The remote and immediate preparations for prayer are very important, especially for beginners. The form they take may vary, of course. Perhaps the best way for the beginner is to start with some such format as I have described. Then, with experience, one can adapt it to one's own temperament and needs. The goal is to come to prayer prepared to hear the Lord, and reverently attentive to his word. To paraphrase St. Teresa, good preparation is whatever most helps us to pray well—whatever most moves us to love God.[7]

---

[6]I have found it important to stress to beginners that good spiritual reading is that which moves the will and not merely the understanding. The purpose of spiritual reading is to inspire us to act—to seek the Lord and commit ourselves to his service. Thus, good biographies of saints, and of great contemporary men and women of God, are excellent spiritual reading.

[7]*Interior Castle,* Fourth Mansions, Chapter 1: "The important thing is not to think much but to love much; do, then, whatever most arouses you to love." As we noted above (p. 63), in speaking of techniques for coming to quiet, the same flexibility should guide our choice of a place and a posture for prayer.

The third stage of the traditional schema of prayer is the actual prayer itself. This is what we have called meditation, and have described as the use of our understanding to come to know God more fully, in order that we may love him more ardently and follow him more faithfully. Actually, in the history of spirituality there has never been any one terminology universally accepted by all authors on prayer. Most use the word "meditation" more or less as we have used it above. Whatever the words chosen, the same essential points about the beginnings of prayer are found in all the Christian masters of prayer. But I have found it helpful to make a distinction here, between meditation and contemplation.[8] The basis of the distinction is this: Man is endowed with an understanding or reasoning faculty and with an imagination, and both faculties can be employed in coming to know someone or something better. Reasoning is more logical, more abstract; it considers causes and draws conclusions, often step by step. Imagination is more concrete, more specific; it sees a single event or situation in its concrete totality. Reason sees the logical links between events or actions ("The guitar is off-key; it must need tuning"), whereas imagination enters into, gets the feel of an actual experience ("What a strange feeling of desolation I get when I hear that guitar playing off-key!").

As we said, all of us are endowed with faculties both of reasoning and of imagination, and both faculties help us to know reality in different, but complementary, ways.

---

[8]The distinction between meditation and contemplation which follows is implicit in St. Ignatius' use of the words in *The Spiritual Exercises.* John of the Cross and Teresa of Avila tend to use the word meditation to cover both activities, because they use the word contemplation to describe a later stage of prayer in which God takes over and we are more passive or receptive. Authors have tried to clarify the situation by distinguishing between acquired contemplation (the beginner's type which we are discussing) and infused contemplation (the more advanced stage of prayer where God takes over more and more). We will say a word about infused contemplation in the Epilogue.

It often happens, though, that one faculty is dominant in a given person. Artists are often said to be more imaginative, and scientists to be more rational—although Bach or Mozart is much more "rational" than Brahms or Beethoven, and a creative scientist like Pasteur or Einstein must possess a strong imaginative faculty. Women are probably more imaginative, as a whole, than men, who tend to be more logical. I have learned that Filipinos—and perhaps Southeast Asians in general—are generally far more imaginative than their more analytical American or Chinese friends. The important point here is that men and women, not only groups but individuals, vary greatly in the mix of reasoning and imagination which they bring to the interpretation of their experience.

This is an important insight for beginners in prayer. We can come to know the Lord via our reasoning or via our imagination, or, more likely, via a very personal blend of the two. This is the basis of the distinction I have suggested between meditation and contemplation. Meditation is the use of the understanding, the reasoning faculty, to come to know God's revelation better, whereas contemplation is the use of the imagination to achieve the same end. Since both are good techniques for coming to know the Lord, and since some people will find one more helpful and some the other, let us discuss each more fully.

We can begin with meditation. And since, as we have said, the primary source of our knowledge of the Lord is scripture, let us take a passage from the Gospel of St. John as an illustrative example.[9] A very beautiful passage is the story of the Samaritan woman at the well in John 4. Jesus has been journeying through Samaria, the region between Galilee and Judea, and has sat down to rest beside Jacob's well. The disciples have gone into the nearby city of Sychar

---

[9]It is very helpful to choose as the subject of our meditation or contemplation the gospel passage from the liturgy of the day. In this way, the liturgy is enriched and made deeper by the reflections of our time of private prayer.

91

to buy food, so Jesus is alone at the well. A woman of the neighborhood comes to draw water at the well, and Jesus asks her for a drink. She is surprised that he would speak to a strange woman in public, especially since the Jews and the Samaritans were enemies. She expresses her puzzlement at his request, and Jesus replies by referring to the far better water which he could give her. This leads into the famous dialogue about the water of eternal life—a dialogue which results in the conversion of the woman and of many of her townmates. It is a very human passage, and one which brings out the simplicity of the woman and the gentleness of Jesus. Let us see how we would meditate on the incident.

Recall that meditation means using our reasoning to come to know God better. Here it would mean reflecting on the behavior of Jesus in this very concrete situation, and on the words he speaks to the woman, to discover more of God's ways with men. Why does Jesus speak to a strange woman, particularly to one who has had five husbands and is now living with a man not her husband, and who must have had a rather low standing in her town? What does this say about the way God judges people, as contrasted with the judgments of men? What implications does this have for the way I should deal with people if I am truly to follow Christ? Again what does Jesus mean by living water?[10] The woman misunderstands him. She thinks he has a secret source of natural water, but he very patiently uses her misunderstanding to teach her about the water of the Spirit. How deeply do I feel the desire for the living water of the Spirit? What in my life corresponds

---

[10]This is an instance where a good commentary—for example *The New Testament Reading Guide* series, Barclay or Peale, can be a great help in preparing for our prayer. "Living water" meant water that was flowing, as from a spring, which was very valuable in a semidesert country like Palestine, where stagnant water was dangerous and flowing water was scarce. Jesus uses flowing, life-giving water as a symbol for the inner "water" which gives life to our souls.

to the five and a half husbands of the Samaritan woman—
i.e., what blocks me from truly encountering Christ in my
life? How has the Lord used that very obstacle to reach
out to me? It is often said that we become most aware of
God when we are weakest and most aware of our sinfulness.[11] But not all sinners hear God's voice. What is there
about the Samaritan woman's attitudes which makes her
very sinfulness the basis for her encounter with Jesus?

The incident in John 4 is a rich and beautiful source
of meditative prayer, and our reflections above have only
scratched the surface of its treasure for the pray-er. But
perhaps we have said enough to make clear what meditation is: a reflective searching of the scriptures to discover
what God reveals of himself in the person of Jesus, and to
learn by analogy how he is speaking in the events of one's
own life. As Jesus tells Thomas, "I am the way, and the
truth, and the life; no one comes to the Father, but by me.
If you had known me you would have known my Father
also . . ." (Jn 14:6-7). Philip still does not understand,
and he says, "Lord, show us the Father, and we shall
be satisfied." But Jesus insists that "He who has seen me
has seen the Father" (14:9). This is the very heart of the
Christian faith: "No one has ever seen God: the only Son,
who is in the bosom of the Father, he has made him
known" (Jn 1:18). Jesus is *the* revelation of the Father for
men of flesh and blood. It is by studying his life—his
values, his attitudes, his ways of dealing with men—that
we learn who God is for us.[12]

In meditation, however, we reflect not merely on the
historical life of Jesus and the experience of the evangelists
and apostles. We also reflect on how God reveals himself
in our lives today. Jesus is the "firstborn of many breth-

---

[11]St. John of the Cross, in the *Spiritual Canticle* (stanza IV,
Exposition), says that we *first* encounter God in our sinfulness, and
only then in the goodness of creatures, and only lastly in himself.

[12]See also I Jn 4:9-15; Heb 1:3; I Pt 2:21; Rom 8:29; 2 Cor
4:4-6.

93

ren," and we are called to "have this mind among you, which is yours in Christ Jesus," to "put on the Lord Jesus Christ."[13] Thus meditation is not merely a reflective historical study of a past figure—no matter how important we may consider that historical figure to be. It is an attempt to discover, by means of the life and teaching of Jesus, how God is revealing himself through Christ in the events of our life today. Some of the questions we raised in our consideration of the Samaritan woman bring out this link between Jesus' early life and our search for God today.

As we have described it, meditation is the use of our reasoning powers. We said earlier that there is another, equally valid, way to come to know the Lord: contemplation. Contemplation is more imaginative, and is often helpful for those who find difficult the type of analytic reasoning we have described as meditation. The story of the Samaritan woman can be useful here, since it lends itself as easily to contemplation as to meditation. Let us contrast the two approaches by seeing what it would mean to contemplate the incident at the well.

Contemplation involves imaginatively entering into the incident we are considering—being present at the event, seeing it happen as if we were actually participants ourselves. This is a much easier task for children of a visual culture such as ours. Movies and TV draw us into an event, a story, in a way which the printed word cannot often duplicate.[14] In fact, I have found it very helpful to explain contemplation by likening it to our experience of a movie. Why is it that we weep at a tragic movie? Surely not because a piece of film is running through a projector, or because certain shadows are appearing on a screen! This is what is actually happening at the time, but there is

---

[13]Rom 8:29; Rom 13:14; Phil 2:5.

[14]It is true that a skilled storyteller, whether live or in print, has always been one who can totally involve his hearers in the story. But even news events have an immediacy, an emotional impact on TV which they never achieve on the front page of a newspaper.

nothing to cry about in that. Why, then, do we cry? Because we ourselves have become imaginatively involved in the story: we relive it in some way ourselves. We make our own the attitudes and feelings of the actors with whom we identify. We know how they feel because we feel and experience with them. We come to experience a long-lasting sense of kinship with characters from our favorite movies. Somehow they become part of our lives.

Contemplation is like this. We bring our human powers of imagination to our prayer, and we seek to relive, not some movie, but the life of the Lord Jesus. In our example, we seek to be present at the well when Jesus meets the woman. Perhaps we are sitting beside him as she comes walking along the road. We notice his face (he is "weary"). We see what a woman looks like who has had five and a half husbands, and who is tired of having to come to the well day after day. We feel the heat of the noonday sun in this semitropical land. We notice the shape of the stones in this ancient well, believed by tradition to date back more than a thousand years to Jacob. And then Jesus speaks to this strange woman. We hear his words, note the tone of his voice, observe the surprised look on the face of the woman. We listen, and look, as their dialogue unfolds—and we imagine how we would have reacted had we been in the woman's place. Perhaps we share her puzzlement at Jesus' reference to living water. Perhaps we find ourselves involved in the conversation, asking the Lord our own questions about eternal life, asking the woman what the Lord really said to her. She tells the people of Sychar that he told her "everything I have ever done"—which goes far beyond the conversation actually recorded in the Gospel. What would it mean to meet someone who tells *us* everything we have ever done? We may even, in our contemplation, find ourselves remaining at the well with Jesus, when the woman hurries off to town to tell the people—and we may learn by experience what it means to have him tell *us* everything we have ever done.

95

Like meditation, contemplation is not merely an imaginative reliving of the past. In experiencing with the Lord the concrete situations of his life, we come to discover how he is living and working in our lives. We too meet him sitting beside a well. We also recognize him in the breaking of the bread (Lk 24:35), and our imaginative reliving of the Gospel event gives way to our own encounter with the Lord. This element of personal encounter, of personal involvement, is what makes both meditation and contemplation different from the knowledge that the theologian or the historian, as such, might have of the same Gospel event. This *personal* knowledge is what makes meditation and contemplation properly prayer—i.e., part of the whole process by which we encounter God in love.

That is why the traditional manuals of prayer recommend that, right from the beginning, we end our prayer with a colloquy or conversation with the Lord. When we begin, the colloquy will be somewhat awkward and stilted, like a conversation with a stranger. But as we come to know God better, the colloquy will become more spontaneous and natural. Gradually the colloquy will become the substance of our prayer, as knowledge gives way to love. Then there will be less and less need for meditation or contemplation. Our primary need will be to be with the Lord, whom we have come to know and love—and that, as we have said, is the essence of prayer.

This makes clear the first important warning we must give concerning meditation and contemplation. They are the beginnings of a good prayer life, but reasoning and imagining are not ends in themselves. Prayer is not simply a lifetime process of understanding the Gospel and making applications to our lives. Nor is it a lifetime of imaginative involvement in the events of Christ's life. Too much stress on speculation and analysis would lead to an abstract and sterile concern with the "logic" of the Gospel. Too much stress on the imagination would lead to a false visionary kind of spirituality, which spent its time discovering what color cloak Jesus was wearing at the well, or how old the woman was. Both would wrap us up too much in ourselves and our own thoughts, and not open us enough to the transforming of God's word in our lives.

Another caution: fruitful meditation or contemplation is an art, and thus is not so much taught as it is learned by experience. Although we use our own faculties of reasoning and imagination, the knowledge we seek is ultimately God's gift. We should be willing to experiment with the approaches I have described, and to discover what is most suited to our own temperament and to the gospel passage we are praying over. Some passages (such as Jesus' discussion with the Pharisees about divorce or the beatitudes) are much more suited to meditation. Other passages (such as the raising of Lazarus or the annunciation) are ideally suited to contemplation. Many passages, such as the woman at the well, can be fruitfully prayed over in either way. These latter passages can be very helpful in learning which approach is more suited to your own temperament and needs.

Too often in the past, meditation has been presented as the *only* way for beginners. As a result, many people have found prayer extremely difficult, and have felt they were unable to meditate. Perhaps the reason why contemplation was avoided is because we thought of the imagination as too physical, too carnal—and too likely to lead us into temptation. But the imagination is an integral part of man, and many of the great pray-ers have been richly imaginative people. Grace builds on nature: it does not destroy it. What we must learn to do is to channel and discipline or imagination and our other faculties, not to kill them. If you tame a wild and spirited horse, you have something of great value. If you tame a timid horse you don't have much. If you kill a spirited horse, you have nothing but a carcass. This is why the active purification of the soul—which, along with the techniques for coming to quiet, is the taming of the wild horse in each of us—must always be employed only insofar as it contributes to our experience in prayer. Dispositive techniques are, as we have stressed before, means to an end. The end or goal is to encounter God and to respond authentically to his love.

Similarly, contemplation and meditation are means to an end. They are ways of coming to know the Lord in order that we may truly love him—not merely in word but in action. As such they will not normally continue throughout a whole life of prayer, just as courtship will not normally continue throughout the whole of married life. To put it more accurately, while the element of coming to know the Lord will continue in some way throughout life —just as a loving husband and wife never know each other "inside out" and are always discovering more about the mystery of each other—still it will later cease to play the dominant role it plays in the courtship period. We will say a word about what happens later in the Epilogue to this book; it takes us beyond this introduction to prayer. What is important here, however, is to realize that prayer is life. Like all life, it changes, it evolves.

There is evolution even within what we may call the beginner's state of prayer. There may be an initial infatuation with the Lord, corresponding to what, in human relations, we call love at first sight. As we seek to learn, by meditation and/or contemplation, who this mysterious person is to whom we are drawn, infatuation or emotional attraction gives way to a more sober knowledge of the Lord. He is *not* what our feelings would like him to be. Human lovers discover that the one they love is flawed and imperfect, and is very different from their romantic image. God is not flawed and imperfect, but he is different from our expectations. Every pray-er must learn, as the apostles did, that God is a very different savior from what they naturally expect. The sons of Zebedee sought glory and he offered them the cross.[15] Peter wanted to remain on Tabor,

---

[15]Mt 20:20-23.

but Jesus led him to Calvary.[16] At the very end of his earthly sojourning among them, they expected a political revolution to liberate Israel, but Jesus ascended to the right hand of the Father and left them, for a time, alone.[17] The God they learned to love was far different from the God they wanted to love! So it must be with us.

Coming to know the Lord is different for another reason also: He does not speak as men speak, with a voice we can hear with our ears. We do not look into his face as a boy and a girl courting can look into each other's faces. For this reason, beginners find meditation or contemplation laborious. Despite their sincere efforts, their attention span is short in seeking to know an invisible God. How often, in retreats, I have proposed to beginners a chapter, such as John 4, which is rich in insight. After an hour they return to say they finished that chapter in 10 minutes—and did not know what to do next! To dig deeper is laborious for beginners, and often seems boring.

The first time I had this experience, in a lay retreat in Syracuse, New York, I felt perhaps I was expecting too much of laymen—or perhaps that the style of prayer I was proposing was too much geared to religious. When the same problem recurred with sister-novices in the U.S., and with seminarians in the Philippines, I began to realize that the problem was a normal one for beginners. When these same people, as I had the chance to work longer with them, began to discover the riches of the scriptures and the God who is there revealing himself, it became clearer and clearer to me that this is a normal problem, and should not cause us discouragement. If we persevere, patiently and peacefully returning to our prayer whenever we become aware of being distracted, our perseverance will ultimately bear fruit. The time will come when it becomes easy and joyous to pray, and when the insights of our meditation and contemplation flow smoothly and almost

---

[16]Mk 9:4-9.
[17]Acts 1:6-9.

spontaneously. The riches of the scriptures will flow easily from the pages of the Gospels. There will be a new depth to our experience which makes prayer a joy. The same chapter which, in the beginning, was exhausted in 10 minutes, will provide more fruitful insights than we can digest in a day. We begin to see links between various gospel incidents. The Gospels become, not a series of isolated events touching diverse themes, but a portrait of a whole and very real person, Jesus Christ. We begin to discover, in him, the face of God for us.

When will this happen, and what does it mean? Each of us is unique, of course, and our experiences vary with our needs and with God's designs for us. But this new ease and joy in meditating will often come within the first year or two of a faithful and persevering life of prayer. It means that we are coming to be at home with the Lord, and that he is responding to our fidelity by guiding and deepening our thoughts. It will seem to us, at this point, that we have truly learned how to pray—that now, in fact, we have mastered the secret of the interior life and are well on our way to holiness. The truth, however, is that "no eye has seen, nor ear heard, nor the heart of man conceived, what God has prepared for those who love him."[18] We are only beginning to discover what the Spirit has to teach us of God—but it is a very good beginning.

---

[18] I Cor 2:9; cf. Is 64:4.

Epilogue:

Prayer Beyond the Beginnings

For some years I have taught a course on apostolic prayer. In one class, not many years ago, there was a sister who belonged to a contemplative community. We became friends, and I was privileged to become her director as well. One day, toward the end of the course, when we were discussing some of the points I had made in class, she said: "I found your lectures very helpful, but I wish you had said more about the *goal* of the interior life—where it is all leading, what the end result will be." I was puzzled and challenged by her comment, and we discussed it several times thereafter. In one sense, I felt I could not say any more about the goal than had already been said; all the saints, including John of the Cross, become strangely inarticulate when they come to describe the state of union with God which is the threshold to eternity.[1] How could I say anything when they were reduced to silence?

In another sense, I knew her question was valid and needed an answer. Knowing the goal of our journey is an

---

[1] See John of the Cross, *Living Flame of Love*, Stanza IV, par. 17.

essential condition of discernment: only if we know where we are going can we be confident we are on the right road. My attempts to formulate that answer—for myself, at least —have proven very fruitful to my own life and to my work as a spiritual director. What can *not* be described, I believe, is the *experience* of God which he gives to those whom he has wedded to himself. St. Paul acknowledged this when he sought to justify his mission by saying that he had once "been caught up into paradise"; he says of his experience that he "heard things that cannot be told, which man may not utter" (2 Cor 12:3-4). Earlier in the same letter (9:15) he concludes an appeal for support for the needy churches by contrasting the donations of the Corinthians with the incomparably greater gifts of God to them: "Thanks be to God for his *inexpressible* gift," which is the surpassing grace of God in them. The fullness of the experience of God is beyond words.

What can be expressed, however, is what the experience of God is *not*—and also what the manifest fruits of this gift should be in the here and now. In Chapter 6, I quoted a passage from St. Teresa's *Interior Castle* which has long been a favorite of mine: "The important thing is not to think much but to love much: do, then, whatever most arouses you to love." Teresa then goes on to clarify what precisely this love is, which we seek:

> Perhaps we do not know what love is: it would not surprise me a great deal to learn this, for love consists, not in the extent of our happiness, but in the firmness of our determination to try to please God in everything, and to endeavor, in all possible ways, not to offend Him, and to pray Him ever to advance the honor and glory of His Son and the growth of the Catholic Church.[2]

---

[2]The *Interior Castle,* Fourth Mansions, Chapter 1 (vol. 2, p. 233 in the Peers edition).

To love in this way—unselfishly, courageously and with a genuine passion for God's will "on earth and in heaven"—is the real goal of our life of prayer. St. Paul spells it out when he enumerates the fruit of the Spirit: love, joy, peace, patience, kindness, goodness, faithfulness, gentleness, and self-control.[3] These are the manifest fruits of a genuine prayer life. If we are growing in these, we are on the right road. To possess them perfectly, by the working of the Holy Spirit in us, is the goal of our prayer. The experience of God is not measured or validated by visions, ecstasies, magnificent insights or floods of tears. These phenomena may have their place for the edification of the Church and the encouragement of the pray-er, but they are not necessary to genuine holiness. In fact they are not even infallibly from God: their genuineness must be tested by the fruits of the Spirit we mentioned above. An ecstatic or a visionary who lacked deep peace and joy, real gentleness and self-control in his or her dealings with others, would make any good director very suspicious!

In this context, it might be helpful to say a word about *infused* contemplation, which we described briefly in a footnote to Chapter 6 (page 90). Recall first that we spoke in the Introduction of those spontaneous moments of prayer when, indeliberately as it were, we are aware of God's presence to us. Such moments may occur, even in the life of a beginner in prayer—in fact, even in the life of someone who would not consider himself a pray-er at all. As we stressed throughout the book, these encounters—these personal encounters with God in love—are the very essence of prayer at every stage of our development. All our talk of techniques, of meditation and (imaginative) contemplation, of coming to quiet and penance and the examen, was based on the conviction that these are the ways we *normally* can learn to respond to God *habitually*—to open ourselves to an *abiding* experience of his presence in our lives.

----

[3]Gal 5:22-23.

We might say that those occasional, indeliberate moments of contact with the Lord of Love which mark the early stages of a life of prayer are precisely God's way of drawing us to a deeper, because habitual, experience of his presence.

Put in this way, the whole point of Part II of this book has been to ask how we can best *respond* to God's initial drawing. "No one can come to me," Jesus says, "unless the Father who sent me draws him" (Jn 6:44).[4] Our efforts are vain unless God first comes to us. But if and when he comes, how do we respond so that his gracious initiative can bear full fruit in our lives? This is the principal question we have sought to answer in this book.

Now, as we respond to God in the dialogue of love which is our life of prayer and service, the time may come when God takes over more and more—when, in terms of our analogy of dialogue, we do less and less of the talking and God does more and more. We become passive (to use the term of the saints); we become more and more like the clay in the hand of the potter (Jer 18:6) to be shaped and molded by him. From the very beginning, God's grace is essential to any prayer, to any response of ours; but the time *may*[5] come when he not only gives us the grace to seek him, but himself does the work in us. This is what is known as infused contemplation, where, according to the theologians, not only is God's grace at work, but our very

[4]See also Jn 3:27; 6:65; 15:16; 17:9. Along with the correlative idea that "no one comes to the Father except through me" (Jn 14:6), this total dependence on God's drawing is a dominant theme of Jesus' preaching in John.

[5]I say "may" here because this passivity is a special and rather advanced experience in the interior life. John of the Cross, the master of higher stages of prayer, insists that it is sheerly gratuitous and that it may not be the experience of all—or even most—faithful pray-ers. For myself, I suspect that it is the normal terminus of a real life of prayer—but it is certainly a sheer gift of God, to which we have no right, and (barring a miracle of grace) it would come only after years of a more active response by the pray-er to God's word.

way of knowing him transcends our human powers of knowing and loving. Because our natural faculties are suspended, it is a "dark night," a "cloud of unknowing."

This discussion of infused contemplation may seem obscure and confusing to a beginner in prayer. If so, it is because this is not yet a part of his own experience. I mention it here, however, to give some faint outline of the road ahead in the life of prayer. Another, and more important, reason is to stress that the goal of *all* good prayer, no matter how elementary or how advanced it may be, is to transform our lives, to deepen and strengthen our love of God in action. Whatever our stage of interior growth may be, the growth in the fruits of the Spirit is the only touchstone of genuine prayer.

This knowledge of the goal of our prayers can help us to understand the way God normally leads us. We said that the way of beginners is usually meditation or contemplation, whereby they come to know who God is—to acquire that knowledge which is the necessary basis of genuine love. Toward the end of the last chapter, we said that the first breakthrough in our life of prayer is when our meditation or contemplation becomes easy and joyous. When we find much fruit in just a few verses of scripture, and when the Lord Jesus begins to be a real person for us. This breakthrough, which may come after a year or two of a serious life of prayer, may usher in a period lasting, with ups and downs, for several years. As I said, we are tempted to think we have truly grown: God is near and dear to us, practicing virtue is easy, and no sacrifice seems too costly if it is for him. We feel quite holy!

For example, at this time, failings in us which have been particularly deep-rooted—envy, irritability, a strong and unruly imagination—may suddenly disappear. We feel that we have finally mastered the dark side of ourselves, and are free of these faults forever. The real situation is quite different. It is not that we have grown so much but that God is spoiling us—in order to win us to himself.

106

The image I often use is that of a father and his year-old child. The baby has learned how to crawl all about the house. He has become a very skilled crawler. Then one day the father decides to carry the baby for a walk. As they walk out the door and down the street, the baby is very excited. Up to now his whole world has been knees and ankles and the bottoms of tables. Suddenly he sees things from his father's shoulder—and moves with the speed of his father's feet. If you have noticed a baby taken for a walk, you have seen that the baby usually thinks *he* is really accomplishing something himself. He kicks and pushes in his father's arms as if his feet were doing the work. When they return home, and Papa puts baby down on the floor again, the baby is frustrated. Left to himself, he can only crawl. It is not merely that the baby is right back where he started. Before the walk, crawling was all he knew and he was contented with it. Now he knows something better is possible, and crawling is no longer enough to satisfy him. He is, in a sense, worse off than he was before he discovered what fun walking can be.

It is like this in the early stages of our life of prayer. God is the father, and we are the baby. When we begin to make progress, it is not because we have learned to walk but because God is carrying us. Like the baby, however, we tend to think we have really accomplished something ourselves. When prayer becomes a joy and our faults disappear, we think it is a sign that we have really learned to walk in the ways of God. The reality is quite different: God is carrying us in his arms. Our faults (our inability to walk) have not been eliminated, but merely temporarily masked by God's grace. He, too, like the father of the baby, sets us down again—prayer becomes difficult and our failings return, and we find our whole situation very frustrating. Once we have known the joy of walking with the Lord, we can never again be satisfied with crawling on our bellies on the earth.

This is a critical and dangerous turning point in our

life of prayer. It is humiliating to realize that, left to ourselves, we are only good for crawling. We are tempted to
feel that our experience of prayer must have been self-
deception, that God has abandoned us, that prayer is a
waste of time for us. None of this is true, of course, but
the devil works overtime to convince us that we are failures.
Sound spiritual direction and regular reading in the masters
of prayer[6] are essential if we are to overcome the devil and
our own wounded pride.

If we recall the goal of the life of prayer—the fruits
of the Spirit grounded in a true knowledge of who God is
and who I am—we can realize that what looks like failure
is really growth. By carrying us in his arms for a time, the
Lord has taught us that there is another world, far better
than the crawler's world of man left to himself. By setting
us down again, the Lord teaches us that this new world is
not within our own power to reach. It is here that our
father-baby analogy breaks down. The baby *will* gradually learn to walk for himself. The day will come when he
is as tall as his father and can walk about the world on his
own strong legs. But in the realm of prayer we are *always*
babies, and we will always be carried on our Father's arms.
The "little way" of the Little Flower, Therese of Lisieux,
is ultimately the only way. This is precisely what she
meant, that holiness is not the result of heroic efforts to
improve ourselves but is the sheer gift of God's transforming love. Once we really learn this, the "dark night" will
end and the Lord will lift us up to carry us forever.

How long will it take for us to learn this? John of the
Cross, who calls the frustrating experience of our own
helplessness and God's absence the "dark night of the
senses," says that it is the lot of most faithful pray-ers for
most of their lives. The Lord will pick us up from time to

---

[6]Boase's *Prayer of Faith*, Teresa's *Interior Castle* (Second and
Third Mansions), John of the Cross's *Dark Night of the Soul*
(Book I), and Merton's *Contemplative Prayer* are very helpful
guides at this crucial stage of the interior life.

time. There will be occasional glimmers of light in the darkness, to reassure us and to strengthen us to persevere. But the principal proof of the genuineness of our prayer—the evidence that we are on the right track despite the darkness—will be the growth in us of the fruits of the Spirit. Do I find myself—today as compared, say, to a year or two years ago—more humble, more sensitive to the needs of others, with a deeper hunger for God and for his justice among men, gentler in dealing with human frailty? If I do, then my prayer is genuine and I am on the right track, for these are the fruits of the Spirit of God. This kind of growth can come only from him.

Given these signs, we can proceed peacefully in darkness and leave all else to the Lord. He alone knows how long the log of wood needs to be scorched and blackened before it is ready to become fire. He alone is the Lord. Teresa of Avila expresses it beautifully in the last of her "Exclamations of the Soul to God":

> Blessed are those whose names are written in the book of . . . life. But if thou are among them, my soul, why art thou sad and why dost thou trouble me? Hope in God, for even now I will confess to Him my sins and His mercies and of them all I will make a song of praise and will breathe perpetual sighs to my Savior and my God. It may be that a day will come when my glory shall sing to Him and my conscience shall be no more afflicted, when at last all sighs and fears shall cease. But meanwhile in silence and in hope shall my strength be. Rather would I live and die in the expectation and hope of eternal life than possess all created things and all the blessings which belong to them, since these must pass away. Forsake me not, Lord; since I hope in Thee, may my hope not be confounded; may I ever serve Thee; do with me what Thou wilt.[7]

---

[7]*Exclamations of the Soul to God,* XVII (vol. II, p. 420 in the Peers edition).

The experience is very different from what we expected when we began to learn to pray. But our God is a God of surprises. To encounter the Lord personally in love is to be captured by him—and to be carried in his arms.

DISCOVERING
VINTAGE
San Francisco

A Guide to the City's Timeless Eateries, Bars, Shops & More

LAURA SMITH BORRMAN

Globe
Pequot

Guilford, Connecticut

All the information in this guidebook is subject to change. We recommend that you call ahead to obtain current information before traveling.

Globe
Pequot

An imprint of Rowman & Littlefield

Distributed by NATIONAL BOOK NETWORK

The Discovering Vintage series was created by Mitch Broder, the author of *Discovering Vintage New York: A Guide to the City's Timeless Shops, Bars, Delis & More.*

All modern photos were taken by Brandon Borrman, with the exception of those for Liguria Bakery, Golden Gate Fortune Cookie Factory, The Magazine, McRoskey Mattress Company, Tommaso's Italian Restaurant, and Swan Oyster Depot, which were taken by the author. All other photos are courtesy of those credited within the essays. Mechanic's Institute photo by Brandon Borrman printed with establishment's permission.

British Library Cataloguing in Publication Information Available

Library of Congress Cataloging-in-Publication Data

Borrman, Laura Smith.
   Discovering vintage San Francisco : a guide to the city's timeless eateries, bars, shops & more / Laura Smith Borrman. — First edition.
      pages cm
   Includes index.
   ISBN 978-1-4930-1264-0 (pbk.) — ISBN 978-1-4930-1402-6 (e-book) 1. Restaurants—California—San Francisco—Directories. 2. Stores, Retail—California—San Francisco—Directories. 3. San Francisco (Calif.)—Description and travel. I. Title.
   TX907.3.C22S36185 2015
   647.95794'61—dc23
                              2015015987

♾™ The paper used in this publication meets the minimum requirements of American National Standard for Information Sciences—Permanence of Paper for Printed Library Materials, ANSI/NISO Z39.48-1992.

Contents

Introduction viii

Alfred's Steakhouse. 1

Anchor Brewing Company. 5

Aub Zam Zam. 10

Benkyodo Company 14

Buena Vista Cafe 19

Cable Car Clothiers. 23

City Lights Booksellers & Publishers 27

Cliff House. 31

Cliff's Variety 35

Dianda's Italian American Pastry Co. 39

Fior d'Italia. 43

Fishermen's Grotto No. 9. 47

Garden Court 52

Golden Gate Fortune Cookie Factory 57

Grubstake 61

Gump's. 65

House of Prime Rib 69

House of Shields 73

It's Tops Coffee Shop. 78

John's Grill 84

Lefty O'Doul's 88

Liguria Bakery 92

Li Po Cocktail Lounge 96

The Magazine 101

Mario's Bohemian Cigar Store Cafe 104

McRoskey Mattress Company 108

Mechanics' Institute Library & Chess Room 112

The Old Clam House 116

Original Joe's 120

The Original Tommy's Joynt 123

Piedmont Boutique 127

Pied Piper Bar and Grill 132

Pier 23 Cafe 137

Red's Java House 142

The Roosevelt Tamale Parlor 146

Sam Jordan's Bar 150

Sam's Grill 153

Schroeder's 157

Scoma's 160

Sears Fine Food 164

Shreve & Co. 167

Swan Oyster Depot 172

Tadich Grill 176

Tommaso's Italian Restaurant 181

Tonga Room & Hurricane Bar 184

Top of the Mark 189

Tosca Cafe. 192

Twin Peaks Tavern .197

Vesuvio. 202

Wilkes Bashford. 207

Appendix A: Featured Places by Category 215

Appendix B: Featured Places by Neighborhood 220

Appendix C: Featured Places by Year of Origin 223

Index 227

About the Author

For Brandon, Sadie, and Dashiell

California native Laura Smith Borrman is writer, editor, and lover of food and drink and the story behind the thing, especially when those things are old. She has worked in many industries, including in bakeries, culinary travel, public radio, research, and the corporate world, and loves sharing people's stories. She's also now a mother of two and lives with her husband and children in Oakland. This is her second book. Read her blog at discoveringvintagesanfrancisco.com.

Acknowledgments

redit goes to many for the completion of this book, a feat that felt impossible when I embarked on the project in the third trimester of pregnancy with my second child. Thank you first to my husband, Brandon, for juggling family and career to make sure I finished this—and especially, for the beautiful photos he took that illuminate my words on these vintage establishments. And to my kids, Sadie and Dashiell, for reminding me of what matters. To all the cafes in San Francisco and Oakland with outdoor tables where I wrote feverishly with a little baby in tow, thanks for your patience. On the same note, Renata and Tom Dorn of Mar Vista Cottages, we are forever indebted for your little slice of heaven. Thank you, as always, to my parents, Roberta and Calvin Smith, for their love and support and extreme dog care, and to my sister, Emily, and my extended family and friends for their awesomeness (especially Cori Tahara, who ate a lot of focaccia with me for research). And to Chiub Saephanh, we are so grateful for you. Thanks to editor extraordinaire Tracee Williams, whose support, positive attitude, flexibility, and critical eye made this both possible and readable. And to Meredith Dias, for her fantastic editorial work. To Hilda Chen, who provoked great thought about the city's history and retail landscape—thank you. And to all of the business owners, longtime employees, devoted patrons, and city protectors—you are the reason a book like this can exist.

Introduction

I remember the famous Tony Bennett song running through in my head as I crossed the Bay Bridge for what I thought would be the last time for a long time nearly 20 years ago. It was the late 1990s, and I was moving away after living in "The City" with a close friend following college. We'd had a marvelous year, and even though we were young at the time, we somehow knew then how special and rare it was to be able to have an experience like we'd had. Childhood friends sharing a gorgeous, bay-window-fronted apartment at the intersection of Haight and Ashbury, a historic street corner that was bustling with activity day and night, all in one of the greatest cities in the world. The time felt full of possibility, in an era before tech-fueled skyrocketing rents, and we were confident, unencumbered by real responsibility, and happy the way you are when you feel like you're on the edge of your future. The chapter was ending—I was going on to a job in another city—and even though it was by my own choosing, I felt nostalgic for the experience we'd just had.

As I hummed about leaving my heart in San Francisco, I looked back at the tightly packed buildings that make up the urban dollhouse-like skyline of the City by the Bay. I suddenly felt like I understood the sentiment of the song that I'd heard so much, but never really thought about before.

Working on this book has revived these feelings, as I live in the area once again, just across the water in Oakland, proud of my new East Bay roots but rediscovering what I've always loved about San Francisco. It's a city of hippies, artists, activists, and great thinkers. It has seen a tech boom—twice. It's the home of countless immigrants from Mexico, Italy, Germany, Greece, Japan, China, and so many other places, and has been the center of important movements, for gay rights, against war, and in celebration of sexual freedom. It is the home of the rich and the poor, the young and the old, the criminal and the law-abiding, and has survived natural disasters of gargantuan size. And it is a place of sheer physical beauty—from its architecture to its hills and glorious sea-surrounded location.

Over the last year, I've learned that the proprietors of each of the vintage establishments featured in this book represent that striking diversity and color, the vivid history, and the ability to survive, and they seem to hold Bennett's song in their own hearts, even if subconsciously.

They are family people, entrepreneurs, and pursuers of the American dream. They are movers and shakers in a city that measures just 7-by-7 miles but is one of the most densely populated in the country. They love business, many of them inheriting their own from family. They are engaged civically and philanthropically, their genuine care for the city apparent in their many extracurricular activities.

Their businesses are at least 50 years old, many of them much older than that. There are a few exceptions, purposely selected to represent some important newer eras that helped define the city. All of these businesses are old by modern standards—even those founded in the 1970s—but still thriving, managing to preserve the past while staying relevant and appealing for modern society. And they are not only a part of the community but they helped shape the way it looks today.

And they are, in some cases, an endangered species. Faced with skyrocketing rents or the lack of a next generation that will take over—and in some cases, both—these special little spots may not be available to visit forever.

What is included in the following pages is not an exhaustive list. There are other San Francisco vintage spots that are just as fascinating and worthy of your attention (check out sfheritage.org/legacy/ for more). But a book forces decision making to fit word counts—not every interesting, old spot could be included—and, therefore, it is by nature subjective. I endeavored for a solid assortment, representing various neighborhoods, communities, and types of business. The list is heaviest on restaurants, as they have the strongest draw for me personally, but there are also bars, retailers, hole-in-the-wall spots, and cultural institutions as well.

And like your children, it's impossible to pick favorites. I've fallen for them all, their passion, their longevity, their ability to transport customers back in time, and their wonderful products—whether those are amazing sandwiches, fiercely potent cocktails, or bespoke suits. They all offer a unique taste of the City by the Bay, the city that holds so many departed hearts. Do yourself a favor and visit them before they are gone. And keep Tony Bennett's words close as you do so.

ALFRED'S STEAKHOUSE

659 MERCHANT ST., SAN FRANCISCO, CA 94111

(415) 781-7058 • ALFREDSSTEAKHOUSE.COM

Join the Club

*T*he smell of meat and char wafting into the alley may be your only indication of the classic steakhouse in your midst when you walk down Merchant Street. There is a sign—two, in fact—for Alfred's, but no windows and barely a door, the typical symbols of an inviting restaurant. Frankly, you would never guess the place was there if you didn't know it. Outside and in, it has the feeling of a private club, one you quickly realize you definitely want to become a member of. (It actually does have a real membership club as well—more on that later.)

Established in 1928 by a San Francisco waiter named Alfredo Bacchini, the steakhouse that was formed mid-Prohibition has thrived through numerous threats to its business—including two major labor strikes, two tech "bubbles," World War II, and the invasion of hypermodern food. It keeps it real in the 21st century as a classic, clubby restaurant that specializes in rich meats, richer vegetables, and stiff drinks to wash it all down.

The restaurant has only moved once, in the late 1990s, from its first address on Broadway to the current unassuming spot on Merchant Street. Here, it is sandwiched between a Chinese elementary school and a Chinese restaurant, in a fire escape–adorned building that hunkers in the shadow of the towering Hilton Financial District hotel across the alley. That alley is the deserted sort of lane that is actually open at either end but somehow feels blocked and secluded, the kind that feels like a dead end but isn't. People could see you, should see you, but don't. There might be a guy speaking Russian in a black SUV

1

parked up at the top of the alley, ominously ignoring you but, I'm sure, keenly aware of your every move. He doesn't care about you or the steak that you're about to order—but it feels like he does. The whole walk up to the restaurant feels all about you and drama and danger, that last bit quickly dispelled once you step inside.

It may be server John Deamicis—his last name is Italian for "friends," he's quick to point out—who opens the wrought-iron gate to greet you or jokes with you warmly once you're seated. A 15-year veteran of the place, John is the kind of waiter who makes you feel right at home, no matter if it's your first or your 50th visit to the restaurant. He's representative of the sort of person who works at Alfred's—professional, swift, and fun—providing expert service that's always there when you need it without being intrusive. Whether in the front of the house or behind the scenes, all employees benefit from an 18 percent service charge the restaurant instituted in 2007 to bring parity between tipped and non-tipped staff. Some people may balk at this sort of forced gratuity, but I appreciate it, keeping in mind that the hard work of operating a restaurant doesn't end with waiters and bartenders. (You are welcome to tip above the automatic gratuity level as well.)

Outfitted in bordello-style red, the interior envelops the diner in a color that matches a good medium-rare steak—or the maraschino cherry in your manhattan. Pintuck red-leather booths are separated from each other by etched glass and provide a super-comfy spot for sinking in and luxuriating in a stereotypically manly meal. There are lots of mirrors and images of old San Francisco on the walls, with massive crystal chandeliers making the ceilings sparkle and jazz of the Artie Shaw variety playing in the background. Service is top-notch and familiar; waiters greet regulars by name and vice versa, quickly making newcomers feel like part of the Alfred's family. Since the 1970s, that family has been Petri—first Art and son Al, the latter's son Marco becoming manager in 2000. The three generations have maintained Alfred's classic look and menu while also adding a few of their own traditions—such as the wonderful Buckaroo Luncheon Club.

A true dinner house from Tuesday through Saturday, Alfred's is open for lunch only on Thursday, and a few decades they ago made that day feel even more exclusive with the institution of the Buckaroo club. Induction involves being bestowed a pin—pink indicates modern membership and yellow denotes old-schoolers (those who've been members since the original Broadway location). Wearing the pink button to Thursday lunch today gets you one free drink, while the yellow scores two—and people are not shy about advertising their membership. Diners secretly still committed to the three-martini lunch pour in on Thursday, many of them proudly displaying their Buckaroo buttons. The ritual itself feels timeless and very squarely from a certain time period simultaneously, a perfect representation of the Alfred's sensibility.

Alfred's menu highlights the meat, naturally, but also offers classic steakhouse favorites, such as oysters Rockefeller, to start. A bright and bracing Caesar salad is my preferred first course, deliciously vinegary with lots of finely grated cheese on top—or an equally delectable classic wedge salad. When it comes to the steak, the Alfred's cut is a bone-in New York strip with marbled fat that almost pops when you bite into it. Super seared on the outside, a tender medium rare on the inside, the meat is a piece of carnivorous loveliness, especially when served with a generous helping of creamed spinach on the side. Steaks range in size from a petite, grass-fed filet mignon—5 ounces, and notably, the only completely grass-fed cut on the menu (all others are finished with corn)—to a massive 32-ounce slab of beef, the Chicago bone-in rib eye. Most are aged 28 days and then grilled over mesquite charcoal from Mexico, described on the menu as "the Iron Wood of the West." And if you're still hungry after all that meat, classic desserts like cheesecake, bread pudding, and ice cream sundaes are available.

"Last night I had oysters Rockefeller, wedge salad, rib eye steak— perfectly medium rare—and creamed spinach, ice cream sundae," former owner Al Petri shared with me, divulging that he alternates between the wedge and Caesar salads. "Sharing a Chicago rib steak is a wonderful experience. In my younger days, I could devour the behemoth by myself."

A retired math professor, Petri is still involved in the business that his son now runs, helping with the books at tax time. Obviously proud of the family business and the third generation of ownership, he describes the place after 87 years "like an old shoe that fits great."

"We are neighborly in a downtown sort of way," he says. I completely agree. And even though it's not in my neighborhood, I am now officially part of the club. You should be, too.

ANCHOR BREWING COMPANY

1705 MARIPOSA ST., SAN FRANCISCO, CA 94107

(415) 863-8350 • ANCHORBREWING.COM

Steamy History

*Y*ou don't have to like beer to appreciate the place Anchor Brewing Company holds in San Francisco's history, or in the history of American beer itself, for that matter. And a tour of the brewery, situated on Mariposa Street in Potrero Hill, just may make you a convert.

Founded in 1896 in San Francisco by Germans Ernst Baruth, Otto Schnikel Jr., and brewmaster Gottlieb Brekle, Anchor remained an independent brewery when nearly every other one in the country closed after Prohibition. Later, in the 20th century, along with Sam Adams, which is a baby compared to Anchor, it became the guiding light of the craft brewing movement in the United States. Throughout it all—the 1906 earthquake, Prohibition, and the start of the craft revolution—Anchor has maintained its independence and traditional brewing methods, even in an era of machine-driven systems and automation.

Giant, gleaming copper kettle-like vessels are at the heart of the brewery, which is where the magic happens. All Anchor beer is still brewed in these 60-plus-year-old structures daily by dedicated brewmasters. Just beyond is the tasting room, which has a wall of windows onto the kettle room, where the tour really starts, and where you learn that there is still no computer automation in this process—humans are still in charge of beer making here. They make an average of six different brews a day in this space, with six hours for each brew in the 125-barrel vessels. And they are all about tradition—even still using Hetch Hetchy reservoir water in the steam beer process.

After a visit to the kettles, the tour continues downward through a maze of stainless-steel machinery and damp floors into the bowels of the multistoried brewery, through each part of the operation, all the way down into the cellar. There's lots of talk of sugars, hops, ancient yeast—they've been using the same strain, similar to a sourdough starter, since 1896, "like the Olympic torch"—and hospital-sounding things, such as "clean rooms" where there's no risk of "infecting" the beer. Large barrels filled with hops line the hallways, and an entire room is full of old burlap sacks dedicated to these dried flowers that give beer its bitterness and fill the air with their piney scent. You'll also see the canning operation, a newer part of the brewery that is slated to grow.

Anchor is best known for its steam beer, which is really simply a San Francisco–style lager (meaning, it uses lager yeast, as opposed to an ale yeast), and most people think the place itself is called Anchor Steam. The steam concept dates back to the Gold Rush and a hot liquid called wort.

"Just a fancy way of saying sugar water," explains tour guide Stephen Ruddy of wort, describing how the boiling liquid needs to be brought down to cooling temperature, around 60°F, to make beer. "The way these old pioneers used to do it is that they would brew, and ferment, up on their roofs in these open vessels, basically shallow swimming pools. You'd have these cold San Francisco night skies, and then this boiling hot wort, which together would create billowy plumes of steam coming off of the buildings."

Hence, "steam beer." The name was "just a nickname," Ruddy says, and "kind of a joke," but it stuck. So there were about 35 steam breweries in the city from 1872 to 1920, all brewing beer the same way. Then came Prohibition, "the dark ages of American history," Ruddy laughs, for which there is no record of Anchor's activity.

"I don't have any cool stories about bootlegging or any boring stories about making root beer," Ruddy says. "But what I can tell you—and you can draw your own conclusions from this—is that in 1933 we picked back up like nothing happened, and those other 34 breweries all failed. Not a single brewery came back in 1933 making steam beer, except for Anchor Brewing."

The company did fairly well after Prohibition for a few decades, until it was saved after hard times in the early 1960s by Fritz Maytag,

heir to the appliance and blue-cheese fortunes, a young, beer-loving recent college grad at the time of his purchase. This is also when the brewery's iconic bottle came about: Maytag bought up a bunch of old bottles "for pennies on the dollar" from another brewery that was going under, eventually buying the stout, short-necked mold, too.

Though steam beer is what made the brewery famous, Anchor very successfully makes other styles as well—a good sampling of which is included in the generous tasting session with the tour. Five nearly full medium-size glasses feature some popular beers and others that aren't even available in a store. Reminiscent of a wine tasting, this session feels a bit looser but is quite educational. Ruddy, who is a fairly recent college graduate and one of the newer employees at Anchor, imparts a wealth of knowledge throughout the tour and into the tasting, like any beer nerd both proudly and sort of dismissively sharing his passion.

His knowledge of and passion for the product is representative of the commitment all Anchor employees seem to have to the company, and they—like others at many of these vintage establishments—stay for decades.

Director of operations Phil Longenecker, one of these longtime employees, also describes having "a lot of pride" in working at Anchor.

His history with Anchor, like most of the employees you meet on the tour, goes back to when he first tasted the beer, in his case, around 1990 in his small Pennsylvania hometown. "The bartender said, 'Try this! This is the best f***ing beer!'" he remembers. Naturally, he still agrees.

And after a tour and tasting at Anchor Brewery, I can say I've joined the ranks of beer drinkers in this country. My favorite that day was the Brekle's Brown—an ale light on hops and heavy on malt, and a very different beer than Anchor's most famous. But I can credit this original steam brewery, named Anchor by Germans purportedly because "it sounded very American," with converting me to one of the country's favorite pastimes. And the beer, well, it's a real San Francisco original.

AUB ZAM ZAM

1633 HAIGHT ST., SAN FRANCISCO, CA • (415) 861-2545

FACEBOOK.COM/PAGES/ZAM-ZAM/1033650

49704534?RF=466120273409194

Exotic Drinkery

She made me the perfect martini. The coldest one you could imagine. Artist and bartender extraordinaire Genevieve Coleman is one of a handful of employees at Aub Zam Zam in 2015, and she represents the history and spirit of the 74-year-old Persian theme bar beautifully.

The place has art—a gorgeous, original mural based on a famous Persian fairy tale, with a storyline similar to Romeo and Juliet, provides the backdrop for the intimate, half-moon-shaped bar. And it sits in a neighborhood populated by many artists, like Coleman.

It has sass—former proprietor Bruno Mooshei, who passed away of prostate cancer in 2000 and whose Assyrian parents founded the bar in 1941, was known for his rigid ways and fervent commitment to process, and he's still a spiritual presence here. You'd better have known what drink you wanted and be prepared to order it upon entry, or you'd be commanded to never return. A 30-year regular, Ed reminisced of an early encounter, where he'd prepped his friend, in vain, for entry into the bar: "You gotta know what you want to drink, 'cause he gets in a mood!" After his friend stumbled through "I'll just have a beer," he was asked not to come back.

Even so, the place has conviviality—it is a neighborhood bar in the best way, all about community, chatting with strangers, and building a circle of confidants. It's where the bartenders bring their friends and bargoers become friends with the bartenders. And it's always been this way.

Finally, it has the iconic drink—the martini is still made the way Bruno insisted, with Boord's (a London dry gin) and a whisper of dry vermouth (rumor has it the ratio is 1,000 to 1). Legendary, late San Francisco columnist Herb Caen immortalized the place as "the Holy Shrine of the Dry Martini." It still is, I can attest.

The neighborhood in which it sits—and has for its entire existence—is the Haight, best known for hippies and street kids and said artists, and if you didn't know the bar was there, you probably wouldn't notice it, even with its striking front entry and minaret-topped roof that looks like it belongs in the Middle East. Tourists seek it out—Anthony Bourdain has been there, after all—but the place is mostly for regulars, many of whom live in the neighborhood and have for decades.

Inside, the bar looks straight out of central casting for a '40s-era movie set in old Persia (modern day Iraq), with narrow, painted cutouts in the walls that look like windows peeking onto an old bazaar and another artfully shaped cubby that today houses a jukebox; in Bruno's day, it was a cigarette machine. Next to it is a mysterious door that opened onto a phone booth until the old proprietor discovered a sailor and a woman having sex inside, at which point he scrapped the booth and locked the door (it's now used for storage). The whole room of the bar—and it's quite a small one—is bathed in red, making you feeling almost as if you're stepping into the chambers of a heart. Barstools are original, still maintained by a couple that lives in the neighborhood. Mounted prominently behind the bar is an ancient cash register that is still used for the cash-only tabs. There are no taps, beer comes in bottles only, and no molecular mixology—they specialize in the classics (like the martini) and are very good at them. There still hangs a curved curtain rod just inside the front door that dates back to the war-era curfew, when it was used to shut out the light and make it appear like revelry had concluded. There is, of course, no television; it's proudly one of few bars in the city that remains without one.

Coleman has worked here for just two years but has been a customer for seven, and she has an impressive passion for and knowledge of the history of the place and the city overall. She also seems to love the hospitality part of the industry.

"Lemon cheesecake, anyone?" she asks, offering her birthday dessert from the previous day to her customers (who are all, it's clear, also now her friends). After dispensing delicious wedges of cheesecake on cocktail napkins, a cutting board full of cheese and sliced baguette appears.

The dark-haired Austin native with a 1940s-style curvy gleam in her eye spent time in Chicago and LA before arriving in San Francisco. She explains that Sundays are now for "noshing." The Zam Zam team—which she describes as being "like a family"—has also decided to resurrect an old tradition of Bruno's: They'll go out for periodic Sunday night dinners at the Gold Mirror, an old Italian restaurant in the Inner Sunset district, just staff and regulars. Their first dinner in the new age was "really cool," she says, and involved several of the regulars who used to go with Bruno.

"It was really special for the old guys," she shares. "They went back in the kitchen and talked with the chef."

The bar is now owned by a former regular—Robert Clarke—who used to live upstairs. In addition to serving as a beloved watering hole for all these years, it actually has seen on the silver screen: It was featured in the movie *Blue Jasmine*. "But they didn't shoot toward the bar!" Coleman marvels, surprised they'd miss the most iconic-looking part of the place.

"[Bruno was] very notorious for only letting people sit at the bar, only letting people drink gin martinis, tables were always closed, he didn't like hippies—if he didn't like you, he'd tell you to go down the street," recounting the tales she's heard about the owner who died before she reached the city, the longtime regulars in the midst confirming her stories.

But to me, it seems he was really kind of a softie at heart. Responsible for creating a space where people felt comfortable and wanted to talk to others, instituting a communal dinner-out ritual, he's left a legacy of togetherness that in some ways is uncommon now. So what if he wanted you to be prepared to place your order? He knew a good drink and insisted you experience things his way. Like any proper proprietor, he was confident in his vision. That vision can still be experienced in a touristy neighborhood that belies the fact that it's truly a neighborhood-neighborhood. Just look for the minarets.

BENKYODO COMPANY

1747 BUCHANAN ST., SAN FRANCISCO, CA 94115

(415) 922-1244 • BENKYODOCOMPANY.COM

Pillowy Perfection

Warm, pillowy dough like a cloud of rice essence, wrapped around a plump, fresh strawberry. I'd never had anything like it before my visit to Benkyodo, a little Japanese confectionery and time-warp deli counter hatched in 1906 and still going strong.

The *mochi*—a traditional Japanese confection made of glutinous rice, pounded into a paste, and molded into shape—at this Japantown shop is unlike any I've ever known. It's a far cry from what you can buy at many groceries these days, for *mochi* seems to be everywhere (even Trader Joe's sells *mochi* ice cream). The confection's typical description as a "rice cake" seems off to me, as the little nonsweet sweet seems to be of its own special breed, and Benkyodo's version illustrates that in a truly lovely way. The phenomenal strawberry flavor has a filling made of fresh strawberries and lima beans—a fact that shocks me, but I soon learn that the surprising variety of ingredients is not unusual for Benkyodo's little gems. The care owners Ricky and Bobby Okamura take in their *mochi* production, gingerly but swiftly forming each piece by hand, and the family history behind this learned art are what makes it so special. Their other specialty is *manju*, a confection with an outer pastry made of rice flour that is steamed, enclosing a filling of boiled, sweetened beans—adzuki are traditional, but Benkyodo makes varieties with other legumes and even comfort-food classics such as peanut butter as well.

Benkyodo is a funny little place—a true gem in the realm of vintage establishments. Serving its regulars daily at the slender, classic deli

counter, it seems to be the Japantown neighborhood meeting place for hot coffee and a white-bread sandwich (like your mom made if you were a kid of the '70s), and a guaranteed warm greeting from one of the owners or longtime family friend and part-time employee Benh Nakajo, who admittedly behaves like the shop is his own.

"It drives me crazy if they close during a big festival in the neighborhood," Nakajo confessed. "All the business we're missing!" He also has a firm idea about how the *mochi* should be presented in the pastry case, fastidiously instructing the Okamura brothers if he sees something he deems in disarray.

Nakajo's commitment to the place is a great example of the extended family bond that has kept the business going for so long. Its original owner—the Okamura brothers' grandfather Suyeichi Okamura—first opened the business in 1906, having to close the shop when the family was detained for four years during World War II's paranoia-fueled forcible evacuation of tens of thousands of Japanese Americans from the West Coast. Not to be deterred, Okamura eventually reopened the business once the family was released. In the late 1950s, his son, Hirofumi "Hippo" Okamura, took over, eventually passing along the business to the boys in 1990.

御菓子調子進優

COURTESY OF BENKYODO COMPANY

"Benkyodo is a gathering place," Nakajo explains, and most of its customers are "neighborhood or ex-neighborhood people." Having a home away from home is important in a neighborhood whose native businesses are in rapid decline. Benkyodo is one of the last remaining original businesses in Japantown, its staying power likely due in large part to the comfort people feel when they walk through the door—as well as those incredible little sweets.

Vintage Spot
PALACE OF FINE ARTS: EST. 1915

With 2015 being the publication date of this book, it is important to note that the year also marks the centennial anniversary of an event that physically transformed the city, leaving a vintage legacy today. That event was the Panama-Pacific International Exposition, which purportedly honored the discovery of the Pacific Ocean and the completion of the Panama Canal, but it also put San Francisco in the spotlight after the earthquake that forced the city to rebuild itself from the ground up. Buildings were erected and neighborhoods were born at this world's fair, leaving behind just a few remnants—the Marina District, included—as evidence of the event today. One of the only structural parts of the exposition itself that remains is the Palace of Fine Arts, a glorious building, theater, and landmark.

The background of wedding pictures, postcards, and movie sets, the Palace of Fine Arts joins the Golden Gate Bridge as one of the city's most iconic and most photographed structures. Designed in the style of a Roman ruin and built expressly to show art during the exposition, the theater today hosts concerts, dance performances, and cultural events—not unlike the original vision for the space. With its columns stemming from a majestic dome, filtering the sun and the fog and all of the serene natural surroundings, it's a glorious piece of architecture, situated on a lagoon and surrounded by cypress trees on the edge of the Marina District and abutting the woodsy land of the also historic Presidio, a former military base on the northern tip of the city. Visit this San Francisco gem, photograph it, or just sit near it and feel as though you're a part of a postcard.

3301 Lyon St., San Francisco, CA 94123;
(415) 563-6504; palaceoffinearts.org

Lines form around the building at the holidays, when regular customers await pickup of their preordered confections. If you're interested in partaking, be sure to order in advance—they sell out for New Year's, when *mochi* is a traditional treat, leaving none available for purchase on the spot. The quaint shop is cash only, which one could guess upon entry into what feels like a blast back to the past. But the amount of cash required shouldn't be of concern when you consider the meaning of the shop's name.

"Benkyodo roughly translates to 'bargain' or 'good price,'" Nakajo explains, after consulting some of the elderly regulars in the vicinity. "Really it means when you come to buy something, we will give you a good deal. You're getting your money's worth." I'd say so, when you can take home petite, edible works of art, freshly made by hand daily on the premises, for little more than a dollar apiece.

It is unclear who will take over the art of *mochi* and *manju* making at Benkyodo when this generation of Okamura brothers decides to retire. The lack of an obvious successor makes me fear that this special little spot is imperiled, like so many other businesses in San Francisco's Japantown, or, when it comes to historic businesses that have been family-run for more than a century and require a lot of daily work, really in Anytown, USA. For this reason—and simply because a visit results in guaranteed cultural deliciousness—I urge you: Go as soon as you can. A tender, delicate little sweet awaits.

A Little Coffee in My Whiskey

*D*on't stir it—you won't hear the end of it!" one enthusiastic patron yells to another on the Saturday before Christmas. It is noon at the Buena Vista Cafe, and it seems as though not another body could squeeze into the famous bar-restaurant on the corner of Hyde and Beach Streets in Fisherman's Wharf. The place is boisterous and festive—and seems so regardless of the season.

The advice giver is referring to the bar's famous Irish coffee—an enticing blend of hot coffee, two sugar cubes, and about an ounce and a third of Tullamore Dew Irish whiskey, with a dollop of whipped cream atop—and the bartender's exacting expectations for how the drink should be enjoyed. Never stirred, the finished cocktail is served in a dedicated glass that resembles half an hourglass figure, and it should be sipped (or gulped, depending on your predilection) as presented, its layers intact. If the drink sits for any length of time, those layers gradually bleed into one another, heightening the creamy, buttery, booziness of the whole thing. Dare I say, it's the perfect writer's drink—coffee to invigorate and whiskey to soften the edges, together opening up the senses in a delightful way.

Romanticizing a drink like this feels natural and makes one understand the mind-set in 1952 of then cafe owner Jack Koeppler. He wanted to recreate the Irish coffee served at Ireland's Shannon Airport and enlisted travel writer Stanton Delaplane to help him do it. After much trial and error, a subsequent visit by Koeppler to Ireland, and work with San Francisco's mayor—who happened to own a dairy also—to find the secret to getting the cream to float properly (they

determined it required aging for 48 hours before frothing), the Buena Vista finally found success. And the team behind it isn't secretive about how they do it. Here is the famous recipe, which remains unchanged to this day, from the restaurant's website:

1. Fill glass with very hot water to preheat, then empty.
2. Pour hot coffee into hot glass until it is about three-quarters full. Drop in two cocktail sugar cubes.
3. Stir until the sugar is thoroughly dissolved.
4. Add full jigger of Irish whiskey for proper taste and body.
5. Top with a collar of lightly whipped whipping cream by pouring it gently over a spoon.
6. Enjoy it while piping hot.

The cafe is so famous for the cocktail that in 2008 it attempted to set the world record for the largest Irish coffee ever concocted. Ten liters of whiskey, 4 pounds of sugar, 10 gallons of local Peerless coffee, and 2 gallons of lightly whipped cream later, the team did it—making it into the Guinness record books. They even tapped the gigantic glass so all those witnessing the record in the making could partake in its success.

First opened in 1916 as a saloon occupying the ground floor of an old boardinghouse, the Buena Vista Cafe has stood in its prime water-adjacent spot ever since. Though it's famous for its Irish drink, and they are very crowded on St. Patrick's Day—making around 4,000 of the cocktails—it is not an Irish bar.

"Just a San Francisco saloon," says manager Larry Silva, who has been at the Buena Vista for a decade—a tenure that's nothing compared to most of the staff there. Bartender Larry Dolan, admonisher of the patron at the start of this story, has been there four times as long (like most, including the dishwasher, who only recently retired at age 77). Dolan estimates he's made more than three million of the famous cocktails over the years. No wonder he's firm about how to drink them.

He is the classic straight-faced, quip-doling bartender you'd expect to find in a place like this. As I watched him deftly dollop the billowy cream over the top of a line of 11 coffees at attention like toy soldiers down the long wood bar, I commented that he could probably make the cocktails in his sleep. "As a matter of fact, I was asleep," he said, unsmiling but with a twinkle in his eye. "You just woke me up."

It is this sensibility—and these potent, delicious coffees—that keep people coming back. One patron shared how her mother had advised her years ago, on the occasion of her first trip to San Francisco, that she absolutely must head straight to the cafe upon arrival. "So every year since then, we always start our trip here. Every year. Go to the Buena Vista, have an Irish coffee."

The walls illustrate this loyalty to tradition, with framed historic photos showing magazine articles about the place and all of the customers who are devoted to it. And that loyalty spans the globe—with people like one "little old lady from Italy" who tugged on Silva's sleeve, Italian guidebook in hand, and asked, in her sparing English vocabulary, if "this was the place the Buena Vista?" This is not an uncommon occurrence. And with the customer demographic split roughly down the middle between locals and tourists, there are many repeat visitors, coming year after year or even week after week.

"People feel at home here," Silva explains, the communal tables complementing the barstools for an openness that breeds camaraderie

Vintage Spot

molinari Delicatessen: est. 1896

Delis aren't much of a thing in San Francisco, the way they are in New York. There's basically Saul's in Berkeley, Genova in Oakland, and Molinari in the city. The latter is the local longtime purveyor of Italian-style cured meats—salame, salame, and more salame, all made in San Francisco since 1896. The flagship location is on Columbus Avenue in North Beach, and it provides wonderful sandwiches and cheese and pantry goods in addition to all those meats. Counter staff is well versed in the ways of cured meat, able to help you distinguish between Toscano, Finocchiona, Sopressata, and Coppa and everything else they make. Ask for advice and a taste—though the latter will likely be proffered on its own. You may find Molinari products in bigger stores, too, or order online for expediency, but for a real San Francisco experience, a visit to the small shop on Columbus Avenue can't be beat.

373 Columbus Ave., San Francisco, CA 94133; (415) 421-2337; molinarideli.net

between both friends and strangers. And, "they recognize the person making their drinks; 20 years ago, it really was the same bartender."

Food Network stars and celebrity chefs Tyler Florence and Emeril Lagasse have both named the Buena Vista Cafe as a favorite spot, along with the millions of lesser-known customers over the years who've been equally, if not more, devoted. They are all drawn to the vintage decor and begrudgingly warm spirit of the place that feels just so San Francisco. It is both international and American, both of morning and night, and it has a way of making people, regardless of their background, feel right at home. Countless brown liquid–filled bottles sit at the ready under the bar, while cable cars trundle by just outside—the sounds of the city providing a background hum to patrons imbibing a beautiful boozy bit of local history, most of the time at 8 a.m. rather than 8 at night.

CABLE CAR CLOTHIERS

110 SUTTER ST., SUITE 108, SAN FRANCISCO, CA 94104

(415) 397-4740 • CABLECARCLOTHIERS.COM

Dapper 101

*J*ovially buzzy. This is the quality of the atmosphere in this men's store in the heart of San Francisco's Financial District, and it feels positively classic. There's even an old-elegance smell to the place, one that makes you wish you had a stout tumbler of good scotch in your hand. You are greeted upon entry through the grand columns of this former bank building, erected in 1907, by a longtime staff member who seems part of the fabric of the place just as much as third-generation owner Jonathan Levin, 37-year-old grandson of founder Charles "Charlie" Pivnick, who passed away at 95, just weeks before my chat with Levin.

"Grandpa Hat" is what Levin called his grandfather as a child, and when he shares the nickname now, there is a fresh tenderness that I feel fortunate to witness. Levin describes the store founder as an ever-polished haberdasher who influenced his own sense of style and appreciation for customer service. It's clear the esteem with which he holds his grandfather, mentor, and former business partner, and the love still bursting at the seams for the man who opened what was originally a war surplus store named Vet's Mercantile more than 68 years ago. (It's actually more than 75, if you count—and the shop does—Pivnick's 1972 purchase of Robert Kirk, a city retailer founded in 1939 that specialized in British goods). In 1954, as military sources diminished, the shop shifted its focus to classic British-style clothing and was renamed for the city's iconic transportation symbol that lumbers by just a few blocks away. Now, after seven locations, the original intent of the business has never changed: to outfit San

23

Franciscans—mostly male, but Levin is careful to caution that there's "no such thing as just a *men's* hat"—in the finest classic apparel and the appropriate lifestyle accoutrement to go with it.

The shop specializes in the total fashion experience for the gentleman, carrying all the traditional brands you'd imagine (Stetson, Southwick, Kent, Filson, and many more) in both "business and dress" and "casual" wear, in addition to hats, footwear, shaving tools and other traditional grooming necessities, belts, cuff links, and, of course, pocket squares. There's even a travel section featuring the kind of sturdy, leather-adorned baggage that lasts a lifetime. To complement all of this, there's an in-house tailor and bespoke custom-suit service—Levin emphasizes they believe in a full-service experience—as well as a 1930s-style barber shop and shoe shine, helmed by "Nicky the Barber," Philadelphia-born Nicky Calvenese, who specializes in "authentic vintage" men's cuts and has styled for the stars—including designing looks for HBO's Prohibition-era crime drama *Boardwalk Empire*. He proudly shares upon our meeting that he's the barber for the San Francisco Art Deco Society, and his own immersion in a total period look and persona—replete with authentic 1930s tattoos—is impressive. (I am uncertain that he wasn't actually born 100 years ago and beamed to present day.) Calvenese seems right at home anchoring the corner of the store, making it feel both more modern and more authentically vintage at the same time.

It's easy to see why the oldest men's retail store in the city has countless regulars—including a handful of celebrities who will not be named here, upholding Cable Car's commitment to discretion and gold-standard service. People are naturally drawn to this treatment as well as the whole lifestyle vision the shop presents—it feels of another era, a better era somehow, making visitors, even casual (and female) ones, like me, want to live the life conjured up in its wall displays and glass cases.

Long before the Internet, Cable Car Clothiers actually made its name known to more than two million people nationwide through its pioneering catalogue business. Pivnick produced his popular catalogue through the 1980s, offering all of the store's high-quality products for mail order. Levin recently upgraded that virtual shopping experience with an online store, bringing Pivnick's catalogue vision into the 21st century and taking it "to the next generation," as he describes.

The young owner is often seen in the shop wearing his hat of choice—a crushable, fur felt fedora—and seems the perfect next-generation stalwart supporter of the timeless style his grandfather so admired. Levin's eyes glisten as he remembers Pivnick, whose kind spirit clearly infuses the character of the shop today. "He was a great man," he says, smiling. Though management no longer makes the staff a daily lunch of tuna and egg salad sandwiches, as the founder once did, it still feels like an old-fashioned family operation that prides itself on respect for the people who make it what it is—dedicated employees and loyal customers. The whole place—with its archetypal products, full-service offerings, and overall approach to running a family business—feels like a perfect example of what happens when modernity and tradition marry and push through the decades.

"In the forties and fifties, everyone wore a hat," Levin states matter-of-factly, sharing the simple principle upon which the business rests: "When you dress well, you feel confident."

And after three-quarters of a century in business, confidence still appeals to Cable Car Clothiers' customers. Though there's been a push toward the casual in the tech-driven culture of the San Francisco Bay Area, there's simultaneously a craving for the classic—a hipster-led harkening back to the era of bow ties and straight-razor shaves. Levin notes the longevity in his grandfather's business.

"People are dressing up again," he says, delighting in the fact that everything old is now new, and that more women are coming into his store these days, shopping not just for the men in their lives but for themselves, too.

Not knowing him personally, I think Pivnick would be so proud of how his grandson is carrying on his legacy. Enthusiasm for the era and finery abounds at Cable Car Clothiers, the little shop that began as a military surplus store so many years ago. Thinking of its evolution from pre-catalogue to online shopping times, I toast this beautiful store. Cheers to Grandpa Hat. May good taste—and a proper outfit—never go out of style.

CITY LIGHTS BOOKSELLERS
& PUBLISHERS
61 COLUMBUS AVE., SAN FRANCISCO, CA 94133
(415) 362-8193 • CITYLIGHTS.COM

Legendary Bookstore

I've put off writing this piece for some time. This vintage establishment feels too big a cultural landmark, too important for a generation, too meaningful to too many people to do it justice in 1,000 words. Its longtime marketing officer Stacey Lewis was too forthcoming, too wonderfully full of information and eloquent thoughts in our interview about how this bookstore and publisher has figured into her own life and the lives of so many others over more than 60 years in business. I have 12 pages of notes from my chat with her alone, not including all the other research available, supplementing my own personal experience with the place. There is just too much to say to really say it right.

That said, as a spot that has both shaped the city, the literary community, and even the free-speech movement since 1953—and served as an outgrowth of all three—it belongs in this book. Which means it needs an essay. So I will try to serve it, its founder, its countless political artist-activists and devoted fans over the years well.

The place is City Lights.

Both an independent bookstore and publishing house, City Lights occupies a skinny, triangular piece of real estate on Columbus Avenue in North Beach, the neighborhood that is defined by both its Italian heritage and its position as a virtual ground zero for the Beat movement of the 1950s. Poet, painter, and activist Lawrence Ferlinghetti, born in 1919 in Yonkers, New York, served as a US

Navy ship commander in World War II and got his doctorate at the Sorbonne in Paris on the GI bill before moving to San Francisco. It was then, in 1953, with sociology teacher and pop-culture magazine creator Peter D. Martin, that he founded this little bookstore—the first all-paperback bookshop in the country. (Previously, paperbacks were relegated mostly to drugstores.) He followed this achievement two years later with the establishment of the associated publishing house.

City Lights is best known as a purveyor of poetry, much with a political or countercultural bent, beginning initially with its Pocket Poets series and going on to carry and promote socially progressive work of all sorts. The book house made a name for itself in 1956 by publishing Allen Ginsberg's *Howl*; the poetry collection's depiction of homosexual sex, among other controversial subject matter at the time, led to Ferlinghetti's arrest, an obscenity trial, and, subsequently, a historic First Amendment case. Ferlinghetti was ultimately acquitted of any wrongdoing, marking a moment in history on the side of free speech, regardless of its perceived salaciousness.

City Lights went on to become a meeting place for artists and writers, including Jack Kerouac, whose name marks the alley adjacent to the store. Though the North Beach bookseller grew up with the other businesses in the 'hood, many of them sharing customers, staff, and artsy histories, the shop's influence spreads beyond the confines of San Francisco. Literary-minded tourists flock to the place as if on pilgrimage to a holy site. "I was told I should come here," young people say upon their first visit from across the country or the other side of the world. (I said something similar as a teenager.) It's a reminder that in this age of online book buying and near instantaneous consumer satisfaction, the independent brick-and-mortar store with character and history is still relevant. "People are still looking for places that they feel connected to and that give them a certain feeling," Lewis says, sharing that City Lights' unique appeal is "a marketing person's dream" that she doesn't take for granted. The shop also has attracted fans across oceans, in no small part because of its connection to the famed English-language bookstore in Paris, Shakespeare & Company, and the longtime friendship between its late owner, George Whitman, and Ferlinghetti. The two became friends during Ferlinghetti's time in the City of Lights, and though there is no financial association

with the Parisian bookstore, the shops are kindred spirits in content, artists, and Beat history.

City Lights was founded on the principle that reading should be for everyone, with books easy to acquire. Ninety-eight percent of the publisher's titles are printed in paperback first and only—"making literature more cost-effective and accessible," Lewis says. Events have always been an important part of the shop's agenda as a way to connect with readers, and they continue to be a strong draw for locals. Past programs have celebrated award-winning fiction authors such as Joyce Carol Oates as readily as new left-leaning voices. And sometimes the events become legendary—such as one poetry reading where a drunken Charles Bukowski reportedly threw beer bottles into the crowd.

Poetry and "politically progressive nonfiction" continue to be important genres for the publisher, but the bookstore has much more than that. It "doesn't have everything," Lewis explains, but this is by choice. What it does have is carefully curated, always with an eye on its unstated but clear mission: to articulate a challenge to authority and to give voice to topics that may be less conventional. City Lights gives off a sense of quiet discovery. Walking through the narrow, mazelike aisles of the multilevel shop feels like a private treasure hunt for the book lover—especially one who fancied herself a free-spirited

hippie in high school, always wishing she'd been born a couple decades earlier. Ahem. There is an entire section devoted to Beat writers, as well as more poetry than I'd ever seen before in one place, along with an exciting promotion of local authors, countless classics, and even a children's section downstairs. The floors creak a bit as those in a revered book house should, and the small, long-tenured staff (most have been there for more than two decades) sits upstairs, earnestly working away on discovering the next big thing in the City Lights canon.

In this, the 60th anniversary year of the publishing house, I recommend perusing its proud aisles, honoring radical voices (even if you're not one), and celebrating a generation that grooved to a different beat. Follow the instructive signs positioned throughout the shop by Ferlinghetti himself: "Sit down and read a book." Know, though, that it is not just about the past. "There's still a place for this spot," Lewis says, pleased that the store has been able to "stay relevant" through the years. She considers whether the store is like a museum of sorts. "Perhaps it's like the ideal museum—it makes you think, and maybe you'll buy something at the end."

CLIFF HOUSE

1090 POINT LOBOS, SAN FRANCISCO, CA 94121

(415) 386-3330 • CLIFFHOUSE.COM

Table with a View

Soaring sea views—though not so much views, really, as you feel more like you're part of the Pacific Ocean, perched atop it, at Ocean Beach on the edge of San Francisco. This is what I first envision when I think of the Cliff House—and it has been the chief defining characteristic of the historic establishment throughout its existence. The space drips with history—from the famous ruins of the Sutro Baths just outside to its connection to San Francisco society— and manages to still feel relevant and fun more than a century after it was first built.

Current proprietor Mary Hountalas documented much of that history in an unmatchable way in her book, *The San Francisco Cliff House*. Hountalas and her husband Dan took over the venerable establishment in 1973—always aware of their role as stewards of a city and, eventually, National Park Service (as of the mid-1970s) landmark, but never quite knowing where those roles would take them.

"The restaurant business in San Francisco is very, very tough, and we're very proud we've kept a successful business and institution going for the 41 years we've been the proprietors," Hountalas says. She and her husband are actually the longest-term operators of the establishment. "We've had our ups and downs, but it's been fun and challenging."

"Ups and downs" is an understatement for the business that dates back to 1863. Over its more than 150 years in existence, the Cliff House has seen fires, earthquakes, destruction, construction, and historical restorations.

"It's been blown up, burned down, shut down for Prohibition, and shut down during World War I because it was too close to an army installation with a VA [Veterans Administration] hospital, so they had to stop serving liquor," Hountalas recounts. "For a lot of people then, that made it the place you didn't want to go to if you couldn't get a beer."

The story of persistence in business is what the Cliff House is all about. Thankfully, the building's third iteration, which opened in 1909, was reinforced with steel beams and positioned to last in the event of another earthquake. The property itself has been owned by various people and entities over the years, including local 19th-century millionaire-philanthropist (and eventual mayor) Adolph Sutro; the owners of the seaside amusement park Playland, George and Leo Whitney, who purchased it in 1937; and in 1977, the National Park Service through the Golden Gate National Recreation Area, which serves as its official steward, with the Hountalases as the day-to-day operators.

The Hountalas family came to the restaurant business from food-service backgrounds—when they married in 1972, Mary was a registered dietician and Dan a sales manager for Consolidated Foods. But this wasn't his first foray into restaurant ownership; in fact, it was the family business. He and his father previously had managed the Cliff Chalet, which was destroyed in 1966 by the Sutro Baths fire. It all seemed to come full circle when the couple was approached by then-owner of the Cliff House, George Whitney (also inventor in 1928 of the popular local sweet treat, the It's-It, perfection in the way of an ice cream sandwich) to, as Mary describes it, "help him do more things at the Cliff House."

"At first we thought, no, no, no, no—we've got good jobs, we're newly married—are we out of our minds?" she recalls. After talking it over, the couple decided to take the plunge. "We're young and foolish, we thought. What the heck?" They first opened what was then known as "Upstairs at the Cliff House," and over the years, they expanded, modified, stripped away, and restored, Most importantly, they listened to customers' requests to keep what was most beloved and authentic about the historic establishment.

"We got so much hate mail and angry phone calls when we tried to change it," says Hountalas of the time, a number of years after taking ownership, they attempted to swap out their unique take on crab Louis salad—which adds fresh, seasonal fruit to the standard presentation of crab and iceberg lettuce with Louis dressing—for something more traditional. There was uproar at the proposition of losing the fruit, which was actually Mary's addition when they first took over. "There are certain things I'm never touching again. That's one of them."

Loyalty extends to the Cliff House employee population as well; many staff members have been there for decades—and for one, more than four decades. The executive chef first began as a bar boy, working his way through culinary school to the lead kitchen position. They even have an employee alumni association that meets regularly for reunions.

The landmark's current setup is essentially divided into three dining spaces: the more casual Bistro eatery, situated in the historic part of the building (this is what most people think of when they think of the Cliff House); Sutro's, the fine-dining establishment downstairs that sits opposite the former public baths, its architecture subtly mirroring that of the baths; and the simple bar space that overlooks Sutro's. The restaurant's longtime signature dishes—like that crab Louis salad; the perfectly eggy-airy-crisp popovers that are a draw on their own; a lovely local classic clam chowder; and the unexpectedly delicious pot stickers—are available at the Bistro and bar, while the fancy spot specializes in more modern California cuisine.

One would expect clientele at such a destination spot to be heavily tourist, but not so here: about 80 percent of Cliff House diners are locals. It has also had its fair share of celebrity patrons—from Rock Hudson and singer and voice-over actor Phil Harris (his classic-film actress wife, Alice Faye, was in the movie *Alexander's Ragtime Band*, which featured exteriors of the property) to Robin Williams, Grace Slick, and, while filming *The Rock*, Nicolas Cage, who always requested steamed clams with no oil—as well as countless local, national, and international politicians. Some longtime employees even claim to have seen a female ghost, prior to the remodel that restored the building to its 1909 state and overhauled the electrical and plumbing systems: "They say they haven't seen her since, so maybe she went down with the old parts of the building," Hountalas says.

On the couple's closeness to the historic restaurant, Hountalas describes it almost as predestined—stemming from her husband's Greek immigrant family's restaurant business. "It's been in his blood his entire life," she says. "Even with the Park Service acquiring the property, we just have felt so close to it for so many years. We consider it our baby."

Given that their son-in-law is now the general manager and their daughter works there on occasion, as do two of their grandchildren, they hope "the baby" will stay in the family when they retire. All I know is that I need the Cliff House to continue to persist in the face of adversity, survive any future catastrophes that may come its way, and thrive as it always has—so that my own children can look forward to cliff-side outings and relish a bit of San Francisco's past.

CLIFF'S VARIETY

479 CASTRO ST., SAN FRANCISCO, CA 94114

(415) 431-5365 • CLIFFSVARIETY.COM

Home of the Hard to Find

From hammers and nails to boas and tiaras" is the tagline of this vintage shop, and the reality lives up to the marketing promise. Dubbed "the home of the hard to find," Cliff's Variety has just about anything a San Franciscan could need when it comes to the home and, really, to life in general, with the exception of groceries and pharmaceuticals. Nespresso machines sit around the corner from children's books, and people with an affinity for dress-up will be especially delighted by what's available at this hardware store and more, given all the wigs, ribbons, and aforementioned feather boas in stock. Originally established as a sort of drugstore without the drugs—carrying magazines, cigars, sewing supplies, candy, and toys—the shop that sells a bit of everything has become a landmark in and of itself for its unique appeal to both handymen and drag queens alike—and for the way it has helped shape the neighborhood over the years.

Cliff's opened in 1936 in Eureka Valley—the Castro District before it was "the Castro," the now well-known heart of the gay community in the city—and "grew up with the neighborhood," says current owner Martha Asten, who operates the shop with her husband Ernie and their family. Martha and Ernie are the third generation to oversee the business founded by Ernie's great-grandfather, Hilario DeBaca, a merchant and schoolteacher from New Mexico. It was DeBaca's son Ernie—the current Ernie's grandfather—who became a repairman with his own shop and ultimately brought the hardware side of Cliff's Variety into being. In 1946, he broke his leg, forcing him to close his

place during a long recuperation, so he set up a miniature shop-within-a-shop at the back of his father's store to stay busy. People brought in all manner of small appliances to be fixed, and the rest is history.

"He had an eighth-grade education but could fix anything," Martha says affectionately of her husband's grandfather, who became a boilermaker with the Santa Fe Railroad at just 15 years old and later helped raise her husband. The younger Ernie "inherited that talent," going on to work at the store part-time as a teenager and eventually taking it over with his now wife, who was just his girlfriend when she started working at the shop, also as a teenager, in the late 1960s. The two are now fixtures there and continue to be involved in Cliff's day-to-day operations. Even with Ernie's Parkinson's disease, he is at the shop every day of the week and continues to be "a font of knowledge" about the store and its history. Martha serves as chief financial officer and keeps up her longtime involvement with holiday buying, a critical role when it comes to Cliff's.

Around the holidays—any holiday, really—you'll see the variety store outfitted in decorations of all sorts, from the storefront outside to the towering stacks of shelving within. The family takes pride in celebration, and takes credit for "starting Halloween in the Castro," which, if you don't know the neighborhood, is a bigger deal than it may sound. It all began at Cliff's with a small children's costume contest in 1946, growing over the years to include pie- and ice-cream-eating competitions; a circus-like setup with musicians, clowns, and jugglers; and a full-blown parade. The tradition ceased after three decades when, in the late 1970s, the innocent ritual focused on kids had evolved, courtesy of the changing neighborhood—fewer families, more single people—into a raucous street party of rowdy adults, replete with fights and broken windows. The DeBacas decided to no longer throw their party. But the family's affinity for celebrating holidays did not cease; if you visit at Halloween or Christmas, you will be treated to glorious window displays—another long tradition at Cliff's—and a store transformed by seasonal decor.

The shop has moved a few times on Castro Street over the years but has been in the same location now since the '70s. It was around that time that Cliff's became the first straight-owned business on the block to hire openly gay employees, and it expanded its product line to match the needs of the changing demographics around it.

"As the neighborhood changed so did the skills required of sales clerks," the Astens explain in the store's documented history, describing how they had to grow the staff beyond just the family. "In addition to a knowledge of hardware, electrical and plumbing, people were needed who could advise with decorating, costuming, cooking, sewing, and entertaining."

The neighborhood had gone from mostly Irish, Italian, and Mexican immigrant families to becoming the home of the gay population in a city that made history with the gay rights movement. When asked about the turning point in its customer makeup, Asten divulges how they knew something had changed when customers starting coming in, sent by the local hospital, to have their stuck cock rings removed, using the hardware tools and expertise available in the shop. "At that time, the emergency room didn't know what to do," she says, laughing at the memory, "but they knew Cliff's. So they sent them here."

As the neighborhood became a gay mecca, it also drew back families, both gay and straight, and today it has a reputation for being one of the most charming, desirable areas in which to live in the city. And Cliff's popularity is as strong as ever.

"I think that's what I like best," Martha says. "It's such an institution. We live in the neighborhood, and the shop is part of my identity. We've traveled the world and run into people who know Cliff's Variety store."

There are two sides to Cliff's: the main store and "the Annex," both full of things you need and probably do not, but it's fun to peruse the aisles anyway. If you look overhead in the Annex, you'll see one of Ernie DeBaca's inventions, in the store's legacy of Mr. Fix It–style innovation: Clever ceiling-mounted machines use metal trays and repurposed bicycle chain to maximize space and store things like ribbon (and candy, in a previous day) in an interactive, dry-cleaning-carousel way. The existence of those machines and the fact that they are still around is like the story of the store itself, and it's one that reads in both black and white and brilliant Technicolor. It's an old-fashioned neighborhood hardware store, with professional repairmen on staff, that came into its own serving the needs of a vibrant community, adding brightly colored wigs to its shelves, amidst the screwdrivers, nuts, and bolts. It represents entrepreneurship and a commitment to the business concept of always meeting customers' needs—even as they change around you.

DIANDA'S ITALIAN AMERICAN PASTRY CO.

2883 MISSION ST., SAN FRANCISCO, CA 94110

(415) 647-5469 • DIANDASBAKERY.COM

Unlikely Italian Sweets

edoretti! A cake-like amaretti cookie creates the base of this pastry of perfection: Upon it sits a globe of rum-perfumed chocolate mousse, the whole thing enrobed in a thin, delicate layer of semisweet chocolate that cracks when you bite into it. *Fedoretti*. Remember it. Seek it out. Devour it immediately upon purchase. Experience bliss for the balance of your day.

An original creation of the family from Lucca, Tuscany, who started Dianda's Italian American Pastry in 1962, the *fedoretti* is an absolute must-taste-before-you-die treat. But it is not alone in its glory at this special little bakery that's now run by several of the longtime employees, none of whom are Italian. When you walk into the small, brightly lit bakery in the heavily Latino Mission District, you are immediately surrounded by glass pastry cases forming a U shape around you—and they are packed side to side and front to back with beautiful Italian cookies, cakes, and confections of every sort, all made fresh daily by long-tenured staff, most of whom are Mexican.

The treats at this classic Italian sweetery are the pinnacle of authenticity and of deliciousness. Italian pastries always seem to embrace color in a way their French counterparts do not, and Dianda's is no exception. Glazed fruits, bright frostings, and electric-red maraschino cherries top many desserts here, adding a rainbow to the beige cream puffs and rolled cakes that sit proudly in their display cases. A classic rum cake features liquor-soaked genoise layered with pastry cream and whipped cream, and is a rich slice of heaven. Almond torte is a delightful accompaniment to a cup of coffee, and petits fours were introduced to the collection about five years ago but are so textbook that they seem like they've always been on the menu: Little cubes, ovals, and diamond-shaped bites enrobed in white, milk, or dark chocolate, each contains miniature layers of cake, sandwiching jams, creams, or more chocolate. Holidays bring special flavors of these—and other confections—but you should not wait for a special occasion to visit.

Enrichetta and Elio were the first Dianda family members in the bakery's history, eventually passing it down to their three sons, one of whom—Pasquale—managed the place until 2004, when he sold it to three employees—Sergio Flores, Luis Pena, and Floyd Goldberg.

"Two Latinos and Jewish guy from Brooklyn, New York," Goldberg laughs, though obviously proud of the way the team has been able to carry on the Italian traditions of their former employer. The current owners have brought a few traditions of their own, however, adding Goldberg's special "New York brownie," dense with walnuts, to the menu, along with *tres leches* ("three milks") cake, a Latin-American favorite.

"Latinos just love their three milks," Goldberg says. "They can't get enough of it. People say they want extra [milk] when they order, but you can't really put extra because it leaks out of our sponge. It's already moist, so it sucks it up right away—any extra runs out, all over the table, all over the floor!"

Most customers now are Latino, in keeping with the neighborhood that has changed over the years from what was once mostly German, Irish, and Italian immigrants. Interestingly, the bakery is also popular with local Ethiopians because of the 20th-century imperialism that led to a prevalence of Italian bakeries in their home country. "They really love custard and cream, and especially like the mille-feuille," says Goldberg. "It's like a napoleon cake. Puff pastry, custard, and whipped cream. They love it."

Goldberg was hired in the cake department 17 years ago, never realizing that he'd one day be a co-owner of the bakery, along with Pena and Flores (the latter has been there nearly 35 years and is considered "a key person," says Goldberg—he was mentored by former owner Pasquale, and his son may one day take the reins). Today, each has distinct responsibilities when it comes to the business, "but we try our best to give the best product and follow the traditions of Dianda's."

They do a wonderful job of sticking with tradition. You can taste the legacy in each crumbly cookie and creamy cake slice; people remain devoted to their birthday cakes and Christmastime panettones. (And Goldberg's chocolate work is phenomenal—the first time I met him, his hands were covered in the stuff.) They remain committed to their employees—keeping the two unions they've always had: one for bakers, another for clerks. The team also understands how to make updates that resonate with customers' changing needs—like that *tres leches* cake. It's a top seller now and comes in six different flavors.

Everything at Dianda's is about consistency, quality, and doing things the old-fashioned way. They're all about keeping customers happy. For a "generational" bakery like this, people have a certain expectation when they walk in the door. They know what they like, what they've always had, perhaps what they ate there as children. And they want each visit to match those memories.

"You need that familiarity that people can rely on," Goldberg explains, pleased with their legacy of employees and products that reliably sell out each day. "They want the same thing, over and over; they expect consistency."

For more than 50 years, Dianda's has maintained that consistency by making every custard and layer of cake from scratch, beginning at 2:30 a.m. daily. And they are delighted to celebrate that fact, as

Vintage Spot
STELLA PASTRY & CAFÉ: EST. 1942

Italian bakeries can sometimes seem a dime a dozen in the city of San Francisco, but there are a few that are worth mention. Stella Pastry & Café is one. With its prominent Columbus Avenue location bisecting North Beach, 1942 founding, and sweet pillar-flanked blue-and-white entrance, Stella offers a worthy experience of Italian treats. Its most famous—and most special—item is the Sacripantina cake, which features layers of cream, zabaglione custard, and rum-doused sponge cake and tastes like a positively dreamy blonde tiramisu. The bakery has even patented the name and dome shape for this cake, which is popular for special occasions but also available in the shop by the slice. Stella has other traditional items, too, including a variety of wee Italian cookies, cannoli, and other cakes starring cream. The shop is tiny, but a few cafe tables on the front sidewalk offer the perfect spot to enjoy a cappuccino and slice of San Francisco–Italian sweetness.

446 Columbus Ave., San Francisco, CA 94133;
(415) 986-2914; stellapastry.com

they did for their 50th anniversary party in the neighborhood in 2012, giving away free coffee and cream puffs—more than 1,000 of the latter—all day long.

"I go to a lot of bakeries in the city and when I travel," Goldberg shares, describing how he constantly notices a difference between Dianda's and other places. "We're still making everything by hand, and everything tastes good. That, I think, is the most important. At most bakeries everything looks good, but when you taste it here, you really taste the difference."

You certainly can; I noticed this even while doing research for this book. Not all cream puffs are created equal. What strikes me about Dianda's—in addition to the array of colors and flavors and admirable commitment to staff and doing things the old-fashioned way—is that you can taste the pride in each bite.

FIOR D'ITALIA

SAN REMO HOTEL, 2237 MASON ST., SAN FRANCISCO, CA 94133

(415) 986-1886 • FIOR.COM

The Real Thing

Small in stature but big in personality, chef Gianfranco "Gianni" Audieri has been on a self-described mission since the 1960s to "teach Americans what Italian food actually is." For the last 30 years, he's been at the helm of Fior d'Italia, a rambling, historic Italian restaurant in North Beach that has the distinction of being the oldest Italian restaurant in continual operation in America. And it is a wonderful place.

In 2012, Audieri took ownership of the establishment where he'd served as chef for three decades, a place that was founded in 1886 by Italian immigrants Angelo Del Monte and "Papa" Marianetti. They first opened "The Fior" to serve the local community, many of whom had come to California in search of gold. Fairly quickly "the Italian flower" gained a following with city residents, even operating in a tent for a year while the city was rebuilt after the 1906 earthquake; just the day after the quake, it fed locals soup out of said tent, like an impromptu Red Cross shelter. Today, its customer demographic is split roughly down the middle—half local, half tourist (some of whom come downstairs from the European-style pension in which the restaurant sits)—all there to enjoy authentic Italian specialties for lunch or dinner.

Over the years, The Fior has had five locations due to various circumstances—the earthquake, a few fires, landlord disputes—but just four sets of owners. A native Milanese, Audieri came into the picture in 1982 as chef, eventually taking over with his wife Trudy, after firmly establishing himself and becoming part of the fabric of the

restaurant. His arrival in San Francisco followed a substantial career traversing the globe for hospitality gigs, beginning when he was 16 and cleaning potatoes, beans, and peas—doing "nothing fancy"—at a restaurant in his hometown. He spent time in Switzerland, England, Jamaica, Grand Cayman, Venezuela, Panama, and all over the US consulting in hotels, working on cruise ships, and leading restaurants. He served for a stint as a US Army medic, delivering three babies during his time in Vietnam and Germany, and has even encountered American royalty: Audieri was selected to wait on President John F. Kennedy when the young culinarian was working at the Four Seasons in New York in the 1960s ("They chose me because I had clearance," Audieri explains, from his time in the army). And it was in New York that he became disheartened by what was passed off as an Italian restaurant in this country.

"It was Italian-American food, not Italian food," he recalls. Even today, "I hate it when people ask for more sauce!" he laughs.

At 77, Audieri is still going strong, a fixture at the restaurant just as much as its classic cream-colored punched-tin ceiling. He is always there and can be seen putting on his chef's coat at the back of the bar at the start of service, ready with a smile. He is all about the customers, often serving them personally.

"We don't try to impress food critics with our food," he says, sharing that he believes in fairly large portions and not having to dress up for dinner—though you'd feel comfortable doing so at his white-tablecloth restaurant. "If 100 people cross our threshold and we satisfy 96 of them, I'm great." His food certainly satisfies.

Fervent about the distinction between "tomato sauce" and "marinara sauce"—the latter has anchovies and lots of garlic—Audieri is responsible for a menu that is mostly Northern Italian but also represents the south, like with that tomato sauce. Linguine with said napoletana sauce is a beautiful, simple *primi* course at lunch to precede a plate of the super-fresh fish of the day (when I was last there, it was a lovely petrale sole that had arrived at the restaurant that morning), ever-so-lightly panfried, golden where it'd been kissed by the hot pan, and served with a drizzle of citrusy olive oil, alongside bright green beans, carrots, and a single roasted red potato. The combination is an example of the reverence the staff takes with fine ingredients, prevalent throughout the menu that is divided between the traditional antipasti, both cold and hot; soups and salads; dry and housemade fresh pastas; as well as rice, chicken, "meat" (which includes lamb), veal, fish, and vegetable dishes. The very crusty bread served at the start has an extremely tender, almost see-through center—ideal for dipping in olive oil. And at the end of the meal, tiramisu is presented "mousse" style—in a glass coupe, but with all the traditional components of the classic dessert, including—surprisingly—petite disks of chocolate hidden amidst the billowy cream. Alongside a scalding hot, deeply invigorating espresso, replete with miniature sugar spoon if you're so inclined, it is glorious.

The full bar offers specialty cocktails as well as a respectable wine list with, naturally, Italian and California varietals primarily. Longtime waiters like Israel, who's worked here for 22 years, can often be seen shuttling drinks swiftly from the bar to awaiting diners—many of whom may have been coming to the restaurant for just as long.

"They've been meeting here for lunch two or three times a month for years," Israel told me of a group of distinguished-looking, gray-haired gentlemen who gradually trickled in, asking, "First one here?" and heading to what seemed to be their usual table. With the casual greeting and tasty plate of "real Italian" food The Fior provides, it's easy to see why some people make it their go-to spot. A series of small, gold nameplates lines the long bar, revealing the support fans of the restaurant have given it over the years.

Sitting in one of the bar's dark wood-paneled booths or at an elegant table in one the sprawling dining rooms, surrounded by walls covered with historic photos of the people who've been involved over the years, feels like sitting at a crossover in time. Framed color pictures of local football hero Joe Montana appear not far from sepia-toned shots of serious-faced Italian men, standing rigid and proud next to a storefront, or black-and-white photographs of wedding banquets at the restaurant, with rows and rows of dandily dressed guests seated at long tables. Sitting among this chronicle of local history and customers through the ages gives the sensation of rubbing elbows with the city's Italian immigrant past while simultaneously partaking in a modern tradition: dining out, perhaps on a regular schedule, with friends. Even if it is just over one of chef Gianni's favorite simple meals: a piece of Parmesan ("cheese is my sin," he shared), a bit of pear, a glass of wine, and some good bread.

FISHERMEN'S GROTTO NO. 9

2847 TAYLOR ST., SAN FRANCISCO, CA 94133

(415) 673-7025 • FISHERMENSGROTTO.COM

Time Warp by the Seaside

A sidewalk barker may entice you to explore the oldest sit-down restaurant on Fisherman's Wharf. Or it may be the sheer size and variety of venues that draws you in—from patio seating behind a classic crab stand to a marvelously colored Venetian Room, decked out like the Italian flag, or a traditional, more sedate upstairs dining room with spectacular views of the harbor, the hills of the city, and the Golden Gate Bridge beyond. Perhaps you're curious about what this fish restaurant has over its neighbors, all crammed into a short, competitive stretch by the water. Whatever it is that brings you to eat there, Fishermen's Grotto No. 9 will not disappoint—in its masculine history, its festive air today, and the sheer deliciousness of its seafood.

The place was founded by Sicilian immigrant Mike Geraldi, whose first foray into the world of fisheries came as a teenager, when he shuttled and sold the catch from local fisherman on the streets of San Francisco. He eventually earned enough to get his own boat and open his own fish stand, on the very site the full restaurant still sits today. "No. 9" refers to Geraldi's stall number of the original 10 on the street, and today's crab stand, selling one of the city's best chowders and fresh crab on ice, represents that first business well.

The business has always been passed down to the men in the family, now on the third generation, which includes Rick Geraldi, one of six co-owners and grandson of the founder. You'll often see him manning the crab stand, but he also runs much of the show behind the scenes, including buying all the fish that makes it to your plate.

Vintage Spot
ALIOTO'S RESTAURANT: EST: 1925

The competition: As if in a perpetual duel, Alioto's sits right next to Fishermen's Grotto No. 9.Every Fisherman's Wharf restaurant vies for its own superlative piece of history and Alioto's is no different. Alioto's is now on its fourth generation of family ownership, and, with its establishment as a fish stall in 1925, it is one of the oldest restaurants not only on the wharf but in the city. Where Fishermen's Grotto No. 9 has been run by male-dominated generations, Alioto's history is female—going back to Rose Alioto. When her husband, Nunzio Sr., the founder, died shortly after starting the restaurant, she took over, and it's her cioppino on the menu and her recipes still featured today. The current owner is third-generation family member Nunzio, bearing the same name as the founder so long ago.

Alioto's also has multiple dining spaces—upstairs, downstairs, and the patio cafe out front, where birds may fly straight from the water to your table. Upstairs, you'll likely hear the sounds of opera playing throughout the dining room, where even the sound system has a vintage feel. This is where I'd recommend eating, while taking in the lovely view and attentive service of the tuxedoed waiters with white waist aprons. Carpeted floors dull the clinking forks and glasses, enabling your full focus on a *frutti di mare* pasta, perhaps, featuring spaghetti, calamari, teensy local bay shrimp, and clams in their shells, all in a simple, subtly sweet tomato sauce. Let your mind wander to the time when the matriarch took over out of necessity and made the place the successful establishment it became through three more generations, never losing its competitive spirit, always vying for the next customer.

No. 8 Fisherman's Wharf, San Francisco, CA 94133; (415) 673-0183; aliotos.com

Today that comes from wholesalers, but up until the 1950s, the family had its own boats with which they brought in their own catch. Talk about fresh; there was even a dock behind the building.

"It used to be that people would come in their boats and pull right up in the back," Geraldi explains, also describing the curb service back in the day. Hence the spirited yelling from representatives of each of the row restaurants, even today, trying to pull in customers to their own waterfront experience. Geraldi is notably reserved for a Fisherman's Wharf hawker—not really hawking his wares at all. He stands quietly behind the crab stand, with a half smile and a lifetime of knowledge about the product. He and his brothers and cousins— the gentlemen with whom he runs the place today—used to run around the dining room and kitchen, working every job as kids. He says many customers have an emotional connection with a certain part of the restaurant.

"There's a lot of people who, for sentimental reasons, like the Venetian Room—they went on a first date there, or a prom, or proposed to their wife at that table," Geraldi says of the red, white, and green space with booths and gondolier-style pillars throughout. But just as many people prefer the expansive, fancier upstairs dining room, which surprisingly used to be a fish wholesale house but now sports white linen tablecloths and that vast view.

With its vivid representation of bygone eras—from the '30s to the '60s—and variety of festive, experiential spaces (there is even a gift shop on-site, along with two dark leather-upholstered cocktail lounges that seem to drip with a period vibe—like where Don Draper might be found), Fishermen's Grotto No. 9 has the feeling of a Fisherman's Wharf Disneyland. It is atmospheric from top to bottom, from Venice to view. For someone like me, who spent a fair amount of time there as a child but hasn't been in 30 years, it's like a rocket of nostalgia to walk in the door. Awesome, really. They even maintained their original logo of a cartoonish fisherman, dressed like the yellow-jacketed Gorton's man, designed by an art student in the '30s. Even Geraldi describes the place as being "like a time warp."

He marvels at the tales of "old-timers" who recall the restaurant's previous eras, and is a solid representation of the hard-working fisherman's family today. His grandfather got his recipes from the Italian fishermen up and down the California coast that he met as a traveling motor-oil salesman, supplying their boats with the energy they needed to get that fresh catch. A true entrepreneur, he opened up his restaurant around the time of the world's fair on Treasure Island (1939), knowing the influx of people meant lots of potential customers. So he took his recipes, his boyhood knowledge of fish, and a love of his homeland, and opened his stand. The place drips with pride in country and a spirit of entrepreneurism.

You might think an establishment so kitschy wouldn't do a good job with the food, but you'd be wrong; it's pretty fantastic, too. Classics are the way to go—the chowder or anything with crab, their area of expertise—and specials such as sole stuffed with Dungeness crab are dynamite, highlighting the best of the season in an old-school preparation (cream sauce, please) with vegetables alongside. A glass of wine from their manageable list could begin the meal, though I'd recommend perusing the cocktail menu that also highlights the best of a previous time—calling out drinks such as Gold Cadillacs and an assortment of fizzes, in addition to the expected martinis and gimlets. Sipping these drinks in the downstairs bar that used to be a breezeway onto the dock brings you closer to that midcentury feel, as you swivel on your leather barstool and await your table. And if you choose to dine outside on the front patio, you become part of the scenery, part of the wharf tapestry that is such a signature San Francisco experience. Tourist families photograph their children skipping on the sidewalk; older couples meander, looking for a lunch spot; and grandparents treat the grandkids to a seaside meal, all the while reminiscing about how when they were young, they drove right up to the dock.

GARDEN COURT

PALACE HOTEL, 2 NEW MONTGOMERY ST.,
SAN FRANCISCO, CA 94105 • (415) 546-5089
SFPALACE.COM/GARDEN-COURT

Majesty for All

The Palace Hotel. The sheer name of the place conjures up all sorts of elegant and romantic images of bygone eras—site of the finest galas, presidential stays, even movie star antics (Sarah Bernhardt purportedly caused a stir when she once arrived with her pet baby tiger). "It's a place where magic and memories are made," describes Renée Roberts, longtime public relations representative for the hotel who is actually so much more, given her start 20 years ago in the catering department, experience working her way through all the other divisions, and genuine affection for, and pride in, the hotel as a result. I have her to thank for my insider's peek at the Palace, a hotel that has shaped and hosted San Francisco high society since its original opening in 1875, only to be rebuilt and reopened in 1909, following its devastation in the 1906 earthquake. Ever since, the hotel itself has remained a beacon for the regal and royals of the city and beyond—plus many more "regular" people, like me, not in small part due to some of its greatest individual treasures, such as the utterly lovely Garden Court restaurant.

It feels limiting to call the Garden Court simply a restaurant. Designated an official San Francisco landmark in 1969 (and the city's only interior landmark), the Garden Court is more like a grand, turn-of-the-century ballroom in which you may dine: The lofty space is flanked by towering marble columns, lined with panels of mirrored doors, crowned with a stunning arched glass ceiling, and overlooked by a squadron of 750-pound Austrian crystal chandeliers. It feels

almost alive in its historic spirit. It is where little girls and boys peek at themselves in the mirrors, dressed in their holiday finest at Christmastime, and where those same kids may come for tea at age 6, or decide at 13 they want to be married there someday. For more than a century, the dining space and its adjoining ballroom have together served as the site of the annual December debutante ball, still a high-society event steeped in tradition but today featuring more tattoos and piercings on its debs. The Garden Court is also the birthplace of green goddess dressing—a divinely creamy, speckled green Northern California classic created in 1923 that has made a comeback in recent years, surging in popularity with the fervor for all things vintage. (The recipe's available on the hotel website.)

Certain items on the menu will never be removed, says Roberts—such as the dressing and the hotel's signature crab salad over which it is served—but the team behind the Garden Court constantly strives to balance the old and the new, the traditional and the modern, with dishes to suit the ethereal aesthetic of the room. Sometimes they do this by updating the classics, like using farm-fresh produce instead of the traditional canned vegetables previously featured in the crab salad, or simply by offering modern dishes altogether—crab cake Benedict, for instance, but with the lightest crab cake you've ever tasted (consisting only of jumbo lump crab, no binder) and a beautiful take on hollandaise, prepared with browned butter to add a nuttiness and deepen the sauce's decadence. The Garden Court features the Palace's logo-embossed silver—the hotel is one of few left that still personalizes its fancy flatware—adding another layer of Old World elegance to the dining experience. Open for breakfast, lunch, and proper Saturday afternoon tea, as well as desserts and cocktails, it is one of the loveliest places in the city to dine and feel simultaneously like a 21st-century cosmopolitan citizen as well as a part of history. This careful balance between the old and the new is a theme that runs throughout the Palace experience.

"That's what's so interesting about our city—and it's just like the juxtaposition of what happens at the Palace," comments Roberts, thinking back to those debutantes. "There is this part that is so old, historic, and steeped in tradition, set against something young and fashionable and trendy. You see these young girls now, they're definitely different than they were 10 or 20 years ago. They come to the balls with their dates, and they are tattooed and very current and relevant, yet they are still partaking in these traditions. Family roots and generational celebrations are still very important to them."

Roberts has seen a lot over the hotel's last 20 years—a third-generation wedding in the French Parlor room, where the children, parents, and grandparents all had posed in the same location at their own weddings; a 70th wedding anniversary for a couple who was married at the Palace. "The things they could tell you, it was shocking!" she recounts. "The woman's face lit up when she shared their memories here."

The restoration of the Garden Court took place in 1989, just before Roberts joined the hotel, and it included stripping away "decorating crimes of the '60s," like salmon-pink paint on the grand marble columns in the space and the reinstallation of those gigantic chandeliers. Roberts describes the size of the crystal pieces of art as almost otherworldly: "[In the pictures of the restoration process,] these big men installing the chandeliers looked like little munchkins next to those crates!" And she herself went from client to catering-department employee to chief ambassador for the hotel—even

Vintage Spot
FERRY BUILDING MARKETPLACE: EST: 1898/2003

Modern treatment of vintage institutions isn't always a bad thing. San Francisco's Ferry Building, for instance, has been standing for more than 100 years (originally founded in 1898), but a repurposing a decade ago, in 2003, breathed new life into a building that has been around the block and back. It feels like an old train station—and it is. Now shiny and new inside but with its architectural integrity intact, this original "transportation focal point" for people arriving by train from the East or from the other parts of the Bay is now a foodie mecca. The airy, skylight-topped, 65,000-square-foot marketplace features permanent restaurants—including some of San Francisco's best, such as the award-winning Slanted Door—and local seafood favorites (such as mine, Hog Island Oyster Company, featuring locally harvested bivalves and an unrivaled grilled cheese sandwich), as well as food retailers organized along a central nave. Smaller kiosks dot the space, too, all focused on the culinary arts. Strolling the central path and exploring its offshoots is a wonderful way to kill an afternoon—and get a great sense of the city's modern culinary scene. Artisanal breads and cheeses (Acme and Cowgirl respectively), gluten-free bakery (Mariposa), chocolates (Recchiuti), coffee (Blue Bottle), fresh juices, a wine bar, and farm-fresh meats and multiple seafood purveyors are on offer, along with a thrice-weekly farmers' market. And it's still a ferry terminal! Boats dock throughout the day at the Ferry Building, bringing people from nearby Bay cities to explore San Francisco and take them back home. There's an energy here that's both old and new, and addictive. I love this place so much I'd want to marry it if I weren't married already. It's a wonderfully vibrant spot, a modern marketplace in a vintage building full of grandeur, with a vintage history, of travel through and arrival in the City by the Bay, to match.

One Ferry Building, San Francisco, CA 94111; (415) 983-8030; ferrybuildingmarketplace.com

helping to oversee its centennial celebration in 2009. She also has the Palace to thank for her husband—it's where they met.

But these unforgettable connections to the hotel and its majestic Garden Court dining space don't seem to require employment there. Whether it's for an indulgent afternoon tea with a grandchild, a business lunch, a vacationing family's breakfast, or a Christmas celebration, experiencing the space lends itself to the creation of special, and delicious, memories. Particularly when that green goddess dressing is on the menu.

GOLDEN GATE FORTUNE COOKIE FACTORY

56 ROSS ALLEY, SAN FRANCISCO, CA 94108 • (415) 781-3956

+≈+

Sweet Fortune

*T*he word *factory* typically conjures up something of great scale, machinery, and rote operation. Not so when it comes to the Golden Gate Fortune Cookie Factory, founded in 1962 in a little alley in Chinatown, where they still do things the old-fashioned way, mostly, that is, by hand. It's a fairly small space for a "factory," just a few yards wide but with high ceilings and a narrow pathway next to the cookie-making operation.

That operation includes a couple of women sitting next to antique iron cookie presses—similar to an upright, oversize waffle iron—and methodically collecting the freshly pressed, golden disks of crisped dough as they drop off the irons. They shape the cookies by hand, inserting the fortunes into each one individually. (If you're wondering, it doesn't seem as though they select specific fortunes for specific cookies, leaving that to fate.) Some unformed disks go into bins for distribution to visitors who are ogling the whole process. The women don't seem to speak much, except occasionally to each other, which is difficult given that they sit in somewhat of a line, front to back, making conversation challenging. They are focused on their work, the work that has happened this way for a half century, and aren't distracted by the countless visitors to the factory who snap photos (for 50 cents, please) and snatch up the free samples of the still-warm unformed cookie disks as they are generously, and constantly, dispensed by a tour guide of sorts—an elderly man stationed near the front door. He also operates the on-site shop, which is really just a shelving unit full of bags of fortune cookies in several flavors (chocolate included),

57

a salty chip option, almond cookies, and those flat disks. "Adult" fortune cookies are available and spied sitting at the back of the pile, near the irons, out of reach of patrons for understandable reasons—schoolchildren are frequent visitors. The company will do custom orders as well—in case you're in need of a thousand fortune cookies for a big event—or want lots of the adult versions for a racy party.

The factory is exactly the sort of vintage spot you'd think of when researching a book like this. It is a San Francisco classic that should be visited by all who come or live here. You may have to patiently shuffle through—and it's not really "through," frankly, more in and out—as it's crowded with small children and tourists alike, but it's absolutely worth it. The price of admission is free; only those photographs will cost you—plus any bags of cookies you can't resist taking home with you (I left with four).

"Best fortune cookies ever!" exclaimed a friend when I brought her a bagful. They really are the best I've ever had; even after sitting on my counter for a week, the cookies are still crisp and fresh and pleasantly, subtly sweet. They taste homemade, like they came from someone's private kitchen instead of a nondescript building in an alley in Chinatown. My 2-year-old daughter calls them crackers and begs for one ("Cucker! Cucker! Cucker!") when she sees them. I will

Vintage Spot

GREAT CHINA HERB COMPANY: EST. 1922

Little shops chock-full of thousands of types of herbs—devoted solely to the curing of ills—still exist in some parts of the country, San Francisco included. I shouldn't be surprised by this; acupuncture is wildly popular today, so why wouldn't traditional Chinese medicine still be a thing? Even so, I was dumbstruck to see the rows and rows of little wooden boxes lining a full wall of this shop on Washington Street, antique scales dangling from some of the drawer pulls, each drawer packed with herbs.

They have thousands at the Great China Herb Company, established in 1922 and still doing a gangbusters business today. Generations of families file in regularly to pick up prescribed herbs to cure numerous ailments, from mild tummy trouble to more serious diseases. The shop has an on-site doctor several days a week to "read" patrons' health and give an on-the-spot assessment and prescription. I met one woman who was visiting the shop with a group of schoolchildren as part of a field trip to Chinatown; she told me a fellow teacher swears by the service.

Things are still done the old-fashioned way here, including using an abacus to tally purchases—though they're also required now to use digital scales in addition to the antiques for precise measurements. English is spoken sparingly and on request, and only by a couple of staff members, but the place welcomes visitors of all languages and homelands. It's a cramped little shop—like many in Chinatown—so best not to bring lots of bags or any cumbersome accoutrement (like a baby stroller). But put it on your list for your next visit to the ancient neighborhood. It's a head rush of an experience—and they no doubt have something for that, too.

**857 Washington St., San Francisco,
CA 94108; (415) 982-2195**

take her on a tour someday, which consists really of a short walk into the place, standing around, and taking pictures, for the hot-off-the-presses version.

Back at the factory, be sure to check your bag upon departure: Mr. Tour-Guide-Cashier may have tucked a few more warm cookie disks in among the packaged stuff. Eat them immediately as you stroll along the smoky, sometimes pungent, sometimes intoxicating, sometimes phlegm-dotted sidewalks of the neighborhood, pondering free tea tastings, trinket shops, Peking duck vendors, and egg-custard-tart bakeries. The cookies won't stay warm for long.

GRUBSTAKE

1525 PINE ST., SAN FRANCISCO, CA 94109

(415) 673-8268 • SFGRUBSTAKE.COM

Dining on the Orient Express

What do an old railcar, incredible pumpkin pie, drag queens, and TV food personality Guy Fieri have in common? They are all part of the history of the Grubstake, a classic late-night diner with a unique Portuguese angle—it's San Francisco's only restaurant that serves Portuguese dishes daily—and a spot that feels like a dying breed in a city focused on the latest and greatest culinary trends.

With Gold Rush references woven throughout its menu—*grubstake* is an old mining term that refers to the "supplies or funds furnished a mining prospector on promise of a share in his discoveries" (according to the dictionary)—the sweet little spot feels both Californian and uniquely San Franciscan at once.

Current owners Fernando and Linda Santos have had the place for more than two decades. Fernando (who actually goes by his last name, Santos) bought it on a relative whim with his cousin, Fernando Oliveira, in 1989—before even meeting his future wife. The previous owners, who'd had it since the 1970s, "wanted out after the earthquake," says Linda, referring to the 6.9-magnitude Loma Prieta shaker that devastated much of the Bay Area. But the history of the restaurant and bar dates back to 1927, when an old railcar that served the Key Line—connecting Berkeley and Oakland to San Francisco—was decommissioned and turned into a diner in the city. Then called "The Orient Express," the diner was taken over and renamed by other restaurateurs in 1967 as the second outlet of their restaurant called "The Grubstake I" in another part of the city. Two decades later, the

Portuguese cousins entered the scene. Linda wasn't in the picture at the time of the purchase—she and Santos didn't meet until 1992—and she never imagined living the restaurant life for so long.

"I didn't realize at first how much was involved," Linda confesses. But, she says, her smiling eyes brightening, "It feels great to be part of a business that's been around for so long. And when people say, 'The food is so good!' it really makes you feel like, yes, it's all worth it." She shares how she once emerged from the tiny kitchen, greeted by applause from the guests of a private, rare breakfast party, and was so touched by the response. She comes across as extremely modest, but her huge role in the restaurant-in-a-railcar is undeniable: Linda, dubbed "the cheesecake lady" by customers, designed the menu, develops (and prepares) the specials, bakes the desserts from her own recipes (many of them, in her own home oven), and even grows some of the featured produce in her own city backyard. I was shocked that in a region obsessed with the hyper-local, they don't advertise—or mention anywhere at all—that last bit.

"Yes, the kale for the *caldo verde* and apples for the apple pie come from our yard," she shared. She and Santos shop daily for the other ingredients, scouring farmers' markets, restaurant supply stores, and even Costco for what they need. The Portuguese dishes are family recipes from her mother-in-law and the "home cook" stuff—scalloped potatoes and meat loaf, for instance—is from Linda herself. The block on which the diner sits feels semi-industrial, with a transmission shop next door and a Vespa dealer across the street, and kitty-corner a Holiday Inn occupies half the block. (Like many areas in the city, there are plans to erect a massive condo building in this stretch soon.) You wouldn't notice the restaurant if you weren't actively seeking it out—perhaps for a cozy family dinner; an after-hours, post-clubbing hangout; or, if you're a cab driver or doctor just getting off your shift, a 3 a.m. dinner or breakfast to end or start your day. Once you get inside, you're greeted with mirrors that make the tiny place feel a touch bigger, and small tables on one side and a bar and handful of tables on the other—the side that is actually an old railcar. The walls are covered with photos of the Grubstake family—the owners, employees, and scores of customers—along with classic party-shop seasonal decor, depending on the time of year.

And like any good nighttime diner, the Grubstake has a wealth of colorful customer stories that have shaped its character over the years. Once, a drag queen returned from the restroom, forgetting to pull up her pantyhose and meandering outside awkwardly with stockings halfway up her legs. An international traveler once emerged—also from the men's room—stark naked; apparently, in his jet-lagged state, he confused the diner for his own home. And one young man, the night before his wedding, visited the diner after the dry hour of 2 a.m. He begged and begged for a beer, only to be denied by Linda, who was committed to upholding the law. His persistent desperation led friends to offer him one of the beer-bottles-turned-floral-vases that sit atop each table, and he chugged the flower water thirstily, to Linda's amused disbelief.

It is likely stories like these, along with the delicious, cozy food and local history, that led the Food Network's *Diners, Drive-Ins and Dives*, starring Guy Fieri, to feature the diner in 2008. While it electrified business, Linda has mixed feelings about big publicity like that. It forced the restaurant to get more "corporate" to handle the increased foot traffic and led to a doubling of its staff. She reminisces about "the old Grubstake."

"We knew all of our customers, and our customers knew all of our staff," she says. "It was like a family." To an outsider, it still feels like a true family business—and the co-owner says they still do their best to operate that way. Most of their longtime staff remained through the transition, and the holiday decor—such as what covered the restaurant for a recent Halloween—includes pictures of customers, the owners, and employees over the years, which gives the effect of a home kitchen fridge, covered with photos of the kids growing up, family celebrations, and milestone moments. On the secret to their success, Linda is definitive: "At five in the evening or three o'clock in the morning, people can come in here and get fresh, good food— whether it's a family of five sitting over here or a group of drag queens sitting over there." Everyone gets along and enjoys themselves. "To see that, and be a part of that, really makes you feel good."

Oh, and Linda's pumpkin pie, while not typically a difficult dessert to make, tasted creamier and more delicious than any I'd ever had— even my own mother's, and that's hard to beat. Linda served it to me nonchalantly while we chatted, just like any mom might when you stop by her home for a visit.

GUMP'S

135 POST ST., SAN FRANCISCO, CA 94108

(415) 982-1616 • GUMPS.COM

+⫘⫘+

Treasure Hunting

There is no other store like Gump's in the city or, as far as I know, in the world. A one-of-a-kind retailer that specializes in the one of a kind, the business was founded in 1861—the same year as The Old Clam House, one of the oldest restaurants in San Francisco— as a mirror and frame shop to outfit the homes of new Gold Rush millionaires. Over time, it has become the place for the well-heeled citizens with an eye for design to decorate both themselves and their homes with unique pieces of art—whether it be clothing, sculpture, or, the store's most exciting department, jewelry. The retailer has changed locations seven times over the years, for various reasons, the 1906 earthquake included; it occupied the most memorable address, 250 Post Street, noteworthy for its near-90-year stint and striking façade, until its most recent move down the street in 1995.

Self-described in a 1924 ad as "The Treasure House of European and Oriental Art," the subhead is apt. Everywhere you turn, the museum-like palace of retail presents another gem of an object, collected by Gump's team of savvy buyers, sometimes from near, sometimes quite far. One of the store's most iconic pieces, a Qing dynasty (1644–1912) gilded wood Buddha, was acquired after the 1906 earthquake in Gump's restocking effort. It still presides quietly over the first floor and is the largest of its kind outside of a museum. The store is built around a grand atrium going up, up, upward, and at Christmastime, the ground floor is like a wonderland of twinkly objects and brightly colored trinkets for children and grown-ups alike. Gorgeous, gigantic chandeliers hang high overhead in that atrium with an orangey-beige fabric draped downward, drawing the eye to enchanting displays of nutcrackers, toy trains, and glass ornaments that reflect rainbows of light, bouncing off of everything else around them. The rest of the year, with the holiday displays gone, you really notice what anchors the ground floor: the incredible jewelry.

The department is staffed by longtime employees, such as Irine Dwyer, whose tenure of 38 years feels like a lie when looking at her young face.

"Yep, I started in the credit office and worked my way up!" says the native San Franciscan, who is one of a handful of sales associates in the department that some argue is the reason Gump's is still in business. Her business card simply reads "Fine Jewelry," but over the years she has built a "black book"—an "old-time industry term"—of customers that likely contains many of San Francisco's richest and most powerful citizens.

In a previous time, like when Dwyer started, associates were required to come to the table with a black book—but she had to "prove herself" since she was starting with no experience. She was drawn to the discipline by her admiration of the senior associate in the department, the venerable Marilu Klar, who has been with the store for more than a half century and is a well-known name in the business.

"Marilu used to come back from her buying trips to the Orient, and [at store meetings] I'd see what she did," Dwyer explains. "It was fascinating! Treasure hunting!"

The hunting included scouring jade markets in Hong Kong and forming relationships with unlikely gem dealers—including one notable man, says former employee, art director, and designer Hilda Chen, who "walks around downtown San Francisco, looking shabby as heck, and has pockets filled with the most incredible stones."

Dwyer describes the process of meeting customers' needs: "First, you need to know what can be gotten. If they say they want emerald green jade tomorrow, it's not going to happen. That is totally a treasure hunt."

That hunt typically originates in Myanmar, where most jade comes from these days—but with the eight-year-long embargo (as of this writing), "the prices of jade have been absolutely bonkers,"

she says. Most vendors with fine jade proactively go to Klar "because they know she has a following."

And lately, because of the embargo, Dwyer explains, "a lot of the jades we have now—which are really fine jades, wonderful jades, really fine colors—are old jades that we had years ago. They've come full circle. We're getting them back in the state."

With merchandise that "wonderful," she says, "you can really accommodate your clients. It's not all about 'what you see is what you get.'"

She's referring to the Gump's Signature line, which has pieces designed expressly by Gump's, exclusively for Gump's customers. They decide which stones to use, how they want them mounted, the types of clasps to use.

"That's where custom work comes into play," she says. "I have a customer who loves these necklaces—and she doesn't like a plain clasp. So you go looking for a really neat clasp, something out of the ordinary, you put the clasp on and she's a happy camper."

"Not even Tiffany's provides this sort of custom service," says Chen.

If you can't get to San Francisco to visit the store in person, the online shop provides much of their enchanting merchandise from just about every department. And if it's custom fine jewelry you seek, contact the department directly. Dwyer or one of her other talented colleagues will be sure to work hard to find what you're looking for.

"It's easy to sell what you love," she enthuses with not a touch of falsity. "You're happy it's going to a good home so you don't have to look at it day after day and want it."

Unless, of course, it's the jade bangles she so adores. "I want one in every color," explaining that there are seven primary and a multitude of bicolors.

"What it actually is, is an oddity of nature," created by the cuts made in a "big boulder with streaks of color," she marvels.

Certainly, if you sported one of these bangles, or perhaps a showstopping diamond-and-emerald necklace, at your next city event, you would certainly be the belle of the ball—noticed in a heartbeat by the Gump's fine jewelry specialist who may be enjoying a cocktail in your midst.

HOUSE OF PRIME RIB

1906 VAN NESS AVE., SAN FRANCISCO, CA 94109

(415) 885-4605 • HOUSEOFPRIMERIB.NET

Meat Zeppelin

When you go out to dinner, you expect something different from what you would get at home, whether it be extraordinary service, fancier cooking, a virtual trip to another time and place, or just a change of pace from a humdrum routine. For delivery on all of these fronts, the people of San Francisco and its visitors have gone to the House of Prime Rib since 1949.

The venerable palace of this classic cut of meat provides a treat of a dining experience—and the 178-seat, five-room establishment is packed nightly from its opening hour of 4:00, 5:00 or 5:30 p.m., depending on the day of the week. When you walk in for the first time at what you think will be the early-bird hour, it is actually jarring to be met with a crowd that you can barely weave your way through to reach the comfortable lounge area and await your table. Gem it is, but not a hidden one—the restaurant has been featured on countless "best" lists and profiled on a number of TV shows over the years, including, more recently, Anthony Bourdain's *No Reservations* travel series; the popular local PBS restaurant review show *Check, Please!*; and as a favorite spot of Olympic figure skater Brian Boitano on the Food Network's *The Best Thing I Ever Ate*. Clientele is diverse and includes celebrities as well as plenty of regular folks; families are as comfortable here as are singles on a date. The only requirement? Must love meat. And the prime rib at the eponymously named restaurant is a true star.

How the beef is prepared there contributes to its succulent flavor: dry-aged in-house, then covered with rock salt and roasted,

69

the method preserves the beef's juicy quality of its luscious marbling while creating a lovely outer crust. During dinner service, the prime rib is wheeled around the dining room as the revered main attraction in its own gleaming, stainless steel zeppelin, ready for table-side carving to each diner's specifications. Four cuts are offered: the "City," for "the lighter appetite"; the "House," a heartier portion; the "English," which comes in three thinner slices (a preference of some diners—my husband included); or the "King Henry VIII," billed as extra-generous and thick, for "king-size" appetites. Notably, this last offering comes bone-in. No matter the cut, you will not leave hungry. All portions are more than ample; as a ravenous eight-months-pregnant woman on my last visit, I still had leftovers from the most petite (cough) "City" cut.

The restaurant stays true to its name by keeping its menu tight; other than a fish of the day, there is, well, prime rib. This makes ordering quite simple, appealing for the diner who can be overwhelmed by choices on extensive menus. You choose your cut and potato prep (baked with all the traditional fixings or the most buttery, puree-style mashed you've ever tasted); everything else is a given—indulgent creamed spinach, billowy-crisp Yorkshire pudding, and a beautiful house salad tossed swiftly, also table-side, in a massive bowl over ice. Dessert options adhere to the classics, too: strawberry shortcake, individual apple crisp, even traditional trifle have all headlined the sweets menu. That is, if you have room in your belly after your enormous slab of meat.

German-born owner Joe Betz took over in 1985, making only minor updates to the menu (like the addition of fish) and look of the clubby spot over the years: "We don't change; we update," he says with a smile. He still loves the unique experience his restaurant offers.

"Prime rib is something that you can't really cook at home," Betz says—at least not without a lot of planning and preparation. So it's something people are more inclined to go out for. And on the quality of the House's beef, he says proudly, "We don't just buy a good product, we buy the best product."

Along with that quality product, service is paramount when it comes to the secret of the restaurant's success. "We are only as good as our last meal," Betz states, explaining that a reputation in the business "takes years to build but only weeks to lose." Based on the expert, attentive service on each of my visits there—replete with the waiter's introduction by name of the chef who carved our meat tableside—this is not something Betz's restaurant is at risk of anytime soon.

After 30 years at the helm, the jovial owner still enjoys himself. "I like what I'm doing, so I don't burn out." Even so, a changing of the guard is at some point inevitable for the 75-year-old restaurateur who's been in the business since age 14. Fortunately, his son Steven has already taken over the day-to-day operations, affording the elder Betz vacation and relaxation time. But he remains engaged. If you don't see him on the dining room floor during dinner service, you may read about his community involvement in the papers. For more than two decades, he has served thousands of pounds—2,000, to be precise—of prime rib at Glide Memorial Methodist Church's Christmas Eve dinner for the less fortunate, and appeared in person in a show with three generations of the Betz family (his sons and grandchildren) at the historic house of worship. The food he donates feeds more than 3,000 people.

"When you get, you have to give," Betz says of his charity involvements, of which Glide is just one. His love for giving back to the community and appreciation of the things that matter—like

family—above all else is clear. "I'm more proud of my sons [than anything else]," he divulges. "They are great dads. It's more important than being a good businessman." And this spirit of goodness shines through in the hospitality he imparts in his restaurant.

It's encouraging that a restaurant devoted entirely to meat has continued to thrive in a city that seems to be home to more special-diet devotees than anywhere else. Its success, it seems clear, is not only a result of the fine food it offers but also the disposition of its owner and his seemingly well-grounded view on life. All are welcome in his restaurant. And as long as you bring a good appetite, you will have a great time.

HOUSE OF SHIELDS

9 NEW MONTGOMERY ST., SAN FRANCISCO, CA 94105

THEHOUSEOFSHIELDS.COM

Place of Legend

*T*he story of this bar isn't just about the founder (Eddie Shields, an infamous bootlegger and gambler who used to organize prizefights on Alcatraz) or other previous owners over the years (including someone else "wanted all over town") or even about the current team (restaurateur Dennis Leary and his business partner and bar manager, Eric Passetti) who has a clear passion for the historic and the restoration they did here. It's about all of these people, as well as the diverse mix of bargoers over the years—from bettors and bookies to bike messengers and bankers—and the tales, true and untrue, that have made the place the legend it is.

Though you'll read everywhere that House of Shields was founded in 1908, including on its own website, Passetti says this isn't actually the case.

"The earliest record we can find—its first listing as a bar anyway—is for 1944," Passetti says apologetically, explaining that the Sharon Building itself, in which the bar sits, wasn't completed until 1912. During the restoration process five years ago, they uncovered records that the space housed a number of businesses over the years, including, for a stint, a famous restaurant, The Old Poodle Dog, one of the first haute cuisine spots on the West Coast.

So even though the 1908 date may not be accurate, I am relieved that it still qualifies as vintage. The bar feels like the embodiment of the word, with its massive walls of gorgeous wood, hefty cherry-wood bar rail, and elegantly curved wood booths; mosaic tile floors; ornate brass Art Nouveau lamp statuettes; striking back bar framed by painted wooden shields that look vaguely Scottish but are more likely of dubious historic origin; and the fact that it was a men's-only spot until 1972. (There's even a sign to this effect over the somewhat jerry-rigged women's bathroom: They split what was originally just a men's room into two, cramped, sloped-ceiling spaces.) It is also rich with rumors about its history, which seems another defining characteristic of any good, truly old establishment, the best being that US President Warren Harding actually died at the House of Shields, not the Palace Hotel across the street, as reported, and was carried by underground passageway back to the hotel.

Passetti also corrects another common misconception: "House of Shields has never had a trough," where, in some old bars, men could urinate while standing right at the bar.

And this is the kind of stuff the classic spots are made of.

The young bar manager hails from a line of bar proprietors—both his great-grandfather and grandfather owned places in the city—and at just 36 Passetti has become somewhat of a go-to guy to open hot spots himself. He and Leary now run several places together, a partnership that began in 2010 when Leary approached him to help restore and reopen the House of Shields after it had fallen into grave disrepair.

"Frankly, it looked like people thought it was sort of ironic to mistreat a place like that," Passetti says, his disdain clear as he describes the broken booths and layer of grime on the back bar. "The floor hadn't been mopped in I don't know how long."

Walking into the bar today, you'd never guess it had once been so downtrodden. The careful restoration resulted in what looks like a pristine vintage establishment, even with its series of six owners over the years. Just about everything is original, including the massive Hinsdale urinal in the men's room, which is apparently a relic in itself.

"I believe this is the only one left on the West Coast," Passetti says, naming New York's McSorley's, the Old Town Tavern, and P. J. Clarke's as the only other places that have them.

Both the Sharon Building and the Palace Hotel were designed by the same Beaux Arts architect, George Kelham, so many of the bar's most striking and most "vintage" interior features are also seen at the hotel (such as the mosaic tile floors in the Pied Piper, the hotel's bar, and the hotel's stunning chandeliers). Also part of the shared

history is the bar's former kitchen, which was in the adjacent building that now houses the Palace's parking garage. The cooking space was walled off by the hotel years ago because the bar owner at the time kept spilling grease on the hotel property, but Passetti still gets e-mails from people asking for a lunch reservation.

Something that remains unchanged in 2015 is that there's still no television or even a clock on the premises, a fact appreciated by its patrons.

Most of those folks are Financial District workers, says affable bartender Monika Koczela-Stillman, Polish immigrant by way of Brooklyn who makes a perfect Old Fashioned. She's worked at House of Shields for three years and describes the clientele as respectful, especially compared to her sports-bar job down the street: "You wouldn't believe some of the things people say to me in there!" Though it was, at a time, just for men, and mostly for betting men, the House of Shields today sees a diverse crowd.

"It's an obvious place for people with suits, but [that group mixes] really well with anyone who has an appreciation for the past, or for woodworking," Passetti says, sharing that when he mans the bar, there might be "a banker, an elevator operator, a lawyer, a judge . . . and of course lots of tech people" all comingling happily.

Modern Vintage Spot

BOURBON AND BRANCH: EST. 1921/2006

A door buzzer on a nondescript corner building in a rough part of town does not typically invite one to press it, unless that person is on the run from the cops or the bad guys. One particular buzzer in the Tenderloin district of San Francisco, however, is the gateway into one of the hottest bar experiences in town—one specifically designed to make revelers feel as if they are stepping back in time.

Modern speakeasy Bourbon and Branch was founded in 2006 by a group of men who have a clear reverence for the historic; the bar lives in the building that once, from 1921 to 1933, housed an actual speakeasy. It was listed in the phone book, they say, as "The Ipswitch—A Beverage Parlor," though who called the number back then is hard to say.

Open every day of the week, from 6 p.m. to 2 a.m., the main bar requires reservations—and a password—for entry. But if you haven't planned ahead, never fear: Bourbon and Branch now offers a no-reservations-required space in its "library," which is filled floor to ceiling with actual period literature. Presenting the password *books* upon buzzing for entry will get you admittance and access to a smaller menu of libations.

Mixology is an art form here—fresh juices and laborious methods are prized to create cocktails that all others should aspire to be. House rules require people to "speak easy," so the noise level is truly kept at a minimum in the dark space, and not to "even think about asking for a cosmo." No cellphone use or pictures either, please—both are prohibited on the premises.

Since opening, Bourbon and Branch has remained wildly popular and responded in kind with cocktail classes and the no-reservations-required space. It may seem a bit precious at first—with the password and all—but the cocktail experience and feeling of traveling back in time are worth booking a reservation.

501 Jones St., San Francisco, CA 94102;
(415) 346-1735; bourbonandbranch.com

Though Passetti's not the owner, his close involvement has contributed to the bar's survival as something truly vintage. His passion for the old and the historic—and the material with which this old, historic place is made ("I revere wood," he tells me)—is undeniable. "If House of Shields were my place, it would be my only place," he says firmly.

That sort of devotion says a lot about the allegiance people form to places like this. Places made of solid material, places with countless legends attached, places with long memories, sometimes buried under layers of filth. As a nod to memory here, and how far the bar has come over the years, the team left a small section of wood near the front entrance untouched, to show the remarkable effect of the restoration.

"My only problem with the House of Shields is that I feel like it never had an operator that really cared about the place," Passetti told me. Until now, that is.

IT'S TOPS COFFEE SHOP

1801 MARKET ST., SAN FRANCISCO, CA 94103

(415) 431-6395 • ITSTOPSCOFFEESHOP.COM

Camera Ready

*J*ust down the street from the venerable San Francisco restaurant Zuni Café, a longtime local foodie darling renowned for its perfectly roasted chicken, sits another establishment that arguably should be given equal respect—though admittedly it's a very different sort of place. Known not for elegant food but good classic diner grub, both day and night, It's Tops Coffee Shop is both a relic of the past and a modern favorite—and a picture-perfect representation of the old-fashioned diner experience. It's been around for more than 80 years and in the same family for almost 65.

Hot cakes, along with crispy bacon that would make my family giggle with delight, are the must-order menu item. A 1932 Wolf griddle dates back to the origin of the restaurant, which opened in 1935, and gives the hot cakes—basically, buttermilk pancakes—and the cafe's other grilled foods a special quality. First called "The Top Cafe" or "The Minute Man's," the coffee shop became known for its griddle and fed hungry locals and travelers a typical selection of diner fare—breakfast and burgers became favorites.

It's Tops came into the current family, the Chapmans, in 1952, after father Richard "Dick" returned from service as a military cook on a ship in the Korean War. He added table jukeboxes and red vinyl booths—all still in place today, though the jukeboxes no longer work—and was always ready with a smile and joke for customers. Current owners Bruce and Sheila Chapman, Dick's son and daughter, first worked on Saturdays in the "height-appropriate" job of gum scraper (at age 10) and front-of-the-house server (at age

13), respectively, eventually taking over the business in 1986 when they were just in their 20s. They've maintained it pretty much as is, with a few exceptions: They dropped the dinner shift but added Sunday, late-night hours on "party nights" (Wednesday through Saturday), espresso drinks, and soju cocktails. But you'd never know it by looking at the place, which still feels like a perfectly preserved 1950s diner, lifted from that era and dropped into modern-day San Francisco.

It's such a quintessential visual representation of a time gone by that it frequently catches the eye of location scouts looking to shoot the latest movie or commercial (one was there when I had breakfast on a Wednesday morning). Red and orange vinyl booths and barstools provide a handful of seats in the tiny diner with its wood-paneled ceiling and lots of linoleum. Vintage ice-cream pictures, newspaper clippings, and 49ers paraphernalia adorn the limited wall space while "Summertime Blues" plays on the sound system.

And it's the kind of place where every customer seems to have a story about his or her initial visit. One counter customer says she first came to the diner decades ago when she was 12, for a milk shake with her family, after they had emigrated from the Philippines. They wanted to show her "the original Denny's." And a server I met pointed to a table where she said she used to come for blueberry pancakes with her dad.

The cafe sees immigrants, lifelong locals, the party crowd, and morning-after-the-party crowd; all are right at home in the spot with just 8 small booths and 12 counter seats. It's hard to believe that the place used to be even smaller in terms of seating, but they've "expanded" over the years by incrementally increasing the booth size, inch by inch, when the booths needed reupholstering. This makes for a tapered look, with the largest booth at the back of the restaurant. It's a funky design element that adds to the charm of the place.

The same menu is on offer day or night, and along with those perfect pancakes are burgers, cheesy egg-and-potato breakfast combos, and a relatively new invention of co-owner Bruce: the It's Tops stuffed waffle, which features crispy, thin waffles produced by the diner's vintage Wells waffle "bakers" (what we call irons) that serve as vessels for sweet or savory fillings. A kitchen that roughly matches the petite size of the seating area turns out all of these diner classics, manned by just a single cook to match the singly-staffed server's shift out front. Even with just two people on the job at any given time, attention to customers' needs is paramount, including helping me lift my baby stroller—unprompted—up the two steep steps from the expansive corner at Market Street and Octavia into the little wedge of a cafe.

You pay at your own pace at the counter, upon which sits an old cash register on display, though modernity is apparent in their acceptance of credit cards. Since staff doesn't rush you out the door with checks delivered speedily to tables, you can linger over your coffee and imagine you're an extra in *Back to the Future*, 1950s tunes playing joyfully from the stereo and a young Michael J. Fox just behind you at the counter.

Shutter windows and a picket fence wrap the exterior of the teensy place that sits on one of the major thoroughfares in the city, a determined testament to a classic time. Like the Little Diner That Could, It's Tops has persisted through the area's countless tumults (including the construction of the neighboring freeway and its destruction in the Loma Prieta earthquake) and remained virtually unchanged, only seeming to increase in popularity in recent years. As the development fervor in the city today feels unprecedented, I

Vintage Spot
ST. FRANCIS FOUNTAIN: EST. 1918

Great vintage signs beckon passersby to enter this classic little soda fountain on 24th Street, now best known for hearty breakfasts that fill the bellies of Mission District locals. Tucked among hipster bars, old Mexican restaurants, dry cleaners, and corner stores is San Francisco's oldest ice-cream parlor, the St. Francis Fountain—and it should be sought out by anyone who likes a diet-busting breakfast, ice-cream sundae, old-fashioned candy counter, or even champagne cocktail. All are on order here.

St. Francis Fountain was opened in 1918 by Greek immigrant James Christakes and subsequently run by three generations of the Christakes family until the year 2000. After falling into some disrepair, current owner Peter Hood took it over with his then-partner Levon Kazarian, and, thankfully, the two restored what was special and original about the place, beefing up the breakfast menu and introducing it to new clientele. Glass canisters dispensing red straws sit proudly on the countertops, and old advertisements and menus adorn the walls of the narrow, high-ceilinged space. The vintage candy counter with packaged sweets enables indulging your inner child, and, for your inner glutton, you'll find something called the "Nebulous Potato Thing" on the breakfast menu—a treatment you can give to any order of country-style potatoes, which adds sour cream, cheese, salsa, and fresh green onion to the spuds. Do it. You must. Vegan options and a soy-milk ice-cream alternative make it obvious that this is a modern soda fountain, but the Borax powdered-soap dispenser over the bathroom sink and offering the same local ice cream (Mitchell's) since 1953 keep it truly vintage.

"We could see the potential for the space," recalls Hood of his decision with Kazarian to buy the joint in 2002, describing how there was "zero kitchen" in what was a "classic counter luncheonette." The self-described "breakfast tour de force," Hood was versed in the art of the morning meal, having established other popular local restaurants before taking on the soda fountain.

"I'm more of a day person than a night person," Hood shares, and he enjoys breakfast because it's "more intimate, more about individual choices." He and his team have done a phenomenal job with the meal here, while still keeping the air of the soda fountain alive and well. Hood has a lot to say about the importance of maintaining historic businesses in cities like San Francisco.

"What is a city without places like the St. Francis Fountain?" he asks, divulging that people come in all the time saying their grandparents met here or that they are part of a multigenerational family of customers. Like other vintage businesses, he says it's important that the establishment continues to anchor the corner of 24th and York; it helps preserve the history of the neighborhood. "Otherwise, it's, 'Remember when this place was here?'"

801 24th St., San Francisco, CA 94110; (415) 826-4210; stfrancisfountainsf.com

keep my fingers crossed that It's Tops continues to fight for its little spot.

Old doesn't necessarily mean good. But It's Tops is one of those places that show how good something old can be. And the second-generation Chapmans have done a remarkable job keeping the experience fresh while maintaining what is authentic and original about the place. The whole experience is like a warm hug from the past—even if it's a past you've only daydreamed—and it's one of the best diner experiences in the city, perhaps *the* best. Some might say, it's tops.

JOHN'S GRILL

63 ELLIS ST., SAN FRANCISCO, CA 94102

(415) 986-3274 • JOHNSGRILL.COM

Film Noir Food

*H*ard-boiled detective tales, a stiff drink, food like your grandmother enjoyed on a night out, the potential for celebrities dining just beyond your elbows, and an overall super old-school, clubby feel—this is all part of the fabric and lore of John's Grill. It feels like the sort of spot where *Law & Order*'s Jack McCoy would've lunched with one of his gorgeous, young assistant district attorneys to strategize about a case. Or the site where high-powered political deals are struck over cocktails and rare steaks (it often is). It is most certainly the place where people in the know go for a famous crab and avocado salad—named for former regular and fitness guru, Jack LaLanne—and a bit of city history. It's one of San Francisco's oldest restaurants, and one of my favorite spots in this book.

The restaurant was boldly one of the first in the city to open after the infamous 1906 earthquake, starting construction that year in the midst of the devastation around it and welcoming its first customers in 1908. Now, more than 100 years later, after another massive earthquake in 1989, at least one fire, and 9/11—all of which halted or slowed the business for some time—the classic bistro on Ellis Street has not only survived but thrived.

Divided into three levels, the bistro welcomes guests onto a ground floor decorated with period furnishings and dark oak-paneled walls that serve as a backdrop for countless photos of famous patrons. Seating is just shy of cramped, but appealingly so, making for a more intimate experience that feels as though you are almost part of those political deals at the next table. Upper floors

are reserved for private parties and special occasions, with private dining rooms named for Dashiell Hammett, the famous noir novelist who frequented the restaurant in the '20s and set scenes from here in his legendary book-turned-Bogart-movie, *The Maltese Falcon*. Today the restaurant celebrates its Hammett heritage, with novel and movie memorabilia positioned throughout and a signature dish named for the author's lead *Falcon* character: Sam Spade's Lamb Chops, served with a baked potato and sliced tomato. The dish was reportedly a favorite meal of Hammett's when he dined here.

Beyond those famous chops, John's does a superb job with seafood—especially the ever-popular petrale sole amandine—along with classic steaks and pastas. Jack LaLanne's Favorite Salad is light, creamy, and lovely—just the kind of starter you'd want before a juicy piece of meat. Bottom line: It's the place to come for a real martini, to get a proper plate of fish, to indulge in a side of creamed spinach or asparagus with hollandaise sauce, to strike a political deal, or even to fall in love.

When a restaurant succeeds over such a long period of time, one naturally wonders about the secret to its success. "It's like magic," says current and fourth owner John Konstin—the second generation in his family to operate the place that was first opened by another unrelated John. He's referring to the unexpected ebbs and flows in the business, how a proprietor plans for and adjusts to them. But I think it's more than just the second sense of a skillful owner that has made the place what it is today. A dedication to the business, commitment to its people, and unwavering allegiance to its original concept—good liquor, local farm-to-table cooking (before that was a thing), and great service—has led John's Grill through its 100-plus years. They've made only small changes over that time, barely perceptible to diners—such as replacing the regular tomato on the Sam Spade plate with a more vibrant heirloom varietal. They don't dare do more. And its well-connected owner certainly has had a lot to do with its recent success.

Native San Franciscan Konstin's open gaze and quiet, steady demeanor belies his acute awareness of all around him. Cool in the presence of celebrity clientele—movie stars (including Michael Caine, Renée Zellweger, Keanu Reeves, and late regular Robin Williams), politicians (too many to count), and of course, the late LaLanne—Konstin seems to appreciate and be genuinely interested in folks from all walks of life. He cares about the community, even serving as cochair of the local community police advisory board, and seems to have a special spot in his heart for kids; the board has worked to improve the safety of the adjacent Tenderloin district specifically for children, with more lighting and the Safe Passage program to protect children walking to and from school, and Konstin speaks of the effort passionately. He is also clearly proud to be carrying on the mantle of the family business.

The restaurant has been in his family for about 50 years; the current owner's first job there was as a dishwasher in his teens. He got the bug and eventually took culinary courses and worked as a chef, but he realized he liked the front of the house best. He eventually took over from his father, and now, decades later, he doesn't look as though the hectic life of a big city restaurant owner has taken a toll. The pictures framed at the reception station when you walk in the door show an indeterminately younger Konstin—but when I met him, I honestly thought maybe just a few years had passed. (By the look of Lauren Bacall and Hillary Clinton—pictured in two shots alongside him—I knew it'd been at least 20.) Must be because he loves what he's doing. And he is enthralled by the history of the joint.

"Someone just left a couple boxes of goodies here, full of pictures, letters," Konstin reveals excitedly. He explains that the "old, old boxes" were left anonymously. Among the treasures was a 37-year-old letter from US senator and former San Francisco mayor Dianne Feinstein that he'll frame, talking about all the times she's eaten there and "'look where it got her'—and that was just when she was mayor!" There was also a photo of famous 1930s film actress and *The Maltese Falcon* star Mary Astor, autographed to Konstin's father. "Just amazing."

"The other day, someone sent me a menu from the '20s," he adds. "It showed 35 cents for a full dinner!"

The youthful proprietor seems to thrive on those stories and ones like it, where people fell in love at such and such a table and are still married. "Makes you feel good." With 500 to 700 tables served every night, I imagine there are thousands of similar stories—and if Konstin has anything to do with it, many more yet to come.

LEFTY O'DOUL'S

333 GEARY ST., SAN FRANCISCO, CA 94102

(415) 982-8900 • LEFTYODOULS.BIZ

American Dream

Team sports, heaping plates of food, and good old-fashioned entrepreneurship—all three are at the heart of one of the oldest and most famous baseball restaurants in the country, which sits on the edge of San Francisco's touristy Union Square neighborhood. It's called Lefty O'Doul's.

The classic-turned-modern sports bar was founded in 1958 by Francis "Lefty" O'Doul, native San Franciscan and baseball legend who pitched (left-handed), played left field in the major leagues, including for the New York Giants (before they became the hometown team), and ultimately coached and managed in the minors, most notably for the San Francisco Seals. O'Doul's legendary status even crosses international borders: He is also the man said to have "brought baseball to Japan" through annual visits and decades of building relationships, becoming an unofficial ambassador of the sport. His near-heroic position was solidified in 1949 when he led the Seals in a postwar series of exhibition games in the country, gaining new fans young and old with his expertise, his team, and the sport itself.

After a successful career in baseball, he decided to pursue another dream, that of restaurant-bar owner. He envisioned a place where people could rub elbows with sports stars in a family-friendly environment. Thus, the *hofbrau*-drinking house that was also a shrine to America's favorite pastime was born.

Today, the place is much like it was nearly 60 years ago, only with some modern elements intermingling with original fixtures. A Starbucks sign now hangs above the old-time stadium-style "Cashier"

sign at the register, but the *hofbrau* components of carving station and sandwich line persist popularly. Sports memorabilia plasters the walls, and Maroon 5 is just as likely to be playing on the sound system as are a myriad of games on the surprisingly unobtrusive 12 televisions positioned throughout the space. Tourists—chiefly European—mix with local regulars, visiting each others' tables and chatting at the bar, showing that the camaraderie of fandom brings people together from all parts of the world. Patrons chat with bartenders, and longtime employee Chuck Davis is one of the best; he might provide an impromptu lesson in liquor, if you're interested (the quick-joking, sarcastic guy is an expert in the field, and he even wrote a trade book on bartending). In line with the overall Americana sensibility, apple pie is in fact on the menu, along with lots of hand-carved meat sandwiches, soups, salads, and specials (corned beef and cabbage and spaghetti and meatballs are available daily, with once-a-week classics like turkey à la king and meat loaf making regular appearances, too). They serve breakfast, lunch, and dinner seven days a week, and the bar stays open until 2 a.m. nightly. The place is a hodgepodge of offerings, but one that works, and it all makes perfect sense when you get to know current owner Nick Bovis and his passion for entrepreneurship and the American dream.

Son of Greek immigrants and entrepreneurs in their own right, Bovis, a mechanical engineer by training, took over the city's restaurant-slash-museum-of-baseball with his parents in 1998, 40 years after its establishment. He'd just received a pink slip, losing his engineering job after designing an earthquake safety system that required no maintenance (and therefore, no engineer to maintain it), when his father called him to ask if he could take over the family business. Though a completely different industry, it felt right—so he went for it.

Bovis is a soft-but-quick-speaking man, full of stories about his family, the restaurant, his favorite spots in San Francisco, and his many passions, which include a series of other businesses. He has a shy energy and obvious pride in what he does. Now, that means not only running one of the most heralded baseball restaurants in the country but also several other bars and food joints, a baseball-themed foundation benefitting local children, and a line of cocktail mixes—headlined by the restaurant's secret Bloody Mary mix—now available in several national big box stores, including Wal-Mart and Costco.

Did I mention he's a children's book author, too?

That last bit he accomplished on somewhat of a lark: He always made up stories for his kids' bedtimes, loosely based on his own family's immigrant tale. One day, he decided to capture the essential plot and wrote *Kokolopoulos Journey to America*, got the help of a friend to illustrate it, published it himself, and, voilà, an author was born.

It's easy to imagine the eager, inquisitive boy Bovis once was when chatting with him today, and his zest for "doing" comes through in his many endeavors and the energy of the restaurant. As a matter of fact, that famous Bloody Mary mix was something the owner used to insist on making himself daily at the bar, even before finding O'Doul's original recipe stashed away in a golf bag among other ancient paraphernalia in the back. He felt he knew what customers liked and got complaints when there was any variation from the classic concoction. Upon discovery of the true original, Bovis was pleased that his own recipe matched Lefty's pretty precisely—and that is what is bottled and available on shelves across the country today. Keeping in line with the major leaguers' commitment to charity—particularly

Vintage Spot

GOLD DUST LOUNGE: EST. 1966

The 2011 eviction notice for Gold Dust Lounge to vacate its original location of more than four decades on Union Square caused a citywide outcry. Would the famous old bar, founded in 1966 by Jim Bovis, father of Nick Bovis (of Lefty O'Doul's)—but with roots much older—be put to rest altogether because of development pressures? Its successful booting was a sad day for supporters; chalk one up to the real estate moguls. Fortunately for fans, it found a new home in 2013 at Fisherman's Wharf, reopening near other vintage spots and bringing much of its original decor—including chandeliers, mirrors, and the signature sign—and cocktail menu along with it. Irish coffees and martinis have always been popular at this place, which was a burlesque club before it was transformed into a classic cocktail lounge and piano bar by Greek immigrants, and it remains so today.

**165 Jefferson St., San Francisco, CA 94133;
(415) 397-1695; golddustsf.com**

to benefit children—a portion of the proceeds from the mixes benefits the Lefty O'Doul's Foundation for Kids.

Bovis has kept up nearly all of what was original and special about Lefty O'Doul's sports joint: the menu, the cocktails, the walls of memorabilia, the spirit of welcome to all sports lovers, and a legacy of kid-focused charity work. "The only things that have changed over the years are the fashion and the prices," Bovis says of his family's commitment to the bar's original vision and owner. And perhaps that Bloody Mary recipe—but who's to know?

LIGURIA BAKERY

1700 STOCKTON ST., SAN FRANCISCO, CA 94133 • (415) 421-3786

+==+

For the Love of Focaccia

*B*are. Upon my first visit to Liguria Bakery, the home of what I'd heard would be the best focaccia I'd ever tasted, the space felt bare but for the woman standing behind the counter, not looking at me, and the other woman, older than the first, sitting across from her, also not looking at me. There were no pastry cases full of golden focaccia, no colorful menus, no signs of food, other than a simple, old-fashioned, black-and-white tileboard listing what read like flavors. I was sure I was either in the wrong place, or too late (at 9 a.m.) for the glorious Italian specialty bread I'd read so much about.

"We hear that all the time," explained owner Mike Soracco when I asked about the ascetic aesthetic. "But it's always been that way. We haven't changed a thing. I figure, if it's not broke, don't fix it."

Soracco is the third generation of the family to own the 103-year-old business that was started in 1911 by his grandfather Ambrogio, who'd emigrated from Genoa around 1907, and Soracco always knew it would be something he could "fall back on." But when he became an owner at the tender age of 24—now, a quarter century ago—it wasn't something he was falling back on. It was an opportunity suddenly in his lap to share ownership in the family business, and he jumped on it. He joined his father, George, as part owner and eventually became the sole owner when his dad passed away a couple of years ago at age 84, after working for 66 years at the bakery. A life devoted to family and bread. The concept seems beautiful and of another time.

Liguria initially was a full-service bakery, offering bread and assorted pastries in addition to the now-famed focaccia and making deliveries in wagons early on. "They were still making bread

when I was a kid," recalled Soracco. In the mid-20th century, the growth of big bread bakeries in the region—like Boudin, Parisian, and Colombo—and their ability to undercut the prices of smaller bakeries forced Liguria to tighten its model and get out of the bread business.

"'Before we give bread away, we'll leave the flour in the sacks,' was always my dad's line," recollected Soracco, describing his father and the man's early business partners as "old Italian types" who refused to be taken advantage of. Thankfully, they decided to focus strictly on focaccia—a now legendary decision in the eyes of countless customers throughout the city.

"Back then, the only people who knew what focaccia was were old Italians," Soracco says. Personally, I'm so glad they took a chance that others would get to know it, too.

Because that focaccia, well, is quite amazing. Life changing, was my first reaction. The raisin rendition specifically—their specialty and one of four original flavors for the bakery, along with plain, green onion and "pizza," which is topped with tomato sauce and onion (they've since expanded to 11 flavors)—is unlike any other focaccia I've tasted. More like pastry than bread, with the essence of a fat, chewy cracker. Best when eaten fresh from the shop, just outside, on a bench across the street at Washington Square Park in the heart of North Beach, the city's traditionally Italian neighborhood.

Liguria relies on its original 1911 brick oven to turn daily-made dough into its final, humble-but-spectacular product. "Seasoned" by 100 years of cooking, the oven represents traditional construction, with sand between the bricks and, for many years, wood and coal as fuel. The owners switched to the "more economical" gas years ago, but the vibrant flavors don't reveal this change. Today, as has been the case for decades, Mike's sister Mary and their mother Josephine are the women behind the counter, with Mike and periodically his two daughters and a nephew all involved behind the scenes and making the focaccia each morning beginning at 4 am. Still in the same location from the day it opened, on the corner of Stockton and Filbert Streets, Liguria is a model of doing things the old-fashioned way. Once purchased, the large flats of focaccia are wrapped in butcher paper and tied up with string—unless you specify that you'll be eating it immediately, in which case your order is cut into smaller pieces and stuffed into a paper bag, with a few napkins, for quick access.

The neighborhood has changed over the years, affecting Liguria's business, like so many others in North Beach. The "old Italians" have by and large moved out, with young families, skyrocketing rents, a "screwed-up parking" situation (with vigilante meter maids enforcing price-gouging city policies), and a spillover of residents from adjacent Chinatown moving in. Fortunately, the Soracco family owns the building in which the bakery sits, so they're not at risk of going under due to a rent increase, but times have changed. Liguria has shorter hours and is no longer open on Sunday, which used to see huge lines after the local church let out. Even with these changes, they remain steadfastly committed to doing things the way they've always been done. And they are very proud of the bakery's legacy.

"It's a family tradition that's gone on all this time," Soracco says. "Everyone knows Liguria Bakery; we're the focaccia place. Hopefully we'll be able to keep it going as long as we can. As long as I'm physically able to do it, I'll stay here."

And relatively speaking, they still have quite a solid business to keep going.

Their pizza focaccia is the most popular, outselling all the other flavors by 10 to 1, followed by their second most popular, the green onion. I am frankly shocked when Soracco tells me that my own favorite, the raisin, is more of a dark horse and the least popular of the bunch. But as one of the original offerings, Soracco says they will never give it up. I pry at what makes it so special. It's more complicated to make, no one else really makes raisin focaccia, he says. What else?

"The other ones all have salt on top. But the raisin has the sugar."

There is a magical alchemy that happens at Liguria in that brick oven, and it seems to have something to do with the methods and recipes as well as something less tangible. A commitment to a family business, a passion for hard work, and a little sprinkle of seasoning and tradition are what we have to thank when it comes to this San Francisco specialty bread. That, and a little bit of sugar, if you're a raisin fan like me.

LI PO COCKTAIL LOUNGE

916 GRANT AVE., SAN FRANCISCO, CA 94108

(415) 982-0072 • LIPOLOUNGE.COM

Really Smooth Juice

*E*at a big slice of fatty pizza before you come." Sage advice from bartender and unofficial PR person–translator Jackie, who typically represents Li Po Cocktail Lounge to the media. But she is reluctant to be part of the story, urging me to focus on the "real" bartenders, longtime employees such as Peter Ng and Daniel Choi, as well as Kenneth Lee, the owner since 1997, who are responsible for the character and soul of the place. She simply began as a fan, a customer herself, until a few years ago, when Lee realized he could use her English skills to his advantage.

That said, she is an insider, and the advice she offers should be heeded. It is intended to prepare potential customers for the subtle smash delivered to the system by the bar's famous cocktail, the Chinese Mai Tai. Only developed in the late 1990s, when Lee took over, the signature drink has become local legend for its rare use of a Chinese liquor and the powerful punch it packs. Three kinds of rum, the Chinese liquor (which on its own has the essence of gasoline with a proof to match), and pineapple juice are the drink's sole ingredients, though most people just think it tastes like juice. Anthony Bourdain apparently downed three of them in an hour while filming his 2012 episode of the Travel Channel's *The Layover* in San Francisco. He reportedly felt it.

"It tastes like really smoooooooth juice," Jackie says, describing the drink's "harmony" when the four shots of hard liquor and pineapple come together. "But then you keep drinking and drinking. . . ." she says. People suddenly feel the inclusion of a lot more than

juice when they try to pry themselves off one of the red leather stools positioned around the bar that snakes along the curves of the narrow but cavernous room.

Established in 1937, Li Po claims to be the oldest bar in Chinatown (even though others claim the same) and is the same age as the city's more famous landmark, the Golden Gate Bridge. Its clientele is a mix of tourists during the day, young Financial District types after work, and local residents into the evening hours. The space itself consists of that curved bar, booth and table seating in the back corner, and a mysterious downstairs that feels almost scary to visit using the treacherous flight of stairs, but it's often necessary, as the bathroom's down there.

Named on many "best bars" lists—both for the city and the country, including an episode of the Esquire Channel's *Best Bars in America* show slated to air in 2015—Li Po Cocktail Lounge is no secret hideaway, but it sort of feels like one. A true dive bar in every sense of the word, the lounge offers affordable drinks—mostly beer, Chinese whiskey, and that famous cocktail—purchasable for cash only; loud, eclectic music playing from a jukebox; great, seasoned bartenders— several of whom are in their 60s or 70s now and have been there for decades; and a mazelike setup that feels unchanged since its

Vintage Spots

HANG AH TEA ROOM: EST. 1920

Billed as "the oldest standing and functioning dim sum house in America," the Hang Ah Tea Room today is a true blend of eras. Nestled on a little alley called Pagoda Place, you expect the inside to look like an ancient tea room of your imagination. You'd be wrong. Though the place was established in 1920, much of the interior feels like it's from the '50s and the '70s, with linoleum, bric-a-brac, and wood-veneer tables.

There are elements of the old—such as framed Chinese script and the classic dim sum baskets—mixed with the new, or newish anyway, including white square-tile floors, a big-screen TV sitting in the corner atop what looks like an old reception counter, and a large jar of fortune cookies for doling out to customers at the meal's end. It's a funny little spot, with delicious food and friendly service—including menu guidance for the uninitiated from a cheerful young waitress.

The combo is a great option for those new to the culinary discipline that, like tapas, is a forerunner to today's small plates craze. It includes a sampling of the most common, palate-friendly dim sum dishes: pork meatball, foil-wrapped chicken (which has the essence of steamed barbecue), the Hang Ah BBQ pork bun, egg roll, fried shrimp ball, and an incredible fried sesame ball that was almost plush inside. The menu goes beyond the most common stuff, though, all served rapidly and fresh from the small kitchen.

While you'll see it mentioned in guidebooks and Google searches, Hang Ah still feels off the beaten path. And it is a great taste of old—and new—Chinatown in San Francisco.

1 Pagoda Place, San Francisco, CA 94108; (415) 982-5686; hangah1920.com

FAR EAST CAFÉ: EST. 1920

There are dozens of restaurants in Chinatown, many of them like each other. Far East Café stands out for its age (founded in 1920), its curtained dining tables alongside the grand main room that is two-stories high, and its seafood combination clay pot—described by one waiter as "very famous here." That clay pot is quite savory and delicious, full of umami flavor and seafood, some of which comes from the tank in the back of the restaurant. And the space itself—with giant framed Chinese paintings hung high on the walls and even bigger dragon lanterns with dangling red tassels that hang downward from the lofty ceiling—feels like you've stepped from a time machine into the middle of a magnificent mid-century Chinese-American banquet celebrating success and possibility in this new country. The look of the place alone makes it worth stopping in. But if that doesn't convince you, let this: steaming hot egg custard buns. I'd never had the traditional Chinese confection, the egg custard tart, warm before, and now I never again want it cold. Far East Café's bun version is so sweet and ethereally delicious, like an all-white Asian éclair from heaven—the white-bread sandwich of your dreams. Consumed beneath ancient lanterns and ornate chandeliers in an old dining palace in Chinatown, even better.

631 Grant Ave., San Francisco, CA 94108;
(415) 982-3245; fareastcafesf.com

opening. What truly makes this dive bar unique, though, is not only its age and that random cocktail, but its Chinese-ness.

Watching over the bar is a large, golden Earth Store Buddha, which serves to purify the spirits of those in hell who feel remorse for their bad deeds. There is lots of red, considered a lucky color in Chinese culture—red lanterns dangling from the ceiling, red decorations leftover from Chinese New Year tacked to the walls, a red front door, and red carpeting. A full-scale wall mural, also in various red hues, depicts a famous work of Chinese literature, the historical novel *Romance of the Three Kingdoms*, chronicling the turbulent times of the Han dynasty near the end of the second century AD, with war and brotherhood its key themes. And the bar itself is named after a legendary Chinese poet—Li Bai, aka. Li Po—a romantic who lived during the Tang dynasty and was known, among other things, as much for his appreciation of the beauty of nature as for his celebration of good drink.

The way the business is run is described as particularly Chinese as well, in that honesty and integrity are chief qualities of importance to the owner—superseding the drive to always be above the natural ebbs and flows in business. Hence, the staff stays a long time because they are trusted, professional, and customer-focused—and the business always has a way of surviving natural downturns.

Perhaps it's a good business model, or perhaps it's the watchful eye of that giant Buddha. Whatever the reason, Li Po Cocktail Lounge has staying power as a San Francisco business that has grown up with the city and offers a unique taste of some of its cultural hospitality. Just remember to fill your belly with something hearty before you take your first sip of that Chinese Mai Tai.

THE MAGAZINE

920 LARKIN ST., SAN FRANCISCO, CA 94109

(415) 441-7737 • THEMAGAZINESF.COM

From Art and Archaeology
to Pinups and Porn

*T*he Internet. This is the thing that is killing stores like The Magazine, and at risk of sounding like a curmudgeonly, out-of-touch, get-off-my-lawn old crow, it's a terrible tragedy.

Even with the ability to read and view just about anything your heart desires online, The Magazine is still in business after more than 40 years, offering actual, tangible versions of every sort of periodical you could think up. Want *LIFE* magazine from the 1930s or any edition of the *Saturday Evening Post*? They've got it. Predilection for archaeology or Frank Lloyd Wright or comics or theater? This shop is your place. Vintage porn or modern erotica? They have tons.

It was that latter category that led me to discover this store; in my research for this book, I looked into the city's oldest sex shops and found The Magazine. Notably, in an online search. Known for its remarkably extensive collection of materials on sex—both old and new, educational and pleasure-driven, classic pinups and modern centerfolds, and in magazine, book, and video formats, The Magazine is actually so much more than its racy stuff. Though it is mostly men that patronize the shop that sits in a building formerly occupied by an optometrist's office—framed by lots of gorgeous wood—they are not just buying the porn. Plenty of film buffs, set designers, artists, students, and old-fashioned collectors come here, too. The total collection is jaw-dropping, and not all is viewable from the main floor. If you descend into the building's basement, only on request I should note, you'll find yourself in a gray storage room that has the feeling

of an evidence locker—not unlike "the stacks" in my college library—
full of neatly arranged piles and piles of old magazines. Twenty-two-
year employee Martin Rosen gave me a tour, showing off all the back
copies of everything, explaining that that's not even the extent of
what they can get.

"Just about everything's available online," he says. Sigh. That's
how they get their inventory, too. But they also accept sales from
walk-ins, so save your old stuff. When he says, "You should never
throw away magazines," my inner hoarder sings. Always bring them
to the shop; they'll either resell or recycle. If it's the *New Yorker* you're
squirrelling away, however, they're all full up, Rosen explains as he
points to a group of teetering stacks near the front door. "We have
a ton of *New Yorkers* and no customers." They do donate what they
can't sell; one regular recipient is a man who teaches art to kids with
disabilities.

There's a beautiful reverence here for the hard copy, for the feeling
of holding a magazine, leafing through its pages and exploring its
articles, images, and the history it represents. I get teased, mostly
by my super tech-savvy husband, for my resistance to e-reading and
change in general. But it's because holding paper, being able to turn
actual pages, provides a different experience than swiping to "read
on." My secret hope is that everyone who reads this book—both men
and women—flocks to The Magazine. Before it's gone. Don't let the
Internet win! (Unless, of course, you're using it to order materials from
the shop; The Magazine has launched an online business to remain
viable in a world dominated by the intangible.)

MARIO'S BOHEMIAN CIGAR STORE CAFE

566 COLUMBUS AVE., SAN FRANCISCO, CA 94133 • (415) 362-0536

Sandwich to Change Your World

S ite of the greatest sandwich ever, no ifs, ands, or buts. Mario's Bohemian Cigar Store Cafe is that site, the sandwich is "the combo," and if you haven't had it, you should run, not walk, to devour one immediately. I could end this piece right here, as the most important information about this little mouthful-of-a-name cafe has been shared, but I should probably say a bit more about its history and how it feels to be there before wrapping up.

Really, though, the combo sandwich. If you remember nothing else about this place, remember the combo.

Nostalgia and modernity blend seamlessly at this funky North Beach cafe that has been owned by the same family since 1971—but with a hazy history that long predates its establishment as Mario's. It has served as a local hangout in many iterations over the years. First, it featured fedora-wearing, cigar-smoking Italian men and their "beer, wine, coffee, and cards." Later, then unknown screenwriter-director Francis Ford Coppola could be seen penning *The Godfather* script at one of its little round tables, and famous poet and City Lights founder Lawrence Ferlinghetti at another. A period in the early '80s saw it as an unofficial headquarters for a neighborhood drug dealer, with foosball tournaments and packed crowds ("three-deep every night"), followed by a rebirth later that decade as a sunny space—afforded by giant, new windows that looked out onto Washington Square Park— where everyone, suddenly women, too, felt welcome.

Though it's a full-fledged cafe—loved for its authentic cappuccinos, tumblers of red wine, and a fairly hearty menu for a place without an

on-site kitchen (everything's made off-site and simply prepped behind the counter by the jack-of-all-trades staff)—Mario's is best known for its focaccia sandwiches, which feature the incredible specialty bread from Liguria Bakery, just down the street. It sounds like hyperbole to say, but the place will make a sandwich convert out of even the most skeptical. How can a sandwich be transformative? As someone who is admittedly typically disappointed by the humble sandwich, it's a question I never thought I'd ask myself . . . until I ate "the combo" from Mario's. Tucked into a tender-crisp hunk of green onion focaccia are thinly sliced pieces of ham and salami, with just enough shaved onion to hint at its presence, melted swiss (which I also usually dislike), and sufficient mayo and mustard for a gooey tang. Oh, and it's warm, making it all the more delightful. Perhaps it was that I first tasted it when nine months pregnant, but I truly believe that this sandwich is perfection in the sandwich world.

Bought in the early '70s by Mario Crismani, former plainclothes policeman from Trieste, Italy, and subsequent paint-tinting specialist at a South San Francisco factory upon his arrival in the States, the cafe was then transformed into "Mario's," and it has been owned and operated by his son Paul since 1979 (just 25 when he took over). In addition to Dad, the entire family has always been involved,

Vintage Spot
Aquarius Records: Est: 1970

Since Mario's has the feeling of an album cover—worn, loved, edgy, and with tales to tell—and it was established around the same time as this record store, it seems fitting to talk about Aquarius Records here. Founded in 1970, Aquarius has a charming yellowed look, with unfinished wood floors that are rough and creaky and provide the perfect platform for the smattering of sawhorse-upheld music racks, a succulent-adorned front counter, and four '80s-era video game machines, including *Tron* at the entrance. Many albums—both records and CDs—have handwritten essays pasted to their front covers, reviews from staff members of the music therein. The assessments are authentic and impassioned, the words of sometimes-obsessive music lovers endorsing great finds to friends.

"We say it's like making a mix tape for a friend," says Allan Horrocks, who co-owns the place with Andee Connors. "You're going to order in a record that you think is fantastic, and you're going to write about it and how great it is. You're happy that it sells because you're making a little bit of money, but you're more happy that it sells because you're like, 'Great, all these people got to check out this thing that I really love, and they love it, too.'"

In this way, the staff forms relationships with customers that can last lifetimes, sharing music they love and turning each other on to new records—all of which come in various packages in the shop. For instance, likely unrecognizable to anyone born after 1990, the team maintains a cassette collection in a glass wall case and offers many samples for online or counter listening.

The oldest independent record store in the city also has had high-profile live acts: Aquarius regularly hosts free acoustic performances by bands such as the Posies, Death Cab for Cutie, and Yo La Tengo, clearing out the music racks to make space for the show and the crowd.

It's a place to get a great recommendation for something old-school or obscure, or to pick up a current album by an independent group. Or daydream about your college days. You may just happen to catch a free show by your favorite artist.

1055 Valencia St., San Francisco, CA 94110;
(415) 647-2272; aquariusrecords.org

with Paul's mother Liliana playing a prominent role, serving as local matriarch to the neighborhood, peacemaker during potential bar brawls, and supplier of fresh ricotta cheese (her secret recipe will never be revealed) for decades. And now it is Paul's wife Debbie who is responsible for the cafe's homemade tiramisu, in all its boozy, creamy glory (no liquor-flavored extracts here, just the real thing).

Paul himself is a classic example of the small business owner—tough as nails, struggling to make a living in a land of skyrocketing costs (chiefly rent), always balancing authenticity to the original concept while keeping up with the times with fervent passion for the people involved. "It's the people that make the place," he said of his staff. "Otherwise, it's just tables and chairs and an address." His belief in loyalty and relationships comes through in simple conversation as well as the longtime commitment to purveyors, like Graffeo's coffee down the street, which the cafe has served for more than 40 years. You can almost see him as a neighborhood kid from a family of Italian immigrants—his mother still lives in the flat they grew up in, a few blocks from the cafe—every empty lot a playground, ribbing friends and scrapping with all the other rug rats in the area. Today, he has two children of his own, and his regard for family over all else is clear. He is helping care for his aging mother—his father passed away more than a decade ago—and speaks of his wife and grown children lovingly, even expressing genuine good wishes about my own second baby on the way (at the time of our chat).

It's people like Paul and his father's eponymous, delightful cafe that I'm pulling for, as I consider all of these old businesses and the dilemmas many of their owners face simply to stay afloat. They are good, salt-of-the-earth folks, responsible for so many memorable experiences for their customers—whether quiet moments, raucous times, or just an outrageously delicious sandwich. They have been a part of history and still thrive in the experience-delivery service. They should be supported, and their businesses patronized, with our senses ever open to the relics of the past around us—like the beautiful black-and-white photographs of card-playing gentlemen on Mario's walls—and the possibilities for the future ahead.

McROSKEY MATTRESS COMPANY

1687 MARKET ST., SAN FRANCISCO, CA 94103

(415) 861-4532 • MCROSKEY.COM

A Good Night's Sleep

Who makes mattresses by hand? And to order, no less? McRoskey's, that's who—for more than 100 years in San Francisco.

Until working on this book, I had no idea handmade mattresses were a thing—and in most areas, they are not. Understandably so: They are costly and time-consuming to make, and machinery and automation have sped up the world of manufacturing in a way that bypasses this slow-food style of bed creation. But, many would argue, at a cost. The cost of quality.

"We really know how to build comfort that endures," says Robin McRoskey Azevedo, current CEO and third-generation leader of the family business founded in the city in 1899. Her grandfather Edward McRoskey started the company with his brother after moving from Chicago and selling mattress-making equipment. And since then, the company has been crafting its own mattress components and assembling them by hand at the same address in the city proper—only recently (in 1999) moving their factory operation to a 30,000-square-foot rented warehouse in a different neighborhood.

Today in that warehouse you can see how McRoskey walks the talk of "handcrafted." The company has only 36 employees, the manufacturing subset of which makes every coil, cover, and layer of filling material by hand, sometimes with the help of machinery that dates back decades. The majority of McRoskey's raw materials are made in the US as well; wire comes from a California company, cotton from California and Texas, and ticking (the strong fabric that

covers the mattress) from the East Coast. Nesting coils are formed in a special hourglass design, laced together, and heat-treated in an oversize blue oven that looks like a small bank vault right there at the factory. A subtle difference in the shape of the McRoskey mattress—more curved at the corners and with a slight billow to the sides, which Azevedo describes as its "hips"—again reveals their uniqueness as compared to others. And when all the components are produced, the team then assembles the stuff—also by hand—in a miraculous display of doing things the old-fashioned way that one just doesn't see anymore.

Before they are stitched together and tufted, each unfinished mattress is a behemoth of pillowy cotton and polyester fibers and layers of springs and fabric stretched around a sturdy wood frame, the whole thing rising several feet tall. It's amazing that these monsters are brought down to normal mattress size in the finished product—and all those layers make a difference in the customer's sleeping experience.

"Manufacturing from scratch means we need to pay attention to everything," says Azevedo, from the equipment they use to the suppliers with whom they maintain relationships to detail at every level in the mattress-creation process: initial customer order, final delivery, and setup. (They even carefully chose their delivery company and always use the same one to ensure quality control at that ultimate stage, when the bed meets its bedroom.)

You can see the whole manufacturing process on a tour of the factory, available by request, or peruse the finished products at the company's original, beautiful showroom on busy Market Street or the second retail location in tony Palo Alto, about 30 miles south. At every turn, it truly feels like McRoskey is all about the customer—the company has even kept records dating back to 1921 of all customer purchases, for ease of meeting client needs in the future. Though these records went electronic in the late '90s, a meticulous card-catalogue-style filing system containing the company's actual customer records from the early days is on display in the back of the main showroom of the building the family has owned for decades.

"Some competitors call us 'old-fashioned,' and not in a good way," Azevedo says, but the McRoskey team is proud of its antiquated ways. They are intent on avoiding the "incremental degradation" that comes with farming out processes, she says, quoting a friend. And frankly, those handwritten customer records are pretty awesome to see, if you're into that sort of thing.

Azevedo, who "wandered into the business" at age 40, in 1980, when her kids began preschool and she looked to reenter the workforce part-time, describes her thought process then: "Who will hire me just a couple of days a week? Ah, Dad!" she laughs. She shares how that time in her life, and her gradual increase from "part-time to full-time to overtime," was like "Mattress U," given how much she learned from her father and uncle, who ran the company together back then. Her passion for the business today is obvious.

"I have a great appreciation for, one, the customers who have loved their McRoskey mattresses, and two, how we make them," she says, as we wander through the surprisingly Zen-like factory, with its relative calm and quiet work under way, admiring the individually formed coils and chatting with the workers forming them, many of whom have been there for decades. She correctly describes the mattress as "the most important piece of furniture in the house."

McRoskeys are warranted for a 10-year period—"but they can last longer than that," Azevedo says, explaining that they advise keeping your mattress "as long as it's comfortable."

"Mattresses wear, and we change, too," she continues, divulging that her current preference is for the Classic line, in the "extra-gentle" comfort choice (three lines and seven "comfort choices" are available). They purposely avoid the term *soft* and instead opt for *supple*, as mattresses should both support and give to the sleeper's body. And all of this is why every mattress life is different—because every customer is unique, and his or her needs change over the course of a lifetime.

This knowledge about the McRoskey's difference is well-known by generations of San Franciscans, many of whose preferences are tracked in that solitary card catalogue that quietly anchors the back of the San Francisco showroom, the founder's name still emblazoned across the top of the building that the family bought long ago. One should note, buying into this premium sheep-counting experience isn't cheap—McRoskey mattresses range from $5,000 to $7,800—but isn't a good night's sleep worth every penny?

MECHANICS' INSTITUTE LIBRARY & CHESS ROOM

57 POST ST., SAN FRANCISCO, CA 94104

(415) 393-0101 • MILIBRARY.ORG

The Quiet Ones

*B*ook nerds and history buffs naturally love this place, but it's a spot that remains relatively undiscovered by the masses, even after more than 160 years in operation. And it is a true gem of the city.

With its mouthful of a name and members-only status, the Mechanics' Institute Library & Chess Room may not immediately draw in the passerby to its headquarters on Post Street. But you should plan to visit it on a Wednesday at noon, during the weekly tour. Though the tour is intended to build membership in this library plus educational organization plus special events and chess club—and it does an excellent job of touting the organization's benefits—it is also a fantastic lesson in the city's history and a wonderful opportunity to see an official San Francisco historic landmark up close.

Founded in 1854, the Mechanics' Institute was established to "serve the educational and social needs of mechanics"—defined as "artisans, craftsmen, and inventors"—and their families. At the time of its founding, near the end of the Gold Rush, the city was still being flooded with people seeking quick riches, joining those who'd already been broken in the gold fields, many of whom were now alcoholics. It was one of several like-minded organizations around the English-speaking world at the time, but today it remains one of the last of its kind. It's now the oldest library on the West Coast designed to serve the public. And who is it for in 2015? I couldn't say it better than the organization does itself on its website: "The Institute today is a

favorite of avid readers, writers, downtown employees, students, film lovers, chess players, and the 21st century nomadic worker in search of a place for literary pursuits, thinking, research and study."

I love the bit about the "nomadic worker," as it captures something that's so appealing not just about libraries but uniquely about places like the Mechanics' Institute. It's a space devoted to thought and creative work, a place for exploring ideas and conversations and the arts, a place to stimulate the brain and socialize with others, a place to learn about yourself and the world around you. It's a place for the quiet ones with big, internal voices.

Librarian, historian, and marketing specialist Taryn Edwards led my tour and is a shining representative of both the organization and the library arts. She's full of knowledge, proud to share it and precise in that sharing, and passionate about the historical gravitas of the place she represents. Her allegiance shows up in comments like this, as she's describing the framed portrait of Andrew Hallidie, cable-car inventor and former president of the Mechanics' Institute: "The cable car—kind of fun, but not super important in my mind. What he should be known as is the father of California libraries."

Hallidie helped pass the Rogers Act that ensures funding for the state's public libraries; he was also president of the Mechanics'

Institute for 14 years and involved with the organization for 40. He and other notable figures in the organization's history are given due respect in portraits placed throughout the building, adding to the feeling of gravity you experience amidst the light and airiness of the place.

On first glance from the library's main entry, the place doesn't seem that big. Multiple levels are viewable from a single floor, and the shelves appear carefully crammed with books, yes, but you don't get a real sense of the space—and how many books there truly are—until you start wandering through the stacks. In and out, up and down, through secret stairways and half levels held up by floors of glass, books are everywhere. Collection size is about 150,000 items, spread over five levels on two floors. Local literature and fiction, science, politics, business, and finance are the library's most popular genres, but it also has a world-renowned collection of materials on chess. The fact that it has a section devoted to chess at all is striking, and it's apparently mobbed by schoolkids on the weekends boning up on the game.

For fans of libraries, this one is a charmer. But the Mechanics' Institute is more than just its collection of books. The building itself, which used to be the tallest in the neighborhood but is now dominated by the office towers of the Financial District, offers an experience on its own. With beautiful arched windows overlooking Post Street and nooks and crannies seemingly around every corner, the structure's most notable architectural element is its spiral staircase. Reminiscent of the signature stairway in the movie *Vertigo*, the one at the Mechanics' has fans of its own.

"People come from all over just to photograph the staircase," says Edwards, encouraging tour attendees to "stand in the curl" at the foot of it for the best view.

Upstairs, the heart of the chess club in the organization's title is the room full of roughly 50 tables, each set up with its pawns waiting patiently for a game to begin. Tuesday and Thursday nights are jammed with players, but most days the room is sparsely populated. And today it looks the way it always has, minus the spittoons that used to sit on the floors by each table.

Special events are geared for and mostly free to members, but almost always they are open to the public for a reasonable fee.

Author talks are common and feature both big names and local writers—sometimes one and the same. Friday nights are devoted to film screenings, each month with a theme (such as noir), and book groups meet regularly and cover a variety of interests, from the more expected (mystery lovers) to the less (Proust, books made into films, and Southern literature). And as one of the "pioneering adult educators" in the state, the institute still offers classes in a variety of disciplines today.

Membership hovers around 4,500, and though the institute doesn't keep close tabs on demographics, the staff recently started tracking age; roughly half of members today are under 40. And they're always welcoming more into the ranks.

Walking the halls of the mazelike space feels like you're walking with history, the whispered conversations and artistic debates of early members almost audible with the dulled clacking of modern keyboards. At a minimum, a tour of this, the oldest library on the West Coast and one of the oldest chess clubs in the country, should be part of every local's and visitor's itinerary. You might just decide to become a Mechanic, too.

THE OLD CLAM HOUSE

299 BAYSHORE BLVD., SAN FRANCISCO, CA 94124

(415) 826-4880 • THEOLDCLAMHOUSESF.COM

Doing Shots

It has the distinction of being the oldest restaurant in the city in the same location—and that location is rather unassuming. Nestled between the US 101 and I-280 freeways on the southeastern side of San Francisco, in the area formerly dominated by the naval shipyard and now the working class Bayview–Hunters Point neighborhood, The Old Clam House is not in a place you would naturally seek out when looking for great seafood. Or great anything, for that matter. But it turns out to be just that—a hidden gem that has provided a tasty, authentic, and local culinary experience to diners for more than 150 years.

Founded in 1861 (the same year Lincoln was inaugurated, they proudly note) as a bar and restaurant called The Oakdale Bar and Clam House that primarily served local waterfront workers, The Old Clam House still feels like a spot where the rough-and-tumble crowd would be comfortable—alongside families enjoying a night out. The seafood joint is famous for its Clam Bake Cioppino—the tomato-based seafood stew associated the world over with San Francisco—but more people talk about its clam juice shooter, a warm treat that begins every meal.

Technically an *amuse-bouche*, as it readies the palate for the food to come, the "shooter" feels more like a naughty-but-nice initiation into a secret club. It is the restaurant's signature, unique starter to the meal—I can't think of another place that offers anything like it—served warm and composed simply of clam juice, which is essentially the steaming water from freshly shucked steamed clams, a little fish

sauce, and scallions. That's it. And it is fantastic. Like the flavor-rich broth at the bottom of a pot of mussels, it becomes the quiet star of the show—making you want just a little bit more, just one more sip, just one more dip of the bread. It's quickly and extremely addictive.

The juice is an original offering at the restaurant, retained by adamant customer demand when current owner Jerry Dal Bozzo took over in 2011. Best known for his garlic-focused restaurant, The Stinking Rose (with locations in San Francisco and Los Angeles), along with his handful of other popular eateries in the Bay Area, Dal Bozzo essentially revived a dying establishment when he acquired The Old Clam House. The restaurateur actually has a passion for saving the seemingly unsavable, explains the company's longtime marketing rep Brandy Marts. "He has an affinity for unique places," she says, sharing how he brought his keen eye for design and was personally involved in the remodel and renovation, keeping the bones and authentic look of the place but creating "nooks and crannies" such as new, curtained booths and other special touches. In some cases, he even rebuilt original features (like the outer structure) to heighten the vintage feeling and "make it look more old." Dal Bozzo brought his own takes on classic dishes as well, like that cioppino, which, at The Old Clam House, is available in individual, couple-, or family-size servings (the

last in a big, cast-iron dutch oven) and prepared in the style of a clam bake—with stubs of fresh cobs of corn and chunky potatoes nestled among the local shellfish and white fish swimming in a spicy tomato broth.

The rest of the menu features a hodgepodge of seafood dishes—including sizzling platters of mussels, shrimp, crab, or all of the above, as well as some of the original recipes from the restaurant itself. The clam chowder falls into the latter category, keeping it real as a true local comfort food—always with sourdough bread, of course. A seafood restaurant wouldn't be worth its salt without a catch-of-the-day menu, and here that highlights the requisite local sand dabs, calamari, salmon, and a white fish—each served with the tiny pearl-like *acini di pepe* pasta, sun-dried tomatoes, and snow peas alongside. Sandwiches, salads, and even breakfast round out the menu—but my favorite (aside from the clam juice) is a simple dish called clams escargot, where the eponymous shellfish is served in its shells, just off the fire, with a delightful garlic and parsley butter à la the French snail version . . . but, dare I say, better? Less squeamish, at least.

The bar is part of the original restaurant and is manned by expert, tenured folks who also know the history of vintage establishments in the city—even giving me excellent recommendations for what other places should be featured in this book. Cocktail names play with the restaurant's theme with cutesy fish monikers, but with classic flavors and liquors in the mix. The cocktails are a great example of how The Old Clam House does a good job combining kitsch and authenticity for a down-home taste of the City by the Bay. So pull up a chair, slurp some clam juice, and imagine the old dockworkers slinging beers and feasting on plates of fish alongside you, more than 100 years ago.

ORIGINAL JOE'S

601 UNION ST., SAN FRANCISCO, CA 94133

(415) 775-4877 • ORIGINALJOESSF.COM

Here's the Beef

*J*f this place isn't a must-visit vintage establishment for the city of San Francisco, I don't know what is. Original Joe's is home to one of the city's most unique comfort-food dishes; has been around for 75 years; has a marvelously confusing history with another now-defunct, similarly named restaurant; and signifies the West Coast Italian-American dining experience. Also, it's just plain delicious.

Opened in 1937 by Louis Rocca and Tony "Ante" Rodin in the now rough Tenderloin neighborhood, Original Joe's was arguably a spin-off of another restaurant called New Joe's that had opened a decade earlier. A falling out between the latter's owners led to the new restaurant, with one of its owners swearing that his was "the original"—hence the name. Over the years, the Joe's name has proliferated in the Bay Area restaurant world, with descendants of each of the early owners opening other locations. The "original"— along with many other spots—is still operated by the third generation of the Rodin family, now the Duggans, with both John Duggan Sr. and Jr. the patriarchal leads. They continue to do a fabulous job of keeping things the way they've always been.

More notable than the murky origin story of the restaurant is its most famous dish, which dates back just as far: Joe's Special.

At first it sounds like an omelet—and legend says this is how it began, with one late-night customer asking for a spinach omelet and "anything else that the chef had left to cook," which turned out to be hamburger. Today, though, the emphasis is truly on the ground beef, a buttery, glistening, plate-size mound of it mixed with bits of

spinach and onion, the egg really only serving as a binder for the whole concoction, all piled high atop the plate. Mushrooms are an add-on option, according to the menu, but an essential component, according to most (including me). A little stainless-steel cup of ketchup sits on the side of the plate and, again, must be used. This one-plate wonder was one of my favorite city meals as a child, and, tasting it recently, it's even better—and beefier—than I remembered.

Perhaps it's because Original Joe's has had a reinvention of sorts; after a flue fire forced its closure in 2007, it eventually reopened, in a different neighborhood, five years later. And the reopening was a big deal. Mayor Edwin Lee declared a day in January 2012 "Original Joe's Day"; US senator and former San Francisco mayor Dianne Feinstein sent a letter of congratulations—replete with handwritten note at the bottom reading, "Great news!"—and award-winning culinary magazine *Saveur* featured the Joe's Special in its October issue. A solid PR team probably helped with all this coverage, but it can't be denied that the restaurant was an institution for a city that collectively felt its loss after the fire. Original Joe's new North Beach location, on a bright corner across from Washington Square Park and other Italian-American businesses, such as Mario's Bohemian Cigar Store Cafe and Liguria Bakery, feels almost more fitting than its original spot—more connected to its roots. Some will disagree, mostly longtime customers fervently devoted to the restaurant's gritty original location. But I think the new space still feels authentic, simply a shinier version of its vintage self.

Giant portions remain the establishment's trademark—one order of the Joe's Special will certainly give you two meals, at least. Signature red leather booths still fill the restaurant that again features an open kitchen—they claim to have invented exhibition-style cooking—and counter seating at the back, and a fireplace-warmed bar is outfitted with deep green leather stools, chairs, and banquettes, the perfectly manly atmosphere for an old-school establishment. And though most customers on a Friday afternoon in the bar are men, women feel comfortable, too, including a group of a certain age lunching happily near the fireplace. Families are also at home in the restaurant, which is probably why mine went so often during my childhood—parents can relax with a stiff, ice-cold manhattan while kids enjoy ravioli with meat sauce on a night out. Local dignitaries, naturally, are frequent customers, like those aforementioned politicians, journalists, and business moguls. The scene is bustling and boisterous, protecting instead of preventing conversation, and the tuxedoed front-of-the-house staff is professional and warm. It's the kind of place my dad loves—one of his all-time favorite dishes is the Joe's Special, which he still refers to as an omelet. It's also the kind of place I hope will be around for the next 75 years so my kids can take their own children for a taste of classic San Francisco, gargantuan piles of ground beef and all.

THE ORIGINAL TOMMY'S JOYNT

1101 GEARY BLVD., SAN FRANCISCO, CA 94109

(415) 775-4216 • TOMMYSJOYNT.COM

Welcome, Stranger

As with many long-standing businesses that have been passed from family member to family member, parts of the origin story for The Original Tommy's Joynt are unclear. Like when was it established? Either 1947 or '48, according to current owner Susie Katzman. "There is some disagreement about that." Why did the founder call it "The Original" when no other similar business followed in its footsteps? "I think he just liked the sound of it," she laughs warmly. But make no matter, the gregarious *hofbrau* with a funny name and funky artwork wrapping its building like a colorful outer shell has been going strong for more than 65 years and provides as much of a good, belly-filling time today as it must have in the '40s.

Gleaming steam trays of giant hunks of meat—barbecued brisket, corned beef, pastrami, ham, and turkey included—catch your eye upon entry; behind them are red-and-white menu boards advertising how you can enjoy those glorious meats—in sandwich or dinner-plate form. Once you get to the front of the roped-off line, be prepared with your order: A friendly, swift moving server wearing an old-fashioned soda-jerk hat is at the ready. A handful of salads are on offer to accompany the proteins or to be ordered on their own, including macaroni and potato and a popular cucumber salad with red onion, cherry tomatoes, and vinegar.

An unusual offering that is less so today but was quite rare at the Joynt's opening is buffalo—in both stew and chili forms.

"Tommy's neighbor on the Peninsula had a buffalo ranch," explains Katzman of her second cousin, the restaurant's founder, Tommy Harris,

and his life on this finger of land that stretches downward below San Francisco. "He told Tommy, 'You need to try this!'" The *hofbrau* man did, liked it, and decided to put it on the menu. It's been there ever since. I can only vouch for the tasty, comforting chili, which is a delicious, slightly more gamey version of the football-watching favorite.

A daily special menu dangles from the ceiling, advertising "Our New Exciting Daily Menu"—though most offerings, except for Friday's salmon, have been available for decades. Appropriately, several types of braised meats are featured—oxtails on Monday, pork shoulder on Tuesday, and lamb shanks on Thursday—along with the popular sweet-and-sour spareribs on Saturday. (That salmon replaced a previous favorite—a red-sauce-based calamari stew—that over the years had fallen out of favor.) All plates come with vegetable or starchy sides and, unless it's a sandwich, bread and butter.

"That was my favorite thing to eat here as a kid—just the sourdough roll and butter," Katzman divulges when I ask about her earliest memories of the place.

Katzman has been at the helm for 16 years, now along with her son Sam; she was asked to join the partnership when previous co-owner Al Pollack died. He'd been running the place with Katzman's father, Billy Veprin, for years.

The founder and all subsequent owners have been native San Franciscans, including Pollack and Veprin, and the place has a uniquely San Francisco feel. Those giant murals that wrap the building bring vivid color to expansive thoroughfare Geary Boulevard where there is none, demanding your attention with a groovy sort of 1960s international hippie vibe. (The building was repainted around that time after the city forced the owners, for reasons that are unclear, to remove its upper stories, one of which had been a boardinghouse.) In one part of the mural, the greeting "Welcome Stranger" encourages passersby that all will be comfortable inside—and this proves true.

Locals make up the majority of the business, but many tourists— particularly groups of German, English, French, and Russian travelers— make pilgrimages for meaty sandwiches and beer. The variety of customers, and the stories they share, is what Katzman loves most.

"We see all walks of life—from the people who can only afford a six-dollar sandwich to those who could go anywhere," she says, sharing that she hears from people who came in as toddlers and now bring their own families, people who met there on a first date 50 years ago and subsequently married, even value-seeking college kids ("This is the only place they can afford!").

Prices are cheap, but portions are generous—one plate of carved meat with sides can easily make two meals. This affordability extends to the bar as well. Naturally, since the *y* in the word *Joynt* is supposed to stand for a martini glass, the place has always had a large, full bar, even featuring a couple of house wines that are still available for around $3 a glass! (I swore I was looking at a vintage sign when I saw the prices on the wall.)

And all of this is very deliberate.

"While the City [*sic*] has been changing year after year, we remain steadfast in our opposition to change," states the *hofbrau*'s unofficial manifesto on its website. "We want things to remain the same because our founders established a reputation in San Francisco; a reputation that promises hot food and cold drink at a price that parries our atmosphere."

That atmosphere, they rightly say, is "like our food, no frills." The no-nonsense mission statement continues: "Want lettuce on your sandwich? Better go to some fast-food shop because we actually want you to taste the meat we carve in front of your eyes. Want a fork to eat those lamb shanks with? Better get up and go get one by the cashier. Want green beans instead of mashed potatoes? Well, you better speak up because we move fast, so we can serve the people fast . . ."

While frill-less and all about getting people fed well and quickly, the environment is anything but plain. The bar-restaurant is absolutely full of stuff in terms of decor—beer steins and ads, old photographs, piñatas, and even a few tennis rackets blanket the deep-red walls and hang from the ceiling while tables are festively draped in red-and-white-check oilcloths. There is a quiet reverence for history amidst the schlock: Relics from previous businesses that had occupied parts of the space—like an old mirror from the barbershop that used to operate in what is now the back of the upstairs dining room—have been preserved and placed among the bric-a-brac. The friendly waitstaff complements the eclectic mix and has longevity—many have worked there for decades. Along with the hearty food, it is a recipe for a gem of a vintage establishment that thankfully continues to thrive under the care of new generations. So the next time you need one meal to last for two, or just want a drink in a convivial atmosphere, go to the place where you could eat "like you had all the money in the US Mint, but lived like a Polk Street pauper," part of the original intent of the owners who were children of the Depression. Be sure to bring cash—they don't take anything else—and a hefty appetite.

PIEDMONT BOUTIQUE

1452 HAIGHT ST., SAN FRANCISCO, CA 94117

(415) 864-8075 • PIEDMONT-BOUTIQUE.MYSHOPIFY.COM

Life of the Party

Oh me, oh my, oh me, oh my—what a lot of funny things go by!" Dr. Seuss springs to mind upon entry into the Haight Avenue store marked by giant, fishnet-clad legs dangling from its upstairs window. But the colors of *One Fish, Two Fish, Red Fish, Blue Fish* frankly seem pale in comparison to the explosive palette filling what feels like a costume shop on acid. Piedmont Boutique looks like a drag queen's dream—and for many, it is—and has been outfitting the folks of San Francisco for parties and performances since 1972.

Amazingly, much of the clothing, jewelry, and feathery accessories in the shop are actually made in-house. The walls are lined floor to ceiling with thousands of pairs of earrings, wigs, stockings, hand-painted hair clips, and lingerie, all in more colors than there are in the rainbow. Bangles, tiaras, and barrettes fill glass cases—in some instances, alongside rows and rows of vibrant false eyelashes, again in colors I didn't know existed. Sunglasses come in multiple metallic shades, in both traditional shapes and more unusual ones, such as industrial-party goggles. Feathers and rhinestones seem to be everywhere, too, some of which adorn masks situated at the back that seem perfect for your next masquerade ball. Tutus are dyed in-house and displayed like girly puffs high on the walls. An extensive collection of pasties makes me suddenly wish I were a burlesque dancer; sequin-laden hearts, stars, and cones galore form the shapes of these festive nipple covers. The shop also seems to carry every type of top and bottom you could imagine wearing, from outerwear to lacy getups intended to be worn underneath—though I imagine

much of the inventory ultimately gets a very public display on the purchaser's body.

"Oh, most of those are skirts, but we've definitely got hot pants in the back," answers lovely seven-year employee Zerelle when I ask about the rack of shiny, and tiny, garments up front. With purple-tinted long, dark hair and a silvery rainbow-colored blouse, she, like other employees, represents the store's fun selection well. The people who patronize the store are what she likes most about her job, like "the drag queens, who are funny, and the teenagers shopping for earrings," and she says no request shocks her anymore.

"Honestly, I feel like when I first started working here, yes [things surprised me], but now that I've been here so long, nothing surprises me anymore," she says, smiling warmly. Zerelle's friendly demeanor matches the magnetic draw of the place—something I'm sure founders and married couple Uti, a "Midwestern farm girl," and German-born Sahaj (they don't use a last name) are pleased about.

"We get tremendous satisfaction in [meeting] the very unusual desires that our customers choose," says Uti, sharing how Piedmont Boutique outfitted the complete wedding party for Annie Sprinkle, former prostitute, porn star, and self-described "artist, sexologist, ecosexual, author, lecturer, educator, and thespian." They also

Vintage Spot

GOOD VIBRATIONS: EST: 1977

The sign out front says it all: "Creating a buzz since 1977." Founded by Joani Blank, intent on creating a "clean, well-lighted alternative to conventional adult bookstores," this female-friendly sex shop has been going strong since then and is best known for its colorful and diverse collection of vibrators in various shapes and sizes, along with a variety of things to "spice it up in the bedroom," says flagship employee and San Francisco native Nikki. This includes items from the relatively tame—massage oils, candles, and feathers—to the more overtly sexual—handles for gripping during sex in the shower, for instance. Erotica books and dress-up attire are available, too, as are kitschier things like boob pasta, board games, and sex-position cards. The shop is cheerful and bright, almost mall-like in its spaciousness, with polished wood floors and neat, tidy product displays. Education is big here, from the helpful service to classes held at each of the eight locations (including three in other Bay Area cities and one in Massachusetts). The Valencia Street (Mission District) shop is considered the original, even with several moves since founding, though other locations have a lot to offer, too. Most notable is the antique vibrator collection housed at the Polk Street store, a vintage offering in its own right. Customers from 18 to 80 (Nikki noted an 85-year-old couple who frequents the place) are welcome and at home here, and all will be offered assistance or casually left alone, if they already seem to know their way around.

603 Valencia St., San Francisco, CA 94110 (plus other locations); (415) 503-9522; goodvibes.com

made custom hologram vinyl suits for the music group Pop Rocks. Uti describes herself and her husband as "vintage" themselves, establishing the store in an era of hippies and disco fanaticism.

"It was only a consignment and vintage store at the beginning, but [we] turned to 'high fashion' at the time, with merchandise from

PIED PIPER BAR AND GRILL

PALACE HOTEL, 2 NEW MONTGOMERY, SAN FRANCISCO, CA 94105

(415) 546-5089 • SFPALACE.COM/PIED-PIPER

Picture Worth 1,000 Words

*B*ars and cafes are not commonly associated with great artists beyond serving as local hangouts for them—Les Deux Magots in Paris and the Algonquin in New York come to mind. But San Francisco's got one with a famous painting at its center.

The Pied Piper Bar and Grill—also commonly referred to as "Maxwell's" and part of the historic Palace Hotel, though its street entrance belies that connection—is named for the painting specially commissioned for the establishment at the bar's opening in 1909. Its artist, popular early 20th-century American painter Maxfield Parrish, known for his neoclassical imagery and dreamily rich colors, was paid $6,000 to create a homage to the legend of the Pied Piper of Hamelin, Germany. The 6-by-16-foot painting weighs more than 250 pounds and is one of Parrish's few works devoted to fairy tales; others include *Sing a Song of Sixpence*, commissioned by a hotel in Chicago in 1910 and sold in 2010 for $2.2 million, and the first, *Old King Cole*, painted in 1895 for the University of Pennsylvania Mask and Wig Club and currently at the St. Regis hotel in New York. Upon close viewing, the faces of both the children and adults in the *Pied Piper* mural are incredibly lifelike—particularly the eyes, which appear to see right off the canvas. Perhaps it's because Parrish painted people he actually knew quite well; both his wife and mistress, as well as his two sons, are purportedly represented in the piece, and the artist himself is rumored to be depicted as the lead character.

Though always a central figure in the space, the mural's major moment came in 2013, when it was nearly removed permanently to sell

at auction. After a city uproar and fervent campaign by the citizenry to keep the mural at the bar, the Palace had a change of heart, deciding to instead ship it to New York for professional restoration, to carefully lift away the smoke and grime that had collected from more than 100 years of sitting in the back of the bar. (Before that, the painting had only been removed two other times: first, during Prohibition, when it was relocated to the hotel's Rose Ballroom, and second, in 1989, to the city's de Young Museum during the hotel's renovation.) The effect of the careful restoration was masterful. Public relations director Renée Roberts will never forget the moment she saw the restored masterpiece for the first time.

"I was one of four people who got to go to the shipping company when the painting came back, to open the crate and see it for the very first time," she recalls, her voice trembling. "I have goose bumps and am almost crying just thinking about it." She was with the hotel's general manager, chief engineer (who'd been with the Palace for more than 40 years), and its carpenter (there for more than 30).

"It was unreal," she continued. "In all my years, never had I been able to stand right in front of it. It'd always been up on the wall. To see the detail with such clarity was amazing . . . and the color was unbelievable." The first unveiling for clients was also dramatic: "When

Vintage Spot
San Francisco Heritage: est. 1971

I have to give due credit to the nonprofit organization San Francisco Heritage for greatly helping, unknowingly, with my research for this book. And it's worthy of more than just a mention in the acknowledgments. The work the organization has done over its 44 years in existence is actually helping to ensure that the city's vintage landscape remains intact. It will likely be in large part because of organizations like this—and today, it's one of few—that someone 50 years from now will be able to write a book about the city's vintage establishments that are still going strong.

Preserving San Francisco's historical buildings and saving them from threatened ruin to make way for new development is how San Francisco Heritage got its start in 1971. But over the years it has expanded its mission to be one that, today, is "to preserve and enhance San Francisco's unique architectural and cultural identity." This means not only documenting what is special about the city's old buildings and businesses but also doing extensive advocacy that rises to the level of political action. Their work led to city legislation to create an official legacy business registry in San Francisco, still under way as of press time. And most exciting, for me and for the purposes of this book, anyway, has been their work on the Legacy Project.

In 2012, after the famous Gold Dust Lounge was evicted from its historic Union Square spot and forced to relocate, and the Tonga Room & Hurricane Bar was suddenly at risk of closure (leading to an ultimately successful fan-led grassroots campaign called "SOS Tonga"), the team at San Francisco Heritage knew something had to be done.

"Increasingly, these long-standing iconic San Francisco institutions were facing foreclosure or eviction because of the booming real-estate industry in the city," says executive director Mike Buhler. "We wanted to raise awareness of the significance of these places and provide a marketing tool for the businesses to remain viable."

So in 2013, they launched the Legacy Project, and it has been a marvel in documenting the city's history in food and drink. The organization has now certified more than 100 legacy establishments—a mix of bars, restaurants, and a blend of the two, along with bakeries and specialty food shops—and the work is not finished. Stipulations for inclusion in San Francisco's list are to have been in existence as a business for at least 40 years; and either to have distinctive interior design or architecture, or significance for the local community.

Staff, naturally, is passionate about the cause. Buhler's favorite legacy establishment is the Pied Piper Bar and Grill; his organization led the successful petition to keep the famous mural at the bar when the owners considered selling it at auction. It's also where he had his job interview, so it holds personal significance as well.

"You hear all the time that San Francisco is a collection of neighborhoods," says Buhler. "One thing I really love about the Legacy list is that each of the businesses in their own way reflects the cultural history of that particular group or neighborhood in the city—even if the neighborhood around it has transformed and taken on a completely different cultural identity in the present day.

"We wanted to identify not only the most significant, most long-standing places, but really a collection of businesses that reflects the mosaic of San Francisco's cultural history—and the various layers of immigrant groups that have come to this city and given it its identity today."

They've done a great job of achieving that goal, and they continue to scour the city for establishments that need a hand in saving.

2007 Franklin St., San Francisco, CA 94109; (415) 441-3000; sfheritage.org

they pulled that drape off, everyone just gasped. The difference in color was so apparent."

To see an American work of art is reason enough to visit the bar and grill, but the classic beauty of the turn-of-the-century space, with all of its rich woods, carved box-beam ceilings, and crystal chandeliers, is another draw. Some fans love the ambling feeling of the place and its long path to the bar at the back where that glorious painting sits; the drinks, comfort food, and live entertainment appeal as well. On the cocktail side, the Pied Piper has kept up with trends—maintaining a classic list of wines and beers with a robust selection of spirits (nearly 40 distinct whiskeys and bourbons were available at last count), while tightening its mixed drink offerings to feature fresh juices and syrups in selections that honor the bar's California location and the past. The Pied Piper Martini is the popular signature cocktail. And as part of the Palace's membership in Starwood's Luxury Collection of properties, a special drink list includes the Market Gimlet—featuring cucumber vodka, freshly squeezed lime juice, and tarragon-infused agave—evoking the historic, local, and modern all at once. The grill menu is a blend of elegant renditions of bar food, such as burgers, truffle fries, and soft-baked pretzel "bites" served with Hefeweizen mustard, and comfort classics, like roasted chicken and shepherd's pie. Live music has come and gone over the years but is experiencing a resurgence at the Pied Piper with mostly acoustic sets. Overall, the atmospheric intent is to be modern, luxurious, and comfortable in an historic setting—a place your grandparents would feel at home sitting alongside your best friend. Definitely not stodgy. And they pull it off.

"We'll never have music booming out and people lined up around the block," Roberts says, careful to add that kind of establishment has its place in the city. But, she says, along with the multigenerational guests of the hotel, the clientele is getting younger with the regional tech boom, and the historic bar and grill built around a famous mural is happy to have them. There's a new "vibrancy" and a hunger for cultural experience "that's refreshing," she says. "While they have this mind looking for the next greatest thing, they also have this appreciation for something that will never go away." And may the Pied Piper himself continue to summon them, and future generations like them, over the next 100 years.

PIER 23 CAFE

PIER 23, THE EMBARCADERO, SAN FRANCISCO, CA 94111

(415) 362-5125 • PIER23CAFE.COM

Vintage Derrieres

ℐier 23 Cafe places part of its vintage history squarely at the front door: The first thing you see when you walk in is a black-and-white photograph showcasing a line of women's pert, bare backsides. The shot captures the ladies of Sally Rand's Nude Ranch, a wildly popular exhibit at the 1939 Golden Gate International Exposition on Treasure Island, situated in the bay just beyond the restaurant. Current owner—sixth-generation San Franciscan Flicka McGurrin, who got the place in 1985 with a friend—says the ladies' connection to the cafe is a bit of a mystery; was former owner Joanie Boyer one of the women in the photograph, or had she simply received it as a gift? One might never know. And its origin doesn't seem to matter much; it just is. It exists as part of the cafe's legacy as a place for live music, good drinks, an incredible waterfront location, and tasty dishes—and a place that has weathered many business "storms": a fire in 1986 and massive earthquake in 1989, for instance, the likes of which have put many a business swiftly to rest. Through it all, the cafe has persevered and thrived, and on a glorious late October day, it's hard to imagine a better place to spend an afternoon in San Francisco.

With the bar-cafe's light, airy atmosphere and friendly welcome from everyone you meet, you feel positively enveloped with warmth and sunshine—and ready to dig into a plateful of seafood, delightfully fried bar food, or the carnitas quesadilla—which McGurrin describes as "to die for"—in the beautiful seaside, summer-like environment. Even a cup of clam chowder to start seems appropriate, given the

Vintage Spot
BOUDIN BAKERY: EST. 1849

San Francisco sourdough—the city and the bread—are in such a close partnership they are often inseparable. Each can be defined in part by the other; each has contributed to the history of the other. Sourdough bread is served at almost every classic restaurant in the city—and at many modern spots, too—before the meal or as a main part of it, such as the perennially popular clam chowder in a bread bowl—and most of it comes from the venerable Boudin Bakery.

Boudin has been baking this lovely, chewy, tangy bread since 1849, nurturing its 150-year-old starter to this day. "Every loaf really does come from the same place," explains chatty nana Jean, tour guide at the company's museum and demonstration bakery, located in an imposing concrete, corrugated steel, and glass building erected in 2004 in the heart of Fisherman's Wharf. A visit to this, the bakery's flagship location, gets you a fabulous education not only about the company and how to make bread—along with a piece of it—but also the history of the California Gold Rush and other San Francisco companies that grew up in the same era. Also on-site are a market and gift shop, a cafe of the sort that has popped up in malls throughout the state, and a full-service, sit-down restaurant—all an indication of the company's success beyond the city proper.

With claims to be San Francisco's oldest continuously running company, the history of Boudin—and sourdough—dovetails with that of the Gold Rush. As people poured into the northern part of the state in search of riches, along came a natural proliferation of businesses to support the new population—including many French bakeries. The French technique of using a wild yeast starter—or "mother dough"—to leaven the bread gained popularity in the region, particularly courtesy of the Boudin family, and the technique is still in use to this day.

And that starter? It was actually saved in the 1906 earthquake by Louise, wife of early master baker Isidore Boudin, who had the foresight to snatch it from the shaking building and toss it into a wooden bucket, whisking it to safety just before the bakery burned to the ground. So it really is the same stuff, the same living yeast concoction, that's responsible for every last piece of Boudin bread I've ever eaten.

The fate of this delicious bread has been carefully managed and nurtured, first by several generations of the Boudin family and, since 1941, by master baker Steve "Papa Steve" Giraudo Sr., who purchased it that year with the family's blessing, saving the business from bankruptcy. Since Giraudo's death in 1997, the bakery has remained with his partners and team, ensuring the preservation of the longtime traditions that have become synonymous with the taste of San Francisco.

Museum, demonstration bakery, and cafe at 160 Jefferson St., San Francisco, CA 94133; (415) 928-1849; boudinbakery.com

cafe's incredibly light rendition, full of delicate, little, tender clams—not potatoes—and topped with a petite sourdough toast. (Do not miss the side of sourdough bread to dip into the soup, or into anything else for that matter; the bread is a San Francisco classic, and the Boudin version the cafe offers is a chewy and addictive city favorite.) And the cafe's allegiance to the Monterey Bay Aquarium's Seafood Watch program means all fish is fresh and sustainably sourced; a tiny morsel of shell still clung to a bit of the Dungeness crab in my Louie salad, a mark of freshness and locality. Striped oilcloths top all the outdoor tables, adding to the very vacationy vibe and French beach-town sensibility outside. During the day, the crowd is a fair blend of business lunchers, workout partners, celebrants of various occasions (including a baby shower on my last visit), friends on vacation, and families traveling from afar. Buckets of upturned wine bottles can be spied on patio tables. With the cafe's Wi-Fi, yet to be discovered by the coffeehouse-magnetized urban masses, and the lack of laptops filling the space, I feel as though I've discovered my new favorite lunch-and-work spot in the city.

Its ideal nature as a daytime place shouldn't overshadow its nighttime heritage, however. The Pier 23 Cafe—positioned on San Francisco's Embarcadero, a stretch of roadway, docks, and businesses that hugs the water—has a strong legacy as a waterfront bar, replete with live music nightly and a rougher past, in line with the formerly rougher neighborhood. In the '60s, long before she owned the place, McGurrin remembers a sawdust-covered floor and strictly ragtime entertainment when she visited with a date. Music still reigns here, in a variety of genres at that—jazz, rhythm and blues, ragtime, you name it—and will for as long as she's involved. The owner's love of the arts is clear—she is a painter herself and, for almost 20 years, has proudly worn a vibrant gold and painted-enamel ring, made by a New Orleans artist friend, featuring the cafe's logo.

McGurrin is unconcerned about the future of the cafe, given that her son, McGurrin "Mac" Leibert, runs the place now, along with her daughter's management of the blog and involvement from all three of McGurrin's children over the years. So the legacy will live on. A woman here and there will continue to complain about the "inappropriateness" of the Nude Ranch photo, and the photo will continue to remain prominently positioned, proudly and defiantly, in the space. Occasional rowdy patrons will continue to jump into the bay just beyond the cafe's dock area and will continue to be calmly booted from the restaurant upon climbing back up, drunk and drenched. And the straightforward waterfront-style food will continue to be served to hungry patrons, locals, and far-flung travelers alike, at the tip of the City by the Bay. What does she enjoy most about being the proprietor of this vintage spot? "The fabulous location—it's still a dream come true and is uniquely San Francisco," she shares.

"We are San Francisco people," she explains, meaning artistic, appreciative of the climate (fog or sunshine), and able to weather the storms—whether those be fires, earthquakes, or the challenges inherent with running a business that's been around for three-quarters of a century. Pier 23 Cafe is all this, and it offers something intangible: a taste of the city and its bawdy history, along with a bit of its breezy, watery outdoors, all set to music, whether from the clink of wine glasses or clang of a butter knife following its use on a hunk of sourdough—or from the upright piano in the bar's corner.

RED'S JAVA HOUSE

PIER 30, THE EMBARCADERO, SAN FRANCISCO, CA 94107

(415) 777-5626 • REDSJAVAHOUSE.COM

Breakfast of Champions

Question: In 1843, Congress granted Samuel F. B. Morse $30,000 to build the first telegraph line between two cities located about 30 miles apart from each other. What were they?"

I'm stumped. I'm standing at the kitchen-window counter of a local historic dive restaurant, not expecting to be tested like this. Wracking my memory of eighth-grade American history, I come up with nothing.

"San Francisco and Sacramento?" I offer stupidly. Wrong on both counts—they are neither 30 miles apart nor was California part of the US then.

"You know Luminosity? We give your brain that same exercise but for free!" intones the olive-skinned manager Rafael, with a huge grin. Turns out I don't need to know the answer (Washington, DC, and Baltimore) to get a burger, which is what I've come for, but the weekly trivia question, scrawled on a chalkboard behind the counter, is a fun tradition of the little cafe that could.

Tucked under the wing of the Bay Bridge, its constant rumble a soundtrack to your lunch, Red's Java House is a must-visit on the list of casual eateries in the city. It sits on the edge of the bay, about halfway between the ballpark and the fancy foodie Ferry Building on Pier 30, and has survived earthquakes, a massive fire, and modern threats in the form of waterfront development. Named for the redheaded brothers who took over the little waterfront eatery in 1955, which had catered to dockworkers and seafarers since the '30s, Red's is a San Francisco institution. It's the place where everyone—yes, Anthony

Combos

Double Cheeseburger & Soda $10 20 +TAX
Double Cheeseburger Fries & Soda $12 20 +TAX
Hamburger or Hot Dog & Beer $9 25 +TAX
Single Cheeseburger & Soda $7 45 +TAX
Double Cheeseburger & Bud $12 35 +TAX
Double Cheeseburger Fries & Lagunitas IPA $15 25 +TAX

Specials

Mon Sausage Sandwich $ +TAX 7.5
Tues Corn Beef Sandwich $ +TAX 7.5
Wed Meatball Sandwich $ +TAX 9.75
Thurs Chicken Parmesan $ 9.75 TAX
Fri Fish & Chips $ 10.76 + TAX
Sat Corn Beef $ 10.76 +TAX
Sun Hash $ +TAX

Breakfast

Two Egg Breakfast Plate $8.9 +TA
Breakfast Sandwich $6.9 +TA
Eggs & Chili Rancheros $8 +TF
Pancakes (2) $6 +T
Pancake Plate w/ 2 Eggs & Bacon
Breakfast Quesadilla $6

Bourdain included (where hasn't he been?)—goes for a taste of a local classic. Here that's a double cheeseburger on a slab of chewy sourdough bread, with pared-down toppings of just pickles, onions, and mustard, all washed down with a beer.

"That's what makes it!" enthuses Rafael about the sourdough bread on the burger. The manager hails from Acapulco but has lived in the city for years and is a great ambassador for Red's. "People complain that we don't have lettuce or tomato on burgers, but this is the European way."

The bread comes from local bakery Wedemeyer, based in South San Francisco and itself a vintage business, established in 1936. Sourdough bread is like a religion in the Bay Area, and Wedemeyer's constitutes a delicious, authentic version.

The meal dates back to the origins of the place, when Franco's Lunch, the cafe's original name, offered a cheeseburger-and-beer breakfast special to longshoremen and sailors. San Francisco natives Tom and Mike McGarvey bought the place in '55, changing its name but keeping its simple foods and just about everything else, including the shack of a building that still remains today, even after a huge blaze leveled almost everything around it in the '70s. (When I was last there, one young man was carefully patching up holes that'd likely been kicked into the side of the building by sidewalk revelers,

Vintage Spot
Java House: est. 1912

Their histories are shared, their locations are just piers away from each other. They have a similar feeling—both waterfront joints, both tiny, both divey. But the Java House is older than Red's and somehow feels like more of a surprising relic today. In the shadow of the AT&T ballpark just yards away, it certainly feels miraculous that it's still standing.

Established in 1912 on Pier 40, the little white clapboard shack that is purportedly the oldest operating eatery on the waterfront has served longshoremen, sailors, baseball fanatics, and waterfront-strolling tourists for more than 100 years. Tom "Red" McGarvey and brother Mike owned the place in the 1950s and eventually opened a different spot down the Embarcadero that became more famous: Red's Java House. After being overseen by several other owners, Java House has been run since the 1980s by the Greek Papadopoulos family, with Philip its patriarch. When you step into the shabby space that seems to house only a bar, kitchen counter (with a grill just beyond your reach), and refrigerated soda case, it's somewhat shocking that it's still around. But it has its fans, famous and not so, and it doesn't try to fool people by updating or doing something different.

The joint serves a simple menu: for breakfast, eggs, omelets, pancakes, and a breakfast sandwich—or a hot dog and coffee, another traditional longshoreman's early morning meal. For lunch, those same hot dogs are on order, plus sandwiches of all sorts, including burgers, a variety of cold sandwiches, and a couple of salads—but who would think of ordering salad in a place like this? The gyro gives a nod to the current family's background. Local signs showing lots of Giants love are everywhere, but nothing blocks the view of the boats bobbing in the marina just beyond the flattop grill.

The shack stands out amidst the modern buildings that have climbed up around it, perhaps because it's all wood or perhaps because it's teensy-tiny and looks ready to be razed at any moment. Don't look past it—it's a funky little spot deserving of your attention and affection.

Pier 40, The Embarcadero, San Francisco CA 94107; (415) 495-7260; javahousesf.com

explaining that they were not allowed to rebuild or do much of anything to the structure besides spot-fix.) As children, long before they were business owners, the McGarveys sold newspapers on the piers and aboard ships docked in the bay, eventually becoming seamen themselves. Later, they owned the Java House down the street before they bought and renamed Franco's, eventually selling Red's in the 1990s. Its several owners since have smartly maintained the status quo.

Though ownership has changed a couple of times over the years, the place has not, making for an authentically Depression-era cafe—with the exception of the prices, of course. Fries were not actually a menu item until this century, a fact that shocks me to learn. Floors creak, and there's a crooked quality to the building that meanders out to an open-air back patio on the pier, a favorite lunch spot for tourists and locals today. Clientele is a total mix—I've seen everything from drunk dudes hitting on married women to bearded, chambray-wearing hipsters, young families, and older workmen, sporting sneakers and sunglasses with neck straps—all lunching at the same time on a weekday. Be sure to grab napkins and a bottle of ketchup on your way outside, and beware of brazen birds—even the little cute ones! They don't hesitate to jump up on your table and try to dine with you.

Along with the cheeseburgers, fish-and-chips is a popular menu item on Friday—and just about everyone, perhaps only kids excluded, drinks beer with their lunch. Nearly all of the other daily specials are sandwiches—sausage (Monday), corned beef (Tuesday), meatball (Wednesday), chicken Parmesan (Thursday)—and corned beef and hash on the weekends. A short list of breakfast items is also available until late morning. If you do dine outside along with the majority, keep an ear out for your order—"single cheese and fries, single cheese and fries"—over the loudspeaker, indicating that it's ready for pickup near that trivia counter.

On a gloriously sunny day, Red's Java House is one of the city's best, and cheapest, al fresco dining spots, ideal to let the light, cool breeze ruffle your hair over a simple lunch. And on a foggy, bone-chilling day, the sort common in San Francisco, a deliciously greasy burger tucked into a half loaf of sourdough can be just the right thing to warm your insides. Especially if consumed like the longshoremen of yore would, with a bottle of beer.

THE ROOSEVELT TAMALE PARLOR

2817 24TH ST., SAN FRANCISCO, CA • (415) 824-2600

FACEBOOK.COM/EATATTHEROOSEVELT

Secret Sauce

Sometimes the best-laid plans become even better when they are altered by life's circumstances. This is what owners Aaron Presbrey and Barry Moore of The Roosevelt Tamale Parlor discovered when they bought the nearly century-old business in 2012.

"It was a good opportunity in right neighborhood at the right time," Presbrey says of the purchase, explaining that they originally had intended to make the old Mexican restaurant, founded in 1919, "something totally different," based on Moore's background in Italian cooking. "But upon buying the place, we pretty quickly realized that it was something we needed to preserve rather than change."

Thankfully, that's the course they pursued, deciding to remake the eatery that had collected many fans over the years but gradually fallen into some disrepair. So they enhanced old recipes and added new takes on classics, including their delicious *"chiva"* tamal, which is a reference to goat (*chiva* in Spanish) and features sweet butternut squash and yams with, appropriately, goat cheese and a vibrant tomatillo sauce. They kept the oversize (read, gigantic) round tamales that the restaurant is known for, with the traditional fillings of pork, chicken, or beef and topping of a rich tomato-based sauce and oozy, melty cheese. The non-tamal portion of the menu still features classic Mexican combination plates—including tacos, enchiladas, chiles rellenos, tostadas, and burritos, all served with beans and rice—and traditional specialties such as pozole and ceviche. Modern dishes have an international sensibility and do the delicate job of avoiding a forced, newfangled feeling while still presenting as fresh and

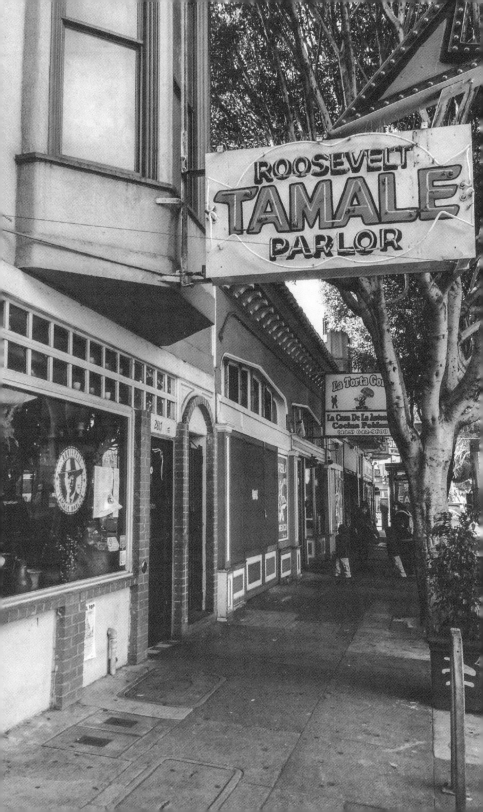

different—including things like a double-decker tostada *colorado* and the *bacalao frito*, a salt cod–potato tamal that is flash-fried before serving, making the masa crisp on the outside. The new team even has a bright Caesar on its short list of salads. And their specials—such as chipotle-barbecued baby back ribs—are a favorite of regulars and often represent something that's less traditionally Mexican.

"We maintain the Mexican influence but are not bound by the idea that everything has to be a tamal or taco," Presbrey explains.

As an *horchata* connoisseur, I order it every time I eat Mexican food for its stupendous ability to counterbalance a spicy meal. The Roosevelt's version of the sweet rice-milk drink is served in a huge, mint-green plastic Coca Cola Classic cup and is the by far the best I've ever had. "Maybe that's because it's the freshest you've ever had," suggests Presbrey, explaining that they use no mix, as some do; they include a lot of cinnamon and a little sweetened condensed milk in addition to the rice; and they prepare it fresh daily. (This is a theme, actually—they also make guacamole fresh three times a day.)

When they first opened under new ownership, Presbrey says longtime customers would come in and see that the place had been sold.

"Their first reaction was, 'Oh no!' We had a hard time convincing some people to even stay and try it," he recalls. But people quickly learned that the food was not only as good as but better than before. "It gives you the same feeling, just elevated."

He has it on good authority that customers are by and large pleased with the new Roosevelt; Presbrey himself has waited the tables "every second of every day since [we] bought the place," so he's been able to hear from every customer what they think.

Fortunately, when they bought the place, they also kept on staff one of The Roosevelt's longest employees, who they respectfully call Doña Maria.

A shy immigrant from Michoacán, Mexico, who came to the city more than 30 years ago, Doña Maria is responsible for many of the traditional flavors that appear in The Roosevelt's dishes—including the authentic sauces that cover the famous tamales. Her secret to deliciousness is not unlike that of countless, brilliant home cooks the world over.

"I work every day happy, with a lot of love," she shares with me through the help of translator Yoana, who works as a server at the restaurant. Doña Maria has stayed through several sets of owners, over decades, first learning how to cook on the job from the previous owner, the reportedly outspoken Rose Carrasco, who used to deny chip refills and loved her local sports teams, and whose family owned the restaurant from the 1960s until the early 2000s when they sold to interim owners. (She also used to live above the restaurant, even as recently as when Presbrey and Moore took over.) Doña Maria has added her special touches to certain original recipes over the years, making for a dynamic partnership with executive chef-owner Moore, who brings culinary expertise and a modern sensibility and creativity to the menu. I joke with her that it's like she's secretly the boss, *el jefe*, since she's been there longer than anyone else. She smiles humbly, embarrassed, and simply says she likes her work—and she promises to cook for me, off the menu, the next time I come in.

Like many places in this book, there's no official written history of the restaurant, only hearsay about how things have transpired over the years, so Presbrey and Moore are doing their best to preserve meaningful traditions as they learn of them. The transplants from Massachusetts and Colorado, respectively, who've now been in San Francisco for decades, have just reinstated the annual calendar poster tradition that was a practice going back at least 50 years, proudly mounting the 2015 installment on the wall. And they relish stories of people meeting spouses there decades ago or coming for dinner with their families as children. Their own connection to the legacy business is subtly profound: It happens to be one of the first restaurants where Moore ate when he moved to the city 30 years ago.

"We are really proud that we've been able to revitalize it and keep it around longer for people," Presbrey says of the palace of steaming hot plates of tamales and Doña Maria's special sauces infused with happiness and secret meals for friends in the back. No one knows how much longer The Roosevelt will be around, but one thing is certain: If you go now, you will not leave hungry.

SAM JORDAN'S BAR

4004 3RD ST., SAN FRANCISCO, CA 94124 • (415) 824-0155

FACEBOOK.COM/SAMJORDANSBAR

Like Family

Stepping into this Bayview bar could feel intimidating if you're not part of the community that calls the place home. Initially that community seems defined by race. In 1963, its founder was the first African American in San Francisco to run for mayor—following his time as a successful light-heavyweight boxer in the professional-amateur league, the Golden Gloves. But you quickly learn that community at Sam Jordan's is not about race, but about regulars.

Some pull up a barstool there twice a day every day, like one man named Kevin, who's been going at lunch and after work for his tequila sunrises and sautéed prawns for 20 years. Newcomers stick out like a sore thumb; people simply know who hasn't been there before. But even if it is your first time, the sense of welcome is palpable and warm, whether from second-generation owner Allen Jordan, who may be in the kitchen preparing barbecued ribs; or the new daytime bartender, a young Croatian man named Carlo; or another member of the Sam Jordan family. It instantly feels like you belong.

The building housing Sam Jordan's dates back to 1883, and it doesn't look like a whole lot has changed since then, except for the modern tinsel and seasonal decor marking holidays—red glittery hearts for Valentine's Day, for instance—dangling from the long, narrow bar. Jordan founded the place in 1959 (though reports of a bar in the space prior to that exist) in what was then still the slaughterhouse-dense neighborhood known as Butchertown. (San Francisco's Cow Palace stadium is right up the street, so-named for obvious reasons.)

Around that time, other industries were moving in as well, and today, though the stockyards are gone, the area is mostly industrial.

Jordan's 1963 run for mayor landed him fourth in a field of eight candidates—pretty remarkable for a political race during the civil rights era. His strong finish was a testament to the popularity he'd gained in his own neighborhood, his unofficial nickname, "the Mayor of Butchertown," underscoring his strong community support. Black-and-white photographs on the walls of the slender, mirror-lined, ho-hum space show the strong founder in his prime, as well as the gorgeous women in his life—the mothers of current owners, brother-and-sister team Allen and Ruth Jordan.

In 2013 the bar-restaurant (and though it has phenomenal barbecue, it feels mostly like a bar) earned San Francisco's historic landmark status—a deserved distinction for more than just its history. It has always been about community, a gathering place, a home away from home. It was in the '60s for Sam Jordan's friends and supporters, and it is today, for the family of the founder and all others who've been dubbed family over the years. Allen's response to my question about the best thing on the menu nicely summed up the feeling people have about the place itself: "Everything's special."

That menu is surprising large for a place this small. It's actually a wonder that it exists at all, coming out of a kitchen almost hidden in the back of what looks strictly like a bar and nightclub (it is very much both). Among "everything" is a whole lot of barbecue—brisket, chicken, ribs, and links—and entrees such as the aforementioned sautéed prawns. Fried chicken and fish (catfish, sole, and red snapper) are popular, too, and traditional sides include potato salad, baked beans, mac and cheese, corn on the cob, and corn-bread muffins, among other options. "Soul Food Sunday" brings out fried pork chops, pepper steak, and salmon croquettes, along with some daily offerings.

Sweet drinks are popular with the crowd, especially "anything made with Cîroc," says Carlo, of the top-shelf vodka available in a multitude of flavors. Kevin confirmed the clientele's affinity for sweet cocktails with his own allegiance to the tequila sunrise. "I don't like to taste my alcohol," he laughs. But a full bar is available, with bartenders versed in making every sort of drink imaginable, with juice or without.

The navy-vet founder was a longshoreman and warehouse worker before he opened the bar. And his boxing-days nickname could have predicted that he'd one day enter the hospitality industry; his tendency to "serenade the crowd after every win" earned him the moniker "Singing Sam." He eventually became friends with Sammy Davis Jr. and other professionals, and he featured performances by big acts of the day right there in the bar. There's a fair amount of singing (karaoke, naturally), dancing, and overall revelry that still goes down at Sam Jordan's, especially on the weekends or during sports events, where customers can cheer together with the games projected on one of several TVs in the intimate space. Though he died more than a decade ago, I imagine he'd be proud to see his children carrying on his legacy—welcoming regulars and newcomers alike, with a song, a sweet drink, or a plate of ribs.

SAM'S GRILL

374 BUSH ST., SAN FRANCISCO, CA 94104

(415) 421-0594 • BELDEN-PLACE.COM/SAMSGRILL

Made for the Movies

This is the kind of place that makes everyone look like someone—though you may see a few actual someones when you're there. The venerable former mayor Willie Brown appeared at the bar as I was telling my husband over lunch one day how everyone in the place looked famous. That sort of sighting is not unusual for one of the oldest restaurants in both the city (second) and the country (fifth), and one that feels ripe with stories that could translate to the silver screen. Just ask Sam's Grill managing partner Peter Quartaroli, who spends the other half of his life as an actor and movie producer.

"Every good restaurant has a story to tell, and Sam's has a great story," he says. With his dark hair, medium build, and warm smile for every customer, Quartaroli looks like a youthful but confident maître d' from a Scorsese movie. You notice his age (50s) because he's significantly younger than the waiters (and, frankly, he looks like he's in his 40s). It's hard to believe the native San Franciscan has been with the place for 22 years, beginning as a waiter himself when the other restaurant where he was working (Bardelli's) suddenly closed. "Someone had just fired a waiter at Sam's, and I had a tux from Bardelli's, so [owner] Paul Lazzareschi came over and said, 'Throw on your tux, run across to Union Square, go into Sam's, and start working! It's the best job in town: They're closed on weekends, they make good money, the guys are great. Give it a shot.'" He did, and the rest, as they say, is history.

It's not often that the actor waiting tables grows up to basically own the restaurant (while simultaneously making movies), but this is just what's happened for Quartaroli, thankfully. When former owner Phil Lyons left in 2014, the restaurant's destiny was uncertain; a group of investors—who happened to be longtime customers—approached Quartaroli, who was the nighttime maître d' at the time, to enlist him as managing partner. After closing for several months and doing a subtle but methodical head-to-toe refurbishment and cleaning (essentially just spiffing up the original setup), Sam's reopened in winter of 2014 to the relief of those regulars and its employees, who resumed service without a hiccup.

Sam's dates back to 1867, when Irish immigrant and oysterman Michael Bolan Moraghan first opened an oyster saloon in what was essentially a permanent farmers' market of that era, called "California Market." Restaurateur Sam Zenovich bought the place in 1922, renaming it the Samuel Zenovich Restaurant—leading to its popular nickname, "Sam's." When Zenovich died in 1937, a man named Frank Seput took over, renaming it again, this time to Sam's Grill and Seafood Restaurant. It then became a true family business, remaining with the Seput family into the 21st century.

It's incredible to see that what began as a Gold Rush–era oyster saloon has evolved into a restaurant that attracts die-hard regulars— some even daily—to dine at one of its smattering of tables or in private, curtained booths. And beyond morphing from saloon into sit-down restaurant, Sam's has changed very little over the years—always with an overt respect for "the old-fashioned," as evidenced by this excerpt from its 1942 menu, included in the menu printed daily today:

> We are Happy to present to you an Old-Fashioned Eating House with Old Fashioned Waiter Service and Old-Fashioned Private Booths together with a newly equipped kitchen for better and faster service.
>
> We want to continue to serve you as we have done in the past and keep our reputation as one of the Good Eating Places of "Old San Francisco."
>
> We are proud of it and hope you will be, too.

Brightly lit, the main room has an almost yellowy hue—like a sepia-toned photograph—and feels somewhat like the unadorned fellowship room of an old church. Except for those in the booths,

people can be seen clearly from almost every angle, sitting beneath hooks that line the walls awaiting a coat or, in former times, a proper hat. (One regular female customer in her 70s reportedly complained of the mostly empty hooks, "No one hangs their hat anymore! Nobody wears hats anymore!") Tabletops are a pillowy vinyl shrouded in white cloth and anchored by funky lamps that appear to be relics from the '60s. Tuxedoed waiters—almost all of a certain age—await diners' arrival at the start of lunch, hanging out near the front of the restaurant in a friendly pack, anxious for the show to begin. The room fills quickly with obvious regulars and Financial District types, mostly men—"a lot of lawyers," according to affable career waiter Capelini, long ago a Maltese immigrant to the city. Like so many people associated with Sam's, Capelini reminds me of someone in a movie.

"They call me Capelini the Champion!" he says, laughing about his tennis obsession and daily habit in the Marina District. His presence in a seafood restaurant is fitting, he explains. "I grew up in the water!" he says, sharing that he ate lots of fish in the summertime as a child. As we're chatting, I'm struck by how it's people like Capelini, his many tenured colleagues, and the devoted customers who eat there regularly that give Sam's the special, authentically San Francisco quality.

"Sam's has a magical feel to me," Quartaroli says. "It doesn't try to be something that it's not. It's a place that's comfortable and a little old-fashioned but true to value. And there are so many San Franciscans who are tied to this place. People have come in here going back to the Gold Rush era. And we have some people that come almost every day; they have their waiters, their tables, their booths." This includes one family that has been coming the night before Christmas Eve for 20 years, he shares.

Things seem to move both delightfully slowly and quickly, simultaneously, at Sam's. It can go from dead quiet to positively boisterous in minutes. It's comforting to see that even amidst modern opportunities for money making and modern trends in the culinary world, a place like this is still selling a lot of romaine seafood salads, shrimp cocktails, and expertly boned fish dressed only with butter. I hope, like many other people do, it sticks around for another century. There are so many more stories that could come through its doors.

SCHROEDER'S

240 FRONT ST., SAN FRANCISCO, CA 94111

(415) 421-4778 • SCHROEDERSSF.COM

German Revival

*E*ating and drinking is fun," says Jan Wiginton, one half of the wunderkind pair of restaurateurs that took over and remade an old German beer hall named Schroeder's in San Francisco's Financial District, and the statement neatly sums up both the historic place and the team's approach to restaurant creation. Fans before they were owners, the two former tech and financial industry professionals used to drink at what was then a dive bar after work—never imagining they'd have the chance to one day own the place.

Andrew Chun is the other half of the partnership, which first opened the popular local wine bar the Press Club in 2008, gaining a following and success with it before taking on the historic project.

It seems there's nothing Wiginton and Chun can't do. These polished entrepreneurs met in Texas in college in the '90s. Though they are not a couple—they actually met through Wiginton's husband—they function like a symbiotic unit in the business. Their expertise in restaurants has been gained mostly on the job, bringing financial and management backgrounds to the work. Clearly, they have a knack for it.

What they've done with Schroeder's after purchasing it in 2014 has astounded many past regulars—including some that frequented the place when it was a men's social club until it opened its doors to women in the 1970s. The Bavarian beer hall was founded in 1893 and has gone through many iterations and owners over more than 120 years in existence. At times it was a restaurant and during others just a drinking joint. When Chun and Wiginton took over, they wanted to

save what was original and special about this, purportedly the oldest German restaurant on the West Coast, but update what was then strictly a bar for a modern crowd.

"People do not appreciate a 1930s bathroom," laughs Chun, explaining how they decided to modernize and restore in pieces. "Decision by decision" they went, says Wiginton, always aiming to strike the right balance between the old and the new. They added a special kind of LED lighting to re-create the warmth of the original candlelight and spectacular restored Hermann Richter murals from the 30s, making them feel suddenly like new additions to the decor. The research has been meticulous, with an eye on preserving what has historic value—such as the sailboat paintings spied throughout— and what was just added to the mix over the years (linoleum from the '50s was nixed). They brought back food with a menu that reads like that of, appropriately, a modern German beer hall—classics like spaetzle and schnitzel and other German dishes updated to suit local, 21st-century tastes. Presentation is artful but deliciously belly filling: The simple *vesperplatte* spread of house-made meats with traditional accompaniments of pickles and mustard is anything but simple, given the work that goes into something like that, and it's a delight to discover. And pretzel knots are a must. (How can you have a proper

German meal without chewy, yeasty dough?) The succinct wine list features Austrian, German, and Californian selections, and a devoted schnapps and German liqueur menu further deepens your awareness of the place's roots. Beer is, of course, the star, with around 20 options on draft alone and the chance to order in pints, steins, or, to really get your drink on, glass boots. Traditional cocktails are complemented by three unique beer-centered cocktails, and, like works of art, the restaurant's classic beer steins are on display in strategically lit glass cases for proper oohing and aahing.

The high-ceilinged space itself is sprawling, its inviting tone set by the gorgeous warmth of wood all around, with a beautiful vintage rosewood bar at the front and the large oak dining room wrapping to the left and filling the back. A buck's head mounted high on the wall greets you upon entry, and other hunters' trophies are positioned throughout the space. There are areas to cordon off for semiprivate dining—ideal for office parties or birthday celebrations—the rooms lit by the warm glow of ring-of-fire chandeliers, transporting diners to another time. What is clear is the reverence for history and the bar's original character that the current owners have—they were selected over several other potential buyers because they wanted to "save the institution" instead of scrapping it altogether and opening a new hot spot—and it seems to thrill them when old regulars stop by approvingly (such as when former owner Max Kniesche's family recently celebrated a 70th birthday there).

"We take it very personally," says Chun of customer feedback and response to the renovation, explaining that it's really the customers who own the place. "That's what comes with a legacy business. There's a sense of stewardship that's really rewarding." Says Wiginton: "I love it when people come in and say, 'It's still Schroeder's!'"

Mostly a place for the young, professional, after-work FiDi crowd, Schroeder's is always hopping with evening activity, and it often requires a bit of elbowing through a boisterous, stein-wielding throng of people to find a spot to stand or place to dine. But as with any good vintage joint, it has deftly won over many new converts, regardless of age or career type, and it still works for old-time fans, too. In this case, anyone who appreciates a good German beer and hearty plate of sauerbraten to go with it. Because why not? Eating and drinking *is* fun, for everyone.

SCOMA'S

PIER 47 ON AL SCOMA WAY, SAN FRANCISCO, CA 94133

(800) 644-5852 OR (415) 771-4383 • SCOMAS.COM

Swingin' Seafood by the Seashore

*T*he welcome you receive from each subtle checkpoint at the esteemed seafood institution Scoma's exudes warmth, with the restaurant's representative in chief, owner, and president Tom Creedon, the absolute embodiment of this genuine spirit of hospitality. A former US Navy man, San Francisco firefighter, and city native, Creedon got into the family business somewhat reluctantly when asked by his father-in-law, Al Scoma, a veteran restaurateur and auto salesman, to "help out" back in 1968. Though he never imagined a lifelong career in a restaurant, Creedon has managed to lead Scoma's into the 21st century while still preserving the swinging '60s qualities that made it a legend in the first place. As it celebrates its golden anniversary in 2015, it is a thrill to highlight one of the city's classic seafood restaurants.

From its anchoring position at the tip of Pier 47, Scoma's provides an authentic Fisherman's Wharf experience to its diners—both locals and travelers alike. Fishing boats and strolling tourists, even a dog riding a skateboard (like I saw on one visit), may all be viewed from your dining table as they pass by outside. Just beyond, across the bay, you may take in the lovely landscape of hilly Marin County. The restaurant feels like old-school San Francisco, with the air of a vacation spot from the mid-20th century. It even has been said to me—twice—by restaurant staff that as soon as I step in the door, my worries and stresses, and sense of time, should melt away. "When you're at Scoma's, you're on vacation," says Nick McGreevy, the smooth Brit who has served as general manager and wine director for nearly 15 of his 20 years with the restaurant. I'm not sure if it was this instruction or a natural occurrence, but McGreevy was right; as soon as I was seated and anticipating my petite Dungeness crab cakes and "Lazy Man's" Cioppino on the way, I felt like I had not a care in the world.

Staff is attentive on every level—from selecting a comfortable table for the diner to giving personal advice on dish selection—and many have been with the restaurant for decades (average tenure is a minimum of 20 years). "We have a lot of really good, loyal employees, really nice people," says Creedon, who himself appears to be beloved by his team. Perhaps it's because he is such an unlikely, and humble, restaurant owner, never expecting to be in, let alone take over, his wife's family's business.

"I got the job by default," he shares, divulging that no one else in the family was interested in management. He continues, "I'm probably less qualified than most people," though to the casual observer, what he's learned on the job over the years has stood him, and the business, in very good stead.

Like many businesses featured in this book, Scoma's has experienced its own ups and downs over the years—contending with the shrinking profitability faced by many restaurants, changing demographics in clientele, and the need to both preserve its original character while updating to reflect the changing times and tastes. The restaurant is in the midst of an interior remodel to "accommodate the next generation," as Creedon puts it—adding bistro tables to the bar for more casual dining, and booths to the main dining room for a more intimate, cozy experience. And Creedon has hired a new chief operating officer to manage the day-to-day operations and big picture as they look to the next 50 years.

The menu will stay true to its roots, with "Scoma's Classics" including a shellfish sauté, two types of Louis salads (both shrimp and crab), and the fabulous aforementioned cioppino—a local classic, dubbed "lazy man's" because shells have been removed from the fish, enabling ease of eating the gems in the deliciously rich tomato-based stew. Local favorites like grilled sand dabs and petrale sole are also popular items, and for non-fish eaters, Scoma's offers a few steaks and pasta specialties (though most of the latter do feature seafood as well).

It is not a surprise to learn that actor Lee Marvin and singers Louie Prima and Al Martino were regulars back in the day, becoming personal friends of the founder (who was "always impressed by celebrities," Creedon shares fondly); the place oozes a finger-snapping vibe of yesteryear hipness. Today the restaurant's clientele is quite mixed, with local dignitaries among the many business folks, special occasion celebrants, lunch regulars, and tourists who frequent the place. When asked about his favorite customers, Creedon doesn't hesitate: the firemen he used to work alongside. "Firemen are different kind of people," he says, sharing how close you naturally become in the profession, spending so many hours together in life-and-death situations. "When the bell dings, you have to be there." Naturally, the restaurant counts local police and fire departments among the charitable organizations it supports, along with the Salesian Boys and Girls Club in nearby North Beach, and is an active member of the community.

Dining at Scoma's is all about deliciousness and city tradition—eating great seafood with an iconic sea (or marina) view right in the heart of Fisherman's Wharf. Knowing the restaurant's backstory—the fact that it's a long-standing family business, started by a passionate businessman and passed on to his reluctant but kindhearted public-servant son-in-law, who has made it what it is today—satisfies on a whole different level. It's a marvel to witness how what was initially a six-stool coffee shop that catered to local fishermen in 1965 has been transformed into a phenomenally successful fine-dining establishment, thanks to first owners Al and brother Joe, and subsequently Creedon and company. I pondered the restaurant's future as I devoured a tiny espresso cup of the creamy, house-made tiramisu at the end of my meal. Looking around the jam-packed room during lunch service on a nondescript autumn day, it was clear that that future is bright in the hands of both the old and new guard. Keeping that in mind, reservations, even for regulars, are always recommended.

SEARS FINE FOOD

439 POWELL ST., SAN FRANCISCO, CA 94102

(415) 986-0700 • SEARSFINEFOOD.COM

Happiness Served Here

A touristy place." Sometimes that phrase has a negative connotation, meaning, "A place locals should avoid like the plague." It's crowded with out-of-towners, overpriced, and, ultimately, not delicious. Other times, though, a touristy place is that way for good reason: It gives a sense of the location in which it sits, is welcoming to strangers, accessible to all, and serves a good meal.

Sears Fine Food falls in that latter category, the good one, and is a place where I cannot imagine anyone being unhappy.

Founded in 1938, the restaurant is situated in Union Square—one of the most touristy areas in the city, with its major hotels, department stores and high-end shopping, and central plaza area that hosts the annual Christmas tree festival and others throughout the year. Inside, Sears feels vintage in a carefully curated way, like many "touristy" establishments that are less earnest in their intent—with wall hangings depicting various aspects of a time that would immediately conjure up feelings of actual nostalgia for some, or of imagined nostalgia for others who may have been born generations later. Even so, there's something more authentic going on here. I think it has something to do with its founders, but we'll get to that in a bit.

Its hodgepodge of old decor includes black-and-white and sepia-toned photographs of children that look like my grandpa's old photos—the ones where little boys are indistinguishable from little girls, both, at a certain age, dressed in gowns and sporting the same hair length. Covering other swaths of wall are lots of World War II-era recruitment advertisements, the kind that glamorized war

and enticed young men to join up. Some make a soft sell, depicting smiling, hugging couples, the women welcoming home their men, with phrases like "He volunteers for submarine service," or a more direct appeal to a desire for opportunity: "Join the air service. Learn. Earn." My favorites brazenly rely on guilt as a tactic, with questions like, "Doing all you can, brother?"

Continuing the period vibe, clanging plates and tinkling forks mix with mostly piano music from the 1940s, playing through a sound system. White honeycomb-tile floors run the length of the spacious dining rooms—of which there are two, punctuated by antique furniture displaying delicate old china and ornately framed mirrors positioned randomly on the walls. There's also a bar area decked out with red vinyl barstools like the kind I impractically coveted for my apartment in my 20s.

The mostly Latino waitstaff's welcome is genuinely warm, including young Soledad, who's worked at Sears a year. She has breakfast there every day, and likes everything but loves the french toast. "It's really good!" she shares, smiling shyly. She says it's a nice place to work. I believe her: There's a sort of pervasive happiness in the restaurant that is uncommon in the tourist-trap dining experience.

Considering Sears' history, the happy vibe makes sense: The place was founded by a retired circus clown! Ben Sears and his wife

Hilbur started the establishment with a special focus on a recipe from the latter's Swedish family for a dish that made Sears famous which remains the star of the menu today. That dish? Swedish pancakes.

Advertised as their "World Famous" Swedish pancakes, the 18 golden, little disks come in 6 petite stacks of 3 each. And there's a reason the pancakes are what Sears is known for: They are both adorable and delicious. Get them with the optional lingonberries for a real Swedish experience, but use the condiment sparingly—it is overwhelmingly sweet in large proportions. (I like mine with butter, syrup, and a touch of the miniature berries in each bite.) The extremely thick-cut bacon makes a perfect, very salty foil for the sweet cakes, and the coffee, while not the greatest, was certainly steaming hot, as advertised on a vintage sign near the table.

Sears serves breakfast, lunch, and dinner daily, making for a large, varied menu that ranges from blue-plate specials and burgers to pastas and pot roast, along with a smattering of seafood dishes one would expect in this city. Really, though, you should just come for the pancakes, available starting at 6:30 every morning of the week.

After your meal, you may just score something extra: The restaurant has a fun, participatory slot-machine tradition. Customers are given a logo-emblazoned gold token to drop into the machine that sits on the front sideboard, pull the lever, and test their luck. Prizes range from free drinks to free meals.

After 65 years in business and several different families running the place, Sears shut down in 2003, saved less than a year later by the team behind Lori's Diner, a local restaurant chain specializing in a period experience. The fact that this is a longtime family business that was ultimately spared instead of killed by a small conglomerate explains the feeling of orchestration mixed with authenticity you get while dining there—and it's encouraging to know that some bigger companies have reverence for unique old businesses. The Lori's gang knew that both tourists and locals need the transportive experience Sears provides. Weary from the frustrations and exhaustion of travel, of traipsing around a city seeing sights and shopping like you'll never see a store again? Or perhaps it's just a super-long week at work? Those Swedish pancakes, with a little piano music from the 1940s, are the perfect antidote. (You may also take home the mix as a souvenir.) The cure from a circus clown, happiness guaranteed.

SHREVE & CO.

200 POST ST., SAN FRANCISCO, CA 94108

(415) 421-2600 • SHREVE.COM

Sparkly Things

J am now saving my pennies not for a rainy day but for an absolutely stunning Art Deco pendant watch encrusted with 2 carats of diamonds. The watch lives in the estate collection at Shreve & Co., San Francisco's oldest and one of its most prestigious jewelry stores. And as a piece of jewelry, a timepiece, and, really, a work of art, it is just exquisite.

Maria Montes, a Honolulu native, hospitality industry professional, and four-year sales associate on the floor at Shreve who showed me the amazing watch, is enthralled by the company's wares—which no longer bear the Shreve name but rather the names of the most elite jewelry and watch designers in the world (including, in the latter category, Chanel, Omega, and Bell & Ross). But the company still maintains this estate collection—part of which is simply antique, the other part, with the most special pieces (in my opinion at least), coming from Shreve's original line.

Shreve & Co. was established in 1852—"just four years after the discovery of gold in the California hills," they note. This is an important fact, considering the company's original target audience: the newly minted millionaires of the state. They made their own timepieces of the finest metals. The company gradually got into the jewelry business, a natural extension of its start, quickly gaining popularity. Shreve initially occupied a couple of other addresses before it moved to its current location in 1906—notably, just before the big earthquake that leveled much of the city. Then that happened.

"Everything was rubble [around Shreve], but the building survived," says Montes, explaining how everything, inside and out, was burned from the big fire that followed the quake. "The vault was apparently too hot to touch for two weeks. But thankfully, all of our goodies were in the vault! So we didn't lose too much."

The company then took two years to repair damage and restore operations, reopening in 1908. It is purportedly the oldest retail establishment in the state and the only jeweler to have survived the historic earthquake. And it has pretty much been a city powerhouse of diamond and luxury jewelry ever since.

The San Francisco flagship (there are also shops in Palo Alto, California, and Portland, Oregon) sits in the Shreve Building, which anchors the corner of Post Street and Grant Avenue in the Union Square neighborhood, on the cusp of the Financial District. Its former grand entry on the street corner has been moved to the flat side of the building, but walking into the space flanked by marble columns still feels regal. There's an office-dedicated upper level overlooking all of the jewels below, and a hushed feeling as you enter the space, all the necklaces, rings, and earrings viewable for easy perusing as you stroll up and down the aisles. There are modern pieces mixed in with the classics, many the sorts of things you'd see on red carpets at award shows. It is clearly the place where most people go—those with money, that is—to buy engagement rings and special occasion jewels, something that Montes loves.

"Besides [being surrounded by] the beautiful and sparkly things, it's really a nice way to be a part of people's lives," she says of working for this iconic store. "People come to us to celebrate, to get special pieces for special occasions, or if they just want to treat themselves."

And it's not just diamonds they sell. Watches are popular, too, sometimes to mark life's major moments. One client, for instance, bought a watch to commemorate the birth of his son, and when his wife got pregnant with their second son, due the same day their first boy was born, the father bought another watch.

"He told me, 'I want to have a photo of me wearing this watch, carrying my son the day he's born, so when I pass it on to him, he'll know it was something I actually had and wore on that day,'" Montes recounts. "Really special."

Vintage Spot

LANG ANTIQUES AND ESTATE JEWELRY: EST: 1969

Lang's has special significance for me, as it was the place where my antique engagement ring—a Victorian-era Russian amethyst—lived until it appeared on my finger. After proposing, my husband took me to see the "jewel box" of a shop, and I fell for the place immediately. "Quaint" doesn't go far enough in describing how tiny the shop was, or the sheer volume of treasures, packed in as many cases and cabinets as could be squeezed into the store. Known for having one of the largest collections of antique and vintage jewelry in the country, Lang was established in 1969 in San Francisco and has served the city's citizenry fruitfully with gorgeous pieces of wearable history over its near half century in business. The shop recently moved two doors down the street to a more modern space, so although it no longer has that nook-of-a-shop, vintage feel, it still offers the same incredible collection of old trinkets and the same impressive group of gem experts behind the counters. A visit is both educational and exciting, if you're into vintage jewelry, and it's also worth getting on the shop's mailing list: Lang's sends hilarious hand-drawn greeting cards by local artist Rich Sigberman for almost every holiday and major event, from Valentine's Day to Christmas, April Fools' Day to Election Day. They are a product line all on their own.

**309 Sutter St., San Francisco, CA 94108;
(800) 924-2213; langantiques.com**

This famous jewelry store fills a special place in many people's lives, going back to its early days, when it was primarily a watchmaker and silversmith, crafting silverware, tableware, and gift items in original Shreve & Co. patterns. "I found a full set of original Shreve silverware and tableware that was used on one of the navy fighter ships in World War I," Montes marvels. Many of their early pre–World War II pieces are platinum, before the precious metal was reserved

for military use only. (My dream pendant watch is platinum.) Another original Shreve piece, an enchanting painted brooch featuring a woman's portrait that dates back to the 1880s, was done in 18-karat yellow gold with platinum tops surrounding the white diamonds that encircle the portrait. This stunner is also in the estate collection, available for viewing on request.

As a jewelry lay person I'm amazed that Montes and her colleagues are not required to wear protective gloves while handling these gorgeous antiques; it's a testament to the solidity and durability of these small works of art and the careful way in which they were made so long ago. She acknowledges my surprise: "They've really stood the test of time."

And speaking of the time—that incredible watch from the 1920s can be taken home for a mere $16,000 and change. For a beautiful, sparkly piece of history, it seems worth it. You know, if you have that kind of money just lying around.

SWAN OYSTER DEPOT

1517 POLK ST., SAN FRANCISCO, CA 94109

(415) 673-2757 • SFSWANOYSTERDEPOT.COM

Local Fishmonger

*M*ost people know it for the long line down the sidewalk, of (sometimes beer-drinking) customers who are awaiting the vacancy of one of just a handful of counter seats at which to sit for lunch. But Swan Oyster Depot is, at its heart, a fish market of the classic persuasion.

Though Anthony Bourdain put the tiny oyster cafe on the modern foodie-TV map with his installment of *The Layover* a couple of years ago, Swan has been around and in the same location for more than 100 years, receiving many accolades over that time—and it remains well-known to locals looking for the freshest catch.

"The main part of our business is the fish market," says Steve Sancimino, part of the family that has owned Swan's for decades. "We don't really consider ourselves a restaurant."

The market carries pretty much any fish you can imagine, headlined by the most popular catch from November through May: local Dungeness crab. Salmon, black cod, petrale and rex sole, and sand dabs are also chiefly local, and tuna and hamachi are flown in from Hawaii, all complementing the critter the store is named for: the humble oyster. Swan has lots, all available raw on the half shell. And they are gobbled up plateful by plateful by diners at one of about 20 counter seats.

There is a line out the door even at 10:30 in the morning on a random weekday, full of people anxiously yet gradually approaching the blue awning over the tiny storefront with gleamingly fresh fish on ice in the front window. Inside, it's even tinier—tight, white tiles

compose the floor that lies under walls crammed with seafood diagrams, medals, old photographs, and "Save Drake's Bay Oyster Farm" posters, referring to the locally renowned oyster provider, threatened and ultimately shut down in 2014 by a federal coastal land-use battle after nearly a century of oyster farming on the Point Reyes National Seashore. (The case went all the way to the Supreme Court.) All the bric-a-brac hovers over stacked plates, and a few sets of tongs dangle from small barrels above the gorgeous front seafood display, fresh crab sitting upright, with claws and legs pointed upward toward the sky, near stainless-steel hotel pans full of plump, pale gray prawns; peachy scallops; petite clams; long, pink fillets of whitefish; and vibrant salmon, both fresh and smoked. Piles of jet-black mussels are tucked between the other offerings, and whole lemons are scattered about, reminding you of how good it'll all taste at home, with a fresh squeeze of citrus.

The market's cafe menu is simple, scrawled in a cartoonish black font on wall-mounted boards that look like they haven't been moved in years. You can get a seafood salad with crab, prawns, shrimp, or a combination of the three, served with a Louie dressing, freshly shucked oysters or clams on the half shell, Boston clam chowder, sometimes sashimi, and a variety of seafood cocktails. Smoked salmon and whitefish are also available, along with less common offerings such as sea urchin roe (or *uni*) and crab fat—which is literally that, served in the rosy crab shell. And it is all the freshest you could imagine.

It has always been that way, ever since 1912 when the business was opened by the Danish Lausten family. At the time, Sancimino's grandfather—whose family had emigrated in the 1890s from Sciacca, an old fishing village in Italy—was a local fisherman. Swan was the go-to spot for selling your catch; the Danish owners were well-known in the area as they were unique in the sea of Portuguese and Italian immigrants in the industry. "[The fishermen] wouldn't say, 'Go to Swan,'" Sancimino describes. "They'd say, 'Go to the Danes.'"

By the 1930s, Sancimino's great uncle—Leo LaRocca—had become one of the largest fish wholesalers in town, and his company, LaRocca Seafood, sold product to Swan. Sancimino's father, Sal—who had an inner ear problem and could never be on a fishing boat—worked for his uncle, alongside a gaggle of cousins. Eventually, in 1946, the family bought Swan from the Danes, and they have continued the generational business to this day.

Sancimino is a kind, no-nonsense guy who, at age 64, what some would consider a lifetime in business, still "hasn't had enough."

"There's a lot of stimulation, being with all the people," he says. "Every day it's something different."

One of the most memorable days was 35 years ago when Margaret Thatcher, then British prime minister, came into the teeny shop with an old friend of his father's.

"My father shook her hand, and when he leaned over to give her a kiss, a Secret Service agent said, 'Oh, no, you can't touch the prime minister,'" Sancimino recalls. "My father just jumped back and said, 'Why not?'" he laughs. "We actually have a letter on the wall from her saying how much she enjoyed her visit 'and meeting that fish man from San Francisco.'"

Lots of food celebrities join politicians in making an appearance at Swan, including Bourdain, who was a counter regular even before his books made him famous. Later, when he wanted to film his TV show there, Sancimino's starstruck daughter asked to stay home from school for the occasion. (Sancimino said no.)

Chef and TV personality Emeril Lagasse also wanted to film a show there a few years ago. "We told him to get here early, before we get busy, so you can really see what we do." Sancimino recounts that he showed up with his "whole entourage" but promptly asked, "Okay, what do you want me to do?" quickly proving himself as a "real down-to-earth, working guy." So they sent him to the wharf with their delivery guy, and Lagasse got right into the morning routine—shoveling ice and picking out fish.

Though plenty of famous people have patronized Swan, San Franciscan families are its primary clientele and "main responsibility," as Sancimino says. "We have five, six, seven generations of families who've been coming here."

And just like those families, Sancimino typically takes his fish to go, bringing home fresh seafood—his favorites are mostly indigenous to the area, including salmon, black cod, rex and petrale sole, and sand dabs—to cook with his family three or four times a week.

This respect for regular people and regular, everyday cooking is clear in the reception you get at Swan, whether you're walking straight up to the counter for a to-go order or waiting an hour or more to dine in. And apparently, it's a conscious effort on behalf of the family who owns the place.

"Like my dad used to say," recalls Sancimino, "when people walk into your business, pretend like they're walking into your home. That's how you should treat them."

TADICH GRILL

240 CALIFORNIA ST., SAN FRANCISCO, CA 94111

(415) 391-1849 • TADICHGRILL.COM

The First

*T*he light in the front space changes as the sun warms the cream-colored, oversize shades in the anterior window, the only one in the place, casting a cheerful midday glow at the head of the long line of noontime customers pressed up against the side wall, waiting for a table. There's a sense of age, of preservation and liveliness all at once up there, with that light creating the look of an old photograph, providing a hazy backdrop to the logo painted in gold on the front window. The sunlight is noticeable because it doesn't reach any other part of the boisterous establishment that is lit primarily by slender Art Deco-style pendant lamps dangling from the ceiling. It traces its roots to 1849, when it was first a "coffee stand," named as such, run by Croatian immigrants selling freshly grilled fish to merchants and sailors from its location on the Long Wharf—an old pier that in the 19th century stretched from downtown into the water. Now the Long Wharf is gone, and the place is a full restaurant, one of San Francisco's most beloved, still owned by Croatians and still serving fresh fish. It's the place where absolutely everyone goes—from city (and world) leaders to locals on a lunch break and tourists who are methodically checking sites off their lists. The place is Tadich Grill, and it's hands down my favorite spot in this book.

Tadich (or Tadich's to many) has an unfair advantage in the favorite department, frankly. It's old, in all of the best ways. It's the oldest restaurant in the city and believed to be the third-oldest in the country—giving it more than 160 years to perfect what it does. It's staffed in the front of the house mostly by older gentlemen,

who simultaneously radiate nonchalance and genuine care, a mix that is strangely so appealing and seems essential in a "vintage" establishment. They provide service with such efficiency and attention it seems they may be lurking right outside your booth (they aren't). And it serves old-school favorites like cioppino and crab cakes and broiled fish and stiff drinks. It still has hat hooks (like its similarly aged peer, Sam's Grill), wooden booths with stained-glass entries and inner doorbells for buzzing your waiter back in the day, and a bowl full of cut lemons on each table. I love all of this oldness and other-era-ness so much that I, in an uncommon occurrence for the place, had my bachelorette party there. Celebration dinners and everyday lunches live harmoniously at Tadich—which is bustling all day, six days a week (Sunday is reserved for private parties).

For instance, on a Friday at 11:30 a.m., just after the restaurant opens, people pour in through the double doors adjacent to that front window. Some look around expectantly, likely thinking they are people of importance who may get special treatment to bypass the line; they will not. Unless you're the president of the United States (such as the first George Bush, whose advance team called ahead to prep the restaurant), in which case arrangements may, just may, be made, celebrities and dignitaries have to stand in line like everyone else. Waitstaff appears to barely notice you but always remembers exactly where you are as you wait for your table. And you will always wait; the restaurant has a firm "no reservations" policy.

They run a tight ship, so here's the process: Upon stepping into the restaurant, give your name to the white-jacketed guy at the corner of the bar, just off your left shoulder (at 10 o'clock). He'll tell you to line up along the sidewall behind you, to your right. You obey and patiently wait for your name to be called. You may get a drink at the impressively long bar in front of you—it is the heart of the restaurant and runs the length of the place—but you may have to reach around people dining there; Tadich prizes its "counter culture" and the way in which the bar seats bring strangers together and enable spontaneous friendships to form.

A few of the tables are contained in the aforementioned wooden booths, which provide marvelous semiprivate spaces in which to dine; about three times as many tables, each backed by its own mirror, sit out in the open, high-ceilinged dining room. If you decide to wait for one—which can easily take an hour, depending on the crowd—you may get a server like 27-year Tadich veteran and Slovakian Marion Pozivenec—the only "Pozivenec" in the US, he claims, besides his offspring—in which case you may receive an unprompted but spot-on recommendation about what you should eat for that particular meal.

"I love the Spanish stew," Pozivenec says, gesturing to me efficiently, right after he takes our drink order, and to my husband, "and our Chilean sea bass." Take his recommendation, and be sure to start with the house crab cake, served with a decadent aioli and topped with an upturned cherry pepper in an endearing presentation.

Pozivenec's tenure is not unusual at Tadich—most people stay for a professional lifetime. Their uniform for decades has been the classic white jacket and long, dark, striped tie—even the few women who work on the floor now don this outfit. And the history of the place was so meticulously documented by the owners a few years ago, it's not worth attempting to replicate here (see its website instead). It should be noted that the Tadich moniker, "The Original Cold Day Restaurant," still emblazoned on the front window, goes back to an 1882 remark by restaurant regular Alexander Badlam Jr., the city's tax assessor, who was running for reelection when the place was still called the New World Coffee Saloon. Badlam reportedly "bragged" it'd be "a cold day" when he'd be defeated, which he soundly was. The city rallied

Vintage Spot

GHIRARDELLI CHOCOLATE [AND SQUARE]: EST. 1852

Founded in 1852, this chocolate company now has the distinction of being the country's oldest continuously operating one, and early on it helped shape the landscape of the San Francisco we know today. The company was founded by Italian immigrant Domingo Ghirardelli after his successful entrepreneurship selling chocolate to gold miners. Now, chocoholics the world over are well acquainted with its products, readily available in its own dedicated shops as well as baking aisles of grocery stores, airports, and shops nationwide. The former factory in an old wooden mill on the edge of Fisherman's Wharf became a tourist destination in its own right and is now on the National Register of Historic Places, with its rambling brick buildings situated on a hill, almost at water's edge. The chocolate "manufactory" and soda fountain are still there, along with specialty food stores, restaurants, retailers, and fancy condos. Touristy but for good reason: It's a lovely place in which to sit, enjoy a square of the famous chocolate, and feel the sea breeze, much like those miners may have done, albeit in a simpler, grittier setting, in the early days of Ghirardelli.

900 North Point St., San Francisco, CA 94109; (415) 474-3938; ghirardellisq.com

around the remark so much that the restaurant owners decided to rename the place the Cold Day Restaurant. It stuck.

The Buich family has owned the place since the early 20th century—Steve, the most recent patriarch, is now in his 80s, and his son Mike is now in charge—and deserves credit for keeping Tadich true to its roots and unchanged over the years and several moves. No one gets a free meal there, "not even my mother," said the elder Buich of his early days at the restaurant. The former owner is kind, generous, shrewd, and clearly tough as nails, even now, explaining, "It's a business!"

But no one cares. With egalitarian treatment and the utmost level of service, Tadich need not consider handouts. It has continued through every boom and bust the city has ever seen, as my husband says—and I'm certain they'll push through many, many more. (Incredibly, they're even on the verge of opening a second location, after all these years, in Washington, DC, at 1001 Pennsylvania Avenue, and I predict it'll fit right in there, too.) I hope, even if they ever have to move in San Francisco again, they will keep everything just as it is: full of the clinks of glasses into which cocktails are poured and the hum of hundreds of conversations, freshly grilled fish quickly shuttled to the myriad tables or those brave souls at the counter. It's a wonderful place, meant for and enjoyed by everyone. The masses wouldn't have it any other way—even, perhaps especially, on a cold day.

TOMMASO'S ITALIAN RESTAURANT

1042 KEARNY ST., SAN FRANCISCO, CA 94133

(415) 398-9696 • TOMMASOS.COM

━┝═══┥━

Italian Hearth

ome of the oldest wood-fired brick oven on the West Coast, this intimate North Beach restaurant specializing in southern Italian cuisine has served as a movie backdrop, annual host to the state governor's birthday party, and site of countless proposals and weddings over its 80 years in operation. It has seen other vintage businesses come and go, weathered the nearby proliferation of sex shops and adult toy stores, and changed very little over the years due to its customers' commitment to nostalgia and demand for consistency. (They even received an open letter from a collection of loyal patrons, begging for the usual, when operators suggested changing a monthly special to something other than the addictive porcini mushroom lasagna.) The restaurant is Tommaso's, and it is one of the city's absolute gems when it comes to vintage eateries.

Run for more than 40 years by the Crotti family, with sister Carmen and older brother Agostino at the helm—they got into the business when they were 16 and 21 respectively—Tommaso's offers the kind of experience you imagine only happens in movies like *Moonstruck* (there's even a poster for the film in the entryway). Front-of-the-house manager Carmen and wine and product chief Agostino have a bickering, loving tone and are "so close it's pathetic . . . we spend too much time together!" complains Carmen, but their partnership over the decades has proven amazingly successful. They are in business with their sister Lidia, who serves as executive chef and "lasagna goddess," according to Carmen, and Agostino's wife,

Anna, who makes the desserts; Carmen's and Agostino's respective children are even involved. And the place has almost always been a family business. It was opened in 1935 by the Cantalupo family, immigrants from Naples, and first known as Lupo's, a name that lasted until its second owner, longtime chef Tommy Chin, took over after being gifted the place in 1971. Chin changed the name to an Italian-sounding version of his own, and it has been Tommaso's ever since.

Stepping down into the restaurant from the street makes you feel as though you've stepped back in time and into a space you won't readily want to leave. Partitioned tables line either wall, providing a bit of privacy for diners and a close view of the murals of Italy spanning the length of the restaurant, and there's a scattering of tables in the center of the room for those who prefer to be in the center of the action (like my dad). Carmen says she's hated the partitions for as long as they've owned the restaurant—they limit the space available for dining—but won't tear them down because customers love them. That famous wood-fired oven burns day in and day out at the back of the space, a testament to the goodness and reliability of tradition and the old-fashioned way of doing things. (Famed locavore and pioneer in California cooking Alice Waters reportedly used the very oven as a model for her own at her restaurant Chez Panisse, as did chef Wolfgang Puck for his restaurants.) It is the only oven in the restaurant, and what it turns out—from many of the entrees to those acclaimed fire-kissed pizzas—is all pretty incredible.

True to tradition and the original concept, the Crottis have made few changes to the menu over the years, except for paring it down a bit for manageability and adding a new flavor combination here and there as palates change. The prices have naturally evolved with time, but longtime diners can still get their favorite pizzas, pastas, and traditional dishes like veal saltimbocca and baked clams. Among their popular newer items are a fresh spinach and Parmesan pie— "like a salad on a pizza, so delicious," says Carmen—and offerings featuring concepts from their annual travel to the homeland or culinary trends, such as burrata. "Until a couple of years ago, no one knew what burrata was," says Agostino. It is in these small ways that the family balances the old and the new, the vintage and the modern, and probably why the oldest Italian restaurant in North Beach is still a hit after eight decades.

"We have to be humble and careful when it comes to change here," Carmen explains, divulging that they've made many refreshments to the decor over the years, but only to restore and brighten what is there, not to make new. Seems like a wise plan for a building still reliant on its original bricks, even after rebuilding following the city's devastating earthquake in 1906.

So go, soak up a bit of tradition, sip a glass of Italian or Californian wine (their finely edited list is a relatively equal split between the regions), and sink your teeth into their tender gnocchi (a guarded recipe is responsible for this twice-annual treat), heavenly béchamel-laced lasagna, or a slice of expertly charred Margherita pizza. Pretend you're a Neopolitan—or one of many celebrities who've alighted on the place—for the night.

TONGA ROOM & HURRICANE BAR

950 MASON ST., SAN FRANCISCO, CA 94108

(415) 772-5278 • TONGAROOM.COM

Tiki Time

A conga line may be circling the inner perimeter of this bar and restaurant on a busy Saturday night, though the party isn't confined to the weekends. Established in 1945, the Tonga Room & Hurricane Bar is a one-of-a-kind spot that forces you to have fun, despite the mood you may be in when you walk through the door, despite the day of the week. It's a quintessential tiki bar that provides a total exclamation-mark experience.

Occupying the bottom floor of the also-historic Fairmont Hotel, the Tonga Room is so much more than just a hotel bar. It is a destination on its own, one that transports you to another time and place. For starters, the Tonga Room's physical space is organized around its sparkling blue central pool. You read that right. An Olympic-size swimming pool is at the center of this bar! And it's put to good use regularly by the live bands that play on its floating stage. Yes, floating stage!

Island Grooves is the wildly popular and extremely talented house band—led by drummer Dean Revelo, with front-man singer, his son-in-law, C. J. Simbre; Nito Medina on guitar; and Nel Tellez on keyboards. They play a diverse set of favorites—going from the Jackson Five to the Beatles to Creedence Clearwater Revival without a hitch—and have the crowd on their feet, dancing and singing as if at the prom you wish you'd had. And at the end of the band's set, as the stage floats backward and they play "Have You Ever Seen the Rain," it rains. Over the pool. It actually rains!

"This is simultaneously the cheesiest and the coolest thing ever!" my husband yells over the blaring music. He has been singing along, despite himself, just like I said. Despite the bad mood he arrived in. Despite his typical disdain for forced fun. And it's because the Tonga Room provides forced fun of the best kind, the authentic kind, the kind fueled by killer-strong fruity drinks with fresh pineapple and straws. The kind made at a bar with a swimming pool and bamboo and thatched roofs and a floating stage. The kind where a band is singing "Play That Funky Music" at the top of its lungs with moves to match, doing call and response with the people who are dancing around the room wearing feathered headbands and cocktail dresses and tuxedos and jeans, arms up in the air like they just don't care.

The Tonga Room offers more than 50 rums, many of which appear in its tiki cocktails that range from modern creations—such as the lychee martini—to the classics—the mai tai, their No. 1 seller, at about 3,000 per month, served in a sweating, chilled coconut mug; the Singapore sling; or the zombie, with its three rums and lots of tropical juice. Those uninitiated to the world of tiki drinking should beware: No matter how fruity the flavors or how cute the umbrellas, these cocktails pack a serious punch. Don't let the straws and fresh

Vintage Spot
TRƏD'R SƏM: EST. 1938

Across the street from a Russian Orthodox cathedral with its dramatic onion-dome towers sits a temple of another sort, another temple to the tiki gods: Trad'r Sam, founded in 1938 on a corner in the Richmond neighborhood, has remained pretty much unchanged over the years, with the exception of an expanded drink menu, says current owner John McGuia, whose family has had the place for about 30 years. And it's a wonderful little spot to experience the tiki trend, and in a quieter way than the Tonga Room & Hurricane Bar.

Tiki bars were all the rage in the 1930s and '40s, and the presence of more than one still in existence in the city of San Francisco is a testament to the fact that they never completely went out of style. It's understandable that the vacation-vibe bar appeals to the masses, even when plane travel is now common, enabling greater ease with reaching these islands of tribute in person. When you step into a bar like Trad'r Sam, with its excess of bamboo—window shades, wrapping the bar and forming arches with notable island names over the tables—you immediately feel like you're somewhere else. Another time, another place. And the fruity and creamy—and quite potent—tiki drinks help to transport as well. More of a neighborhood bar than the showier Tonga Room, Trad'r Sam gets mostly older regulars during the day (it opens most days at 10 a.m.) and a younger college crowd at night. McGuia, who's been a bartender for all of his adult life (from 21 until now, in his late 60s) has seen it all—from the rowdier Mission District spot in his early days to the more sedate tiki establishment his parents bought in the '80s—and he seems ready for some downtime himself. But he still puts on a smile, greets his regulars (three days a week these days), and is ready to whip up a tropical drink—or pour a shot—for anyone who asks.

6150 Geary Blvd., San Francisco, CA 94121; (415) 221-0773

mint deceive you. Go gently and sip slowly, while you take in the ambience of this historic place.

The establishment has always had food, which wasn't its strong suit until a recent overhaul brought fresh fish and more vibrant flavors to what was previously known as just "overpriced, imitation Chinese," explains the team at the Fairmont. Now, the Tonga chef spends face time with his Hawaiian fishmonger to be sure of what he's getting.

In addition to the signature pool—which operated as the hotel's actual pool, called "The Fairmont Terrace Plunge," and hosted Olympians in training and countless celebrities from 1929 until the bar's opening in 1945, when it became a lagoon—the decor includes canoes hanging from the ceiling, carved wood pillars throughout, strings of lanterns everywhere, and bamboo and wood as far as the eye can see. The whole place has the feeling of a giant ship floating in some nondescript, imaginary collection of islands in the land of merriment. And a real shipwreck, the SS *Forester*, even forms part of the dance floor, which features its mast, steering wheel, and two outriggers.

"Tiki people are a special breed," says Melissa Farrar, the hotel's public relations director. "They can be really critical, but when they like it, they talk about it." She shares that Tiki Oasis—a West Coast gathering of tiki lovers—"they're like trekkies, but with ukuleles!"—has been held at the Tonga Room.

The site of countless bachelor and bachelorette parties, memorable wedding proposals (both good and bad!), 21st and 80th birthday parties—anything that is focused on fun and celebration is appropriate here. Celebrities make frequent appearances—Tony Bennett is a regular, and the Beastie Boys and Red Hot Chili Peppers have performed—and they do buyouts, too (both *Wall Street Journal* tech columnist Kara Swisher and MC Hammer feted their 50th birthdays at the Tonga Room).

"It feels so random to have a tiki bar in a luxury hotel, but it serves as an excellent stress relief for guests," says Farrar. "It's a totally foreign environment. And for locals who may not be able to travel, the bar brings the foreign or ridiculous to them. It's the closest to the islands you can get without leaving the city."

COURTESY OF MELISSA FARRAR, FAIRMONT HOTEL

The city has grown up around the hotel and its famous tiki bar, quite literally: The hotel was established in 1907 and sits atop Nob Hill, overlooking the rest of San Francisco and its beautiful bay. And for 75 years, people from near and far have flocked to the place that offers a tropical vacation for the night, without the long flight.

Hotel general manager and Fairmont regional vice president Tom Klein reflects on the customer demographic—a strong mix of repeat visitors and international travelers, along with local fans. "Everyone needs a mai tai!"

Even you. Seriously. Test my theory: Go in a bad mood. I guarantee you'll be singing before the band's next set, tropical cocktail in hand.

TOP OF THE MARK

INTERCONTINENTAL MARK HOPKINS SAN FRANCISCO,
999 CALIFORNIA ST., SAN FRANCISCO, CA 94108 • (415) 392-3434
INTERCONTINENTALMARKHOPKINS.COM/TOP-OF-THE-MARK.ASPX

Keeping Tradition Alive

*K*issing your sweetheart good-bye at the top of the world is what this next vintage establishment has been most known for throughout much of its 75 years in operation. It has a strong US military history that it still honors to this day, and it offers visitors one of the outright best views in the city of San Francisco. It is called Top of the Mark, and it sits, well, at the top (the 19th floor) of the Mark (that is, InterContinental Mark Hopkins San Francisco).

This classic sky lounge—one of few remaining—sits atop Nob Hill in the northeastern part of the city. Its position on a hilltop in one of the most beautiful cities in the world makes it feel like it's at the center of that world. The walls of windows provide an incredible panoramic view of the city and surrounding bay; whether to watch departing navy ships in a bygone era or incoming cruise vessels today, the lounge provides the perfect perch for envisioning what lies ahead in one's life. Shortly after it was established in 1939—the year of the Golden Gate Bridge International Exposition on Treasure Island—what lay ahead for many was World War II, thus the bar quickly became a place for girlfriends and wives to bid adieu to their departing servicemen. The northwest point earned the moniker "Weepers Corner" for all the women who'd gather there to watch the ships, and their beloveds, sail away.

"It was either the first place or the last place they'd see them," says Joe Ferragamo, the hotel's earnest food and beverage director, who in just his few short years at the Mark Hopkins has developed a

passion for its history. "It's as historic as the Golden Gate Bridge," he says proudly.

While the US Navy base at Treasure Island closed in 1997, and those big military ships are no longer ritually departing from the waters below the hotel, the bar continues to be a beacon for active and veteran military members today. It still keeps a "squadron bottle" of bourbon in a prominent position at the front of the bar, available for returning servicemen (and servicewomen) to drink from the bottle for free after signing the label. Their only commitment: The person who takes the last drink must replace the bottle, ensuring the tradition is alive for the next visiting unit.

Ferragamo shows me the book that accompanies the squadron bottle, full of heartfelt notes from members of the military who are honoring their unit or fallen friends, many of whom had visited the Top of the Mark before going to war, though now, instead of World War II, it's Iraq or Afghanistan. It's a moving tribute to tradition and to patriotism, and I tear up as I read the scribbled words.

I'd had no idea about this aspect of the beautiful hotel lounge that I'd visited on special city trips as a kid with my parents. We'd been for Sunday brunch (which they still do) and cocktails (Shirley Temples for us kids) a number of times during my childhood, and I always looked forward to it, dazzled by the 360-degree view and feeling of grown-up elegance. My distinct experience shows how good the bar is at connecting with its diverse customers—whether they are military or civilian, celebrity or regular folk, adults or children. The Top of the Mark—and the hotel overall—is particularly adept at serving this last class of customer with its "Magical Tea" at the holidays, which features a magician, cookie station, toy donation, a colorful spread of treats, and, of course, Santa Claus. Ferragamo even brought a petting zoo to the lobby one year. Kids, however, are not permitted past 10 p.m., when music fills the space; the lounge has live acts most nights of the week.

Celebrities do make regular appearances as customers—I saw Jerry Springer on my last visit—but as it should be at a top-notch hotel, service is professional, discreet, and respectful, regardless of one's level of fame. People from the neighborhood and around the world come for cocktails or a light bite to eat, taking in the view of the ocean and the sky, pondering their days and what may lie ahead. I can't recommend highly enough participating in this old San Francisco tradition and thinking about who may have imbibed, celebrated, or even wept at the table before you.

TOSCA CAFE

242 COLUMBUS AVE., SAN FRANCISCO, CA 94133

(415) 986-9651 • TOSCACAFESF.COM

Night Out

For a historic bar with a serious edge, known for its connection to the most legendary writers, artists, actors, and politicians from its 1919 founding onward, Tosca Cafe is a surprisingly welcoming place, even to regular people, almost 100 years later. When you walk into the dark, narrow room that ultimately pools out into a slightly larger dining room in the back, the last thing you'd expect is for the place to be family friendly.

But it is. Every staff member—from servers to bussers, hosts, and bartenders (and I'm sure cooks as well)—radiates a genuine kindness toward the cumbersome family with two under two, bringing cheesy pasta proactively and flirting with the babies. The Tosca team is phenomenal at handling the chaos that accompanies such a gaggle of diners, which is funny because, for the majority of its existence, the place has been known as a smoky bar (even after a firm smoking ban was instituted in the city). This modern adeptness at dealing with the unexpected is a testament to the new owners' experience with restaurants—and a sign that the vintage place has been able to morph just a touch to stay alive and keep with the times.

Historically, though, and even today, this is not a place meant for children.

Sean Penn, Rudolf Nureyev, Bono, Kid Rock, Henry Kissinger, Mel Brooks, Lauren Hutton, and countless Beat poets are all famous past (and some of them perhaps present) customers, and there seem limitless stories about the rule-bending that happened in the backroom, along with a famous Prohibition-era coffee drink that

has no coffee in it. The place almost shut down a couple years ago following a landlord dispute involving claims of back rent, but the bar was purchased from 30-year proprietor Jeannette Etheredge by famed New York restaurateur team April Bloomfield and Ken Friedman (of the Spotted Pig, the Breslin, and more), and saved from near ruin. Bloomfield and Friedman have successfully transformed the third-oldest, and still thriving, bar in San Francisco into a thriving bar-restaurant—even one nationally recognized for its food (*Bon Appétit* included it on its Best New Restaurants list in 2014).

And it still has that edge.

The team updated the kitchen because it hadn't been used to prepare food in decades, but they kept much of the look loyal patrons had been accustomed to—rust-and-black-colored tile flooring, red leather barstools, and a Wurlitzer jukebox that still plays. Your first entry is directly into the bar, which cuts a narrow path, dense with drinkers, to the high-ceilinged but snug main dining room, which contains just about six booths and the same number of tables—none accommodating more than four to six people at one time. There's a second, smaller, brighter dining room down sort of a secret passageway in the back—and it's a wonder for that family with small children (such as mine). An upright piano still sits in the main space, assumedly ready

Vintage Spot
CAFFE TRIESTE: EST. 1956

Best known for its patronage by famous beatniks and creative types—Francis Ford Coppola was said to have written much of *The Godfather* script here—Caffe Trieste easily blends a coffeehouse, cafe, bar, and music venue into one small space and still offers a great setting for thought and discourse in the modern day. Founded in 1956 by Italian immigrant Giovanni Giotta, the cafe was reportedly the first authentic espresso house on the West Coast. Today, it has spawned a small local franchise operation, with outlets across the bay in Berkeley and Oakland as well as to the south in Monterey—and they're always looking for more. The North Beach original also has an adjacent store, offering Caffe Trieste merchandise, mugs, music, and its famous espresso—also available online. In-house concerts are a regular occurrence and if you're set on attending, arrive early; calling the space "intimate" is an understatement. Be sure to bring cash—credit cards are not accepted, and their on-site ATM isn't always functional. Though the flagship menu is small compared to the other locations, you'll want to be prepared to buy a snack—perhaps an indulgent chocolate-peanut butter bar—to accompany your coffee.

601 Vallejo St., San Francisco, CA; (415) 392-6739; caffetrieste.com

for any impromptu merrymaking by guests. Enchanting murals line the walls, with lighting that draws the eye upward to view scenes of Venice and old Italy. Where there aren't murals, there are framed photos of all the famous people who've crossed the threshold over the years, many posing with arms around Etheredge, herself an important character in the story of Tosca, always described as convivial and candid and adept at forming friendships with her customers. Her presence remains today with her image on coasters, showing her signature wavy blond bob and prominently placed cigarette.

Over that revamped kitchen hangs a massive rectangular mirror, putting diners' movements on display, with the white glow of the open kitchen window serving like a petite center stage. A backlit wall of wine stands at attention to the right, reminding you of the restaurant's origin as an Italian-neighborhood bar, as does the cappuccino machine at the front; the House "Cappuccino," that Prohibition-era concoction made of Ghirardelli chocolate, steamed milk, and brandy, is still served today (though with a different local chocolate).

Bloomfield's menu honors the Italian-ness of the spot and the neighborhood well while also remaining reminiscent of her

Vintage Spot
SPECS' TWELVE ADLER MUSEUM CAFE: EST. 1968

Tucked into a little alley around the corner from Tosca Cafe, this bar does not have an equal within or outside the confines of San Francisco, as far as I know. Specs' Twelve Adler Museum Cafe is a bar, a museum of sorts, and a hangout joint that's been part of the poet-artist-bohemian-rabble-rouser circles for decades. Founded in 1968 by Richard "Specs" Simmons, the bar is tiny and dark in a mysteriously inviting way and crammed with stuff. It sits on what is now called William Saroyan Place—the newer name for Adler—and coincidentally, Saroyan's play *The Time of Your Life*, about a bar in San Francisco, was reportedly part of Simmons's inspiration for Specs. In addition to a bar, it's a curiosity shop of the uniquest San Francisco sort, with old photos, political paraphernalia, and oddities from around the world. "The bar looks and feels like it's sweating out the ghosts of the Barbary Coast," wrote author and television host "Broke-Ass Stuart" Shuffman in his precise piece on the founder, and I couldn't say it better. If you go, don't order a fruity cocktail. You might be laughed out of the place.

12 William Saroyan Place, San Francisco, CA 94133; (415) 421-4112

other restaurants in spirit—bold, comforting flavors and a penchant for fatty foods (fried pig tails are a highlight among the appetizers, and the hangar steak entree features perfectly medium-rare hunks of meat positioned over olive oil-whipped potatoes and mushrooms like a New Age Stonehenge). Pastas are both innovative and textbook—a bucatini with *guanciale*, tomato, and chile oil is like a grown-up version of spaghetti with red sauce, and the *lumaconi*—featuring an oversize macaroni-style noodle, cream, lemon, *puntarelle* (which is part of the chicory family), prosciutto, and

bread crumbs—becomes your new favorite comfort food. Bitterness is a flavor well represented throughout both food and drink at Tosca, with roasted (and then vinegar-doused) Treviso radicchio and killer negronis to whet the appetite even before perusing the menu.

The whole thing feels very Italian, very San Francisco, very old and very new, all at once. The presence of music—whether live on the piano, or '70s, '80s, and '90s tunes blasted through the sound system—the drinks and the drinks that pretend to be other drinks, the old murals and new wine wall. The bitter and the sweet, all on offer harmoniously in the same cafe on Columbus Avenue. It's a fantastic spot for late-night revelers with minimal responsibilities at home or an early evening dinner for a family of four. If you fall into that latter category, be sure to request the back room.

TWIN PEAKS TAVERN

242 COLUMBUS AVE., SAN FRANCISCO, CA 94133

(415) 986-9651 • TWINPEAKSTAVERN.COM

Coming Out Party

From its origins as an Irish pub that opened its doors in 1935, the bar on the corner of Castro and Market Streets ultimately found its place as part of the gay history of San Francisco—serving as advocate, safe space, and simply a good watering hole for those already "out" and those not yet public about their sexual identity. Twin Peaks Tavern—an official historic landmark as designated by the city in 2013—has stood as a beacon on the iconic corner of the famous gay neighborhood, "the Castro," since 1972. Its current owners—two longtime bartenders of the establishment, along with their partners— are proudly continuing the tradition begun by two businesswomen who likely had no idea the impact their decisions about their new bar would have on the community more than 40 years later.

Mary Ellen Cunha and Peggy Forster already owned other bars— the now defunct Golden Cask in the Haight-Ashbury neighborhood and Blue and Gold in the Tenderloin district—when they bought Twin Peaks Tavern. They decided to transform it into a fern bar—marked by living plants and Tiffany lamps—for the gay community and let the light in on the place, so to speak. They stripped away whatever had covered the near floor-to-ceiling windows before and created a completely transparent environment, letting both the patrons look out and the passersby look in—a setup unheard of during an era when people still feared losing their jobs due to their sexual orientation. The tavern reportedly became the first gay bar in the nation to feature windows like this. It was a bold and ultimately empowering move by the owners and for their clientele.

Still affectionately referred to as "the girls" by friends, including the current owners, Cunha and Forster created an establishment that is now known as "the Gay Cheers"—friendly and welcoming to both gays and straights. Many of their original customers still occupy barstools there today, albeit a little grayer—clientele tends to run a bit older, though all ages are welcome—and warmly greet obvious newcomers (like me) upon entry.

George Roehm and Jeff Green, along with their respective partners, Fred Hosking and Day Gallas, own the business today, for 11 years heading its operations, community relations, and serving as some of the friendly faces greeting customers from behind the bar. Roehm began his relationship with the bar as a customer himself in 1979—"the girls were my friends," he reminisces, and they always had a small TV on the fridge behind the bar where he could catch sports. Ten years later, Green became a bartender there, two years after moving to San Francisco from New York City and using Twin Peaks as a sort of home office for filling out job applications.

"It becomes like a customer's home away from home," Roehm and Green explain of the bar's draw, both then and now. For Green, he was still "10 feet in the closet" when he started coming to the bar. "I've come along with the community."

Some regulars come daily, others once a week. But even on your first visit to the tavern, you feel comfortable and relaxed. Music is deliberately kept at a moderate level to encourage conversation and maintain the social atmosphere of the space that is framed by a mezzanine, pre-Prohibition back bar, and curved wood bar, with stained-glass Tiffany-style lamps hanging from the ceiling. Within the turn-of-the-century building that has a 1923 Mediterranean Revival-style facade, the decor hasn't changed much over the years, aside from a bit of updating to replace carpets, paint, jukeboxes, and such—and the bar's original structure and furnishings are part of what led to its success in winning landmark status from the city. That, along with its historic role in supporting the lesbian, gay, bisexual, and transgender (LGBT) community in the latter half of last century.

The San Francisco Planning Department's Historic Preservation Commission Case Report that served as part of the tavern's road to landmark status puts the bar's significance in context:

> San Francisco's nighttime entertainment industries are significant in the formation, expansion and diversification of modern LGBT subcultures. Nighttime entertainment including bars, played an important role in the development of social networks and the creation of an "out" community starting with the repeal of Prohibition and culminating with the opening of the Twin Peaks Tavern's windows in 1972. The influence of nighttime entertainment and community-building organizations such as the Tavern Guild of San Francisco had a consciousness raising effect in society as a whole. Together these enabled collective resistance against persecution by the local, state and military policing agencies.
>
> The Twin Peaks Tavern is significant for its contribution to the evolution towards modern LGBT society and culture. The success of the Twin Peaks Tavern was a combination of several factors. First, it was located in the Castro, where a community of LGBTs was forming. Second, house rules as well as the organization of the physical space established

Vintage Spot

HORSESHOE TAVERN: EST. 1934

Self-described as "the 'non-Marina' Marina bar," the Horseshoe Tavern sits among chichi boutiques, high-end major retailers, and bro bars in the city's ocean-side district. It sticks out like a sore thumb among its newer neighbors, but for more than 80 years it has been going strong with a loyal following of locals, sports fans, and folks who appreciate a good neighborhood bar. Established in 1934 by Vic Ramos, a former US Marine and football player for the San Francisco Clippers, which served as the precursor to the 49ers, the bar has for decades been a haven for drinkers and, in the early days, seemingly gamblers, based on the peephole-protected secret rooms in the maze upstairs above the bar.

Current owner Stefan Wever is a former pro baseball player who has run the bar for 25 years, a length of time that surprises even him. He and friends Robert Walker and Brenda Turner bought the place from Ramos in 1991 after becoming regulars themselves, getting to know the owner and others who frequently occupied "the Shoe's" barstools. Ramos attempted to sell in fits and starts for years, always refusing in the 11th hour.

"He was really concerned about his regulars," Wever recalls, hence the trio's plan to fully understand the business and its customers before making an offer. Once they were ready to buy, they surprised "the old guy" with an offer, and it felt like a foregone conclusion.

The straightforward bar is all about down-to-earth bartenders; a good, cold beer; pool tournaments; and sports lovers watching games. On its future, the owner is uncertain. His young adult daughter jokingly refers to herself as the "heiress of the Horseshoe," but Dad is unsure of what will happen to it when he decides to do something else. In the meantime, he knows one thing for sure: The bar will maintain its "no Marina douche bags" policy—attempting to limit the presence of the stereotypical drunken frat guys that have become associated with the neighborhood—for as long as he's in charge.

2024 Chestnut St., San Francisco, CA 94123; (415) 346-1430; horseshoetavern-sf.com

the culture of the bar that encouraged personal bonding. Third, the lessons learned and advances made in LGBT recognition and political power in the 1960s by the Tavern Guild cleared the path for an "out" gay bar. Lastly, the normalization of an English pub in a social sense to a gay bar was attributable to the personalities and tastes of Cunha and Forster as "out" lesbians.

"To own such a bar is a privilege," Roehm reflects on their association with the vintage business. "We felt shocked when they gave us the opportunity," referring to the girls' selection of the young men as new owners. He and Green have honored the history of the place and added homey traditions of their own over the years—displaying thousands of nutcrackers (from Roehm's own collection) over the gorgeous wood bar at Christmastime and hosting holiday parties for both staff and customers, as well as performances of the popular San Francisco Gay Men's Chorus (the world's first openly gay men's chorus). The bar has always been actively involved in local charities as well, sponsoring countless local baseball teams as well as a highly successful San Francisco AIDS Walk team for more than 20 years, raising more than $30,000 in 2013 alone for the cause.

Most folks, though, come to the tavern not for community events but for a just-plain-good bar experience, which includes their variety of cocktails—from the secret recipe–based Bloody Marys on the weekends to a blend of standards (Irish coffee is their most popular drink, along with hot buttered rum in winter and martinis and manhattans at any time of year). It's easy to see why Twin Peaks Tavern has had such staying power, not only in San Francisco's famously gay neighborhood but in any neighborhood in the city or another: good drinks, a comfortable space and friendly faces. Oh, and all those nutcrackers. What more could one want in a bar?

VESUVIO

255 COLUMBUS AVE., SAN FRANCISCO, CA 94133

(415) 362-3370 • VESUVIO.COM

Beatniks Forever

I'd like to live at Vesuvio, or at least become part of the club that plays chess at a front table by the window while drinking red wine out of tumblers, or scribbling poetry in a cozy corner in the back. This classic San Francisco saloon, founded in 1948, just five years before its kindred spirit—the City Lights bookstore—opened next door, evokes an undeniably artistic vibe that is such a part of the North Beach neighborhood and the city overall. Its art-covered walls drip with history and a vibrancy that shows the establishment has been able to both preserve its original vision—as an "art bar"—and keep up with the times and to continue to be a hangout joint for locals and destination for travelers from the world over.

The bar's founder was a French-speaking Swiss man and, as current part-owner Janet Clyde describes him, "bon vivant bartender" named Henri Lenoir. As the origin story goes, Lenoir purchased a failing restaurant named Vesuvio in the middle of last century to transform it into a gathering place for his bohemian friends and other artistic-minded folk to hang out.

"He made it a place for his pals," says Clyde, also a longtime employee, whose love and respect for Vesuvio and its history is obvious in our conversation. Describing it as a "quintessential San Francisco place," she talks about how it fits into the city's "deep bar culture," sharing that there was once a bar on practically every corner. "It was the working man's living room and social club," something particular to cities of a certain age. And Vesuvio captures that communal living-room feeling in a way that so many other bars do not—with eclectic

artwork covering every open space, mismatched seating tucked into each corner of the roughly triangular room, a random upstairs area, a warm greeting from the person behind the bar (sometimes offering homemade snacks such as spiced popcorn), and an overall sense that the place belongs to everyone.

Clyde began as a morning bartender in 1980, working the "shift that no one else wanted" for years before becoming assistant manager in the mid-1980s and eventually a partner in 1997. (Lenoir sold the business long before that, in 1968, to a man named Ron Fein, who died in 1985 but whose family still co-owns it today.) Clyde herself has become part of the bar's fabric and lore; even a song ("Janet Planet") is devoted to her on current owner Ron Fein Jr.'s *Vesuvio Jazz Trio* album, his musical tribute to his family's famous bar. Music has long been a part of the Vesuvio culture, likely due to the affinity its owners over the years have had for jazz and the natural concentric circles into which music and art fall. But it is its literary links that put the bar on the map in an irrevocable way.

"Companionable businesses," as Clyde calls them, Vesuvio and City Lights essentially grew up together. Separated only by an alley, they were established just a few years apart and attracted similar clientele: "People buy books and then walk next door, get a glass of wine, and read." The not-uncommon symbiosis between drinking and writing likely helped, and the bar's proximity to the burgeoning hub of a special generation of writers made Vesuvio's link to the Beat movement seemingly predestined.

The connection was cemented in 1955 when Neal Cassady, two years later immortalized as Dean Moriarty in Jack Kerouac's *On the Road*, stopped by the bar on his way to the now-legendary Six Gallery poetry reading, where City Lights owner Lawrence Ferlinghetti discovered Allen Ginsberg and other Beat writers first got truly noticed. Kerouac started coming in, famously drinking one night away in 1960 when he should've been on his way to see Henry Miller at Big Sur. Others followed suit. The bar became a hangout for these countercultural writers and artists—a sensibility that continues today. Almost 70 years later, Vesuvio still seems to pulse with creative energy.

Art is everywhere you look in the little two-story bar, with decoupage creations under the glass tabletops and even in the bathrooms, beautifully etched mirrors behind the bar, framed provocative quotes and paintings of all sorts, often rotating to feature different artists, lining the walls. It's not often that your corner bar has an artist on staff, but Vesuvio always has. From the late muralist and decoupage artist Shawn O'Shaughnessy, whose work can be seen throughout the building, to current in-house painter Conrado Henriquez, the bar's employment of artists-in-residence underscores the seriousness with which Vesuvio's stewards take the original vision for the place.

"We're staying true to that vision and not being pulled off that because of trends," Clyde says.

Even the bartenders are artists, including Josie Ramos, who is responsible for some of the mesmerizing liquor-label decoupage covering the bathroom doors, among other pieces over the years. Ramos, the morning bartender at Vesuvio for a seemingly impossible 25-year tenure, is the personification of hospitality. (She was the one doling out popcorn.) She has a twinkle in her eye and sparkling stories about encounters with famous customers to match.

Over the years, she's poured for and become friendly with a number of actors, in the stranger-best-friend bartender way, including Luke Wilson and Jim Caviezel. Caviezel was "very kind," and Wilson, who reportedly "had a girlfriend up the hill" at the time, would come in and drink Heinekens at 8 in the morning. "But we don't judge," says Clyde, reminiscing about all the celebrities who've stepped over the Vesuvio threshold over the years. Robert De Niro, Susan Sarandon, and Jennifer Lopez have all paid visits. Sean Penn held a meeting there. U2's "The Edge" stops by regularly when he's in town. And Johnny Depp, who Clyde says happens to be somewhat of a Beat scholar, purchased a bunch of artwork off the walls once, enamored by the work of illustrator Craig LaRotonda. Josie couldn't believe she'd missed him.

While celebrities can be exciting, they are on equal footing at Vesuvio with its regulars—who are just as likely to come from the other side of the world as from down the street. It's a place for travelers, for locals, for the well-known and the unknown. Everyone gets the same respect, the same welcome, and if you're lucky, the same homemade bag of snacks.

Clyde says it's "a great privilege" to be involved with the bar that's been able to stay consistent with "who we are" and that means so much to so many people. "People have scattered friends' ashes here—and I have a feeling a few families were started here," she reveals with a smile. This knowledge of intimate moments, the celebration of life, and the marking of death, all happening in this quirky, crammed, lovely little space, suddenly makes the legend and import of Vesuvio grow in my own mind.

"The physical environment here is beautiful," Clyde says, with a quiet glow. "The light through the window is outstanding. But what I enjoy most are the people—the staff, the customers, the local school kids researching San Francisco's history. It's the people that have made the place."

I think Jack Kerouac and Neal Cassady would agree.

WILKES BASHFORD

375 SUTTER ST., SAN FRANCISCO, CA 94108

(415) 986-4380 • WILKESBASHFORD.COM

Class Act

A real stand-up guy. This is how the gentleman whose name has represented fine fashion through his eponymous luxury-clothing store for nearly 50 years in San Francisco strikes me upon our first meeting. He is thoughtfully and classically dressed, of course, with tasteful tones of purple and gray woven throughout the look, all finished off by blue-shaded tortoise-shell glasses, and his kindness and loyalty are apparent in all that he does. His name is Wilkes Bashford, and it's nearly impossible to separate the man from the store as the two are undeniably interlinked, the spirit of each influencing the other on a daily basis.

A thick stack of opened envelopes sits atop his desk in a small, basement-level back office, representing all the charity events and fund-raisers to which he's been invited—just for a single week. He tries to attend as many as he can. "I'm out at least four nights a week," he divulges, because he's committed to customer loyalty. Most of these invitations come from close friends, many of who began as customers at his store. Willie Brown, former mayor of the city and notable style icon in his own right, is the closest.

"He's my best friend," Bashford states, describing how they go back 30 years and have been lunching nearly every Friday since, at the same restaurant, Le Central, the city's oldest French bistro. (The weekly meal also used to include famed local columnist Herb Caen before his death at age 80 in 1997.) The company Bashford keeps reveals a bit about his connection to, and place within, the city of San Francisco. He sits on some of the most preeminent boards in

the city, including that of the War Memorial, whose members serve as the trustees of some of San Francisco's most treasured cultural institutions (the San Francisco War Memorial & Performing Arts Center chief among them). You have to be appointed by the mayor for this board; Bashford is its president. Did I mention that he is connected?

A New York native, the man who ultimately became part of the social fabric of San Francisco opened his luxury menswear store in Union Square in 1966. His official foray into the business world followed stints in Cincinnati (for college at a co-op school, where he split his time between studies and work rotations in retail), San Francisco (where he moved after college and worked for the White House, a fine department store reminiscent of those in Paris), and New York for another year before he realized how much he missed the City by the Bay and working in an actual store. Soon thereafter, Bashford became one of the first people on the West Coast to carry the up-and-coming designers of the time—"no-names" like Ralph Lauren, Giorgio Armani, and Gianni Versace.

"It was the late '60s, early '70s—a period of flower children and hippies—no one was really doing what we were doing in the store," Bashford recounts, explaining the fortuitous timing of opening a store at the same time that high-end designers were beginning to launch lines. "Our businesses grew up together," including offering womenswear simultaneously; Bashford introduced it to the store in 1978.

He describes his interest in fashion as "something innate." As a child, "I was always concerned that my shorts went with my T-shirt"; he confirmed his passion for retail during his collegiate work-study assignment with Federated Department Stores—"a mutually happy" arrangement. Today, his commitment to the classic, dapper look continues, even into his 80s. It should also be noted that one of his most frequent, and devoted, accessories is a dachshund. An ardent animal lover (PAWS—Pets Are Wonderful Support—and Muttville are two of his pet, no pun intended, causes), he has brought his pup, always a dachshund, with him to work daily for decades.

Still passionate about his profession, Bashford points to the diversity of activity as the thing he enjoys most about what he does. "Buying, selling, advertising, interacting with the clientele—it's never

Vintage Spot
WAR MEMORIAL OPERA HOUSE AND VETERANS BUILDING: EST. 1932

Opened in 1932, the War Memorial Opera House and Veterans Building, both part of the Performing Arts Center, are not just about war and not just about the opera. They are also about art, architecture, and the birth of a pioneering international body. These stunning examples of Parisian Beaux Arts architecture, popular in the early 20th century in the US and spotted throughout the city of San Francisco, have dominated a stretch of Van Ness Avenue along with their partner, the glorious gold-adorned and dome-capped City Hall, for more than 80 years. They anchored the city's arts scene, starting with a sellout run of Puccini's *Tosca*, despite the Depression that ravaged the country at the time. The opera house has naturally remained the home of the San Francisco Opera, founded just a decade before the building's opening. And it has always been home to the San Francisco Ballet, formed on-site as the San Francisco Opera Ballet in 1933. It is the country's oldest ballet company and also among its largest. The Veterans Building has always been devoted to arts and veterans organizations and today houses the administrative offices of the Performing Arts Center as well as the Herbst Theatre. In 1945, however, that theater—then the Veterans Auditorium—was the site of a major global moment. For several months that year, heads of state from around the world gathered in San Francisco to discuss and plan the organization that became the United Nations (UN). The birth of the international body was made official with the signing of the UN Charter on stage in the Veterans Auditorium that June.

The Herbst Theatre is undergoing a renovation, but will reopen for business in late 2015, and you should put it and the other buildings in the Performing Arts Center on your tour agenda. These structures are grand, as one would expect, with their series of towering columns and arches and elegant construction, and they provide glorious spaces in which to soak up the city's current arts scene—whether music or dance (my favorite recent experience there was watching the ballet's production of the Hans Christian Andersen's *The Little Mermaid*, a dark, tragic tale so beautifully told by the ballet and consumed from the cheap seats at the tippy top of the steep, steep upper balcony). Now when I go to the opera house, I will always think of my childhood ballet teacher and close family friend, Gail Jones, who passed away in 2014. She so loved the city, and even more, loved attending SF Ballet performances; she saw many, often with her eldest daughter, Wendy, and sometimes with me and my own mom. Gail also revered history and politics, and I can't imagine the historical nature of the opera house space and its neighbor was lost on her. So I encourage you, go to the ballet, take in the opera, plan an event, whatever it takes to make a date with the War Memorial Opera House and Veterans Building. Drink in the city's culture, salute the dance teachers in your life, and ponder moments in history that changed the world.

301 and 401 Van Ness Ave., San Francisco, CA 94102; (415) 621-6600; sfwmpac.org

boring," he says. "There's no limit on the creativity. And as society changes, and what people want changes, as cities evolve, we do along with them."

As I said at the start, it's impossible to separate Wilkes Bashford the man from Wilkes Bashford the store, even with the latter's 2010 purchase by the Connecticut-based Mitchells Family of Stores. The sale saved what, at the time, had become a struggling business for Bashford, and enabled a small but significant expansion of his empire, now with stores in the tony Northern California cities of Palo Alto and Carmel. Bashford the man continues to be a constant presence in the business, still in his office daily and showing no signs of slowing down anytime soon.

His flagship store, today a seven-story town house (or, better, palace) on Sutter Street, complete with high-end menswear, womenswear, gorgeous jewelry, and fine home furnishings, is a treat-filled experience for the visitor. Ogling the beautiful clothing, jewels, and specialty collections—including on one visit a series of vintage World War II bomber jackets, all restored to a manly luster—is made even more appealing by luxe lounges (including a television that floats in a floor-length mirror in the women's room), fireplaces, and even bar service on the penthouse level. Nothing too edgy can be spied on the Wilkes Bashford racks, given that the store specializes in conservative classics. And while it caters to the well-heeled San Franciscan, the store's impeccable customer service extends to anyone walking in off the street. There seems a special lift in the air of the shop upon entry—a surprising lack of snootiness where one might expect it. Rather, kindness and a precision in service pervade. It's easy to see why the business has weathered the storms over the years.

"Of the high-end specialty stores in the city that were here when I opened—there were about 60 that were indigenous to the Bay Area—not many are still around," Bashford refers to old San Francisco classics like I. Magnin and lesser known relation J. Magnin, along with his former employer, the White House. "Today it's a menu of stores that are all around the world." For instance, a Banana Republic now sits in the former White House space.

The expense of running an upmarket store is greater than that for a mid-market shop, he explains, as the expectation for luxury runs throughout every element of the business: better store windows, fancier shopping experience, finer packaging. But Bashford has been able to deliver. On the future of the business, he envisions it being "the same, but different." The store launched its first online shop in the fall of 2014 and now caters to some of Silicon Valley's high-tech elite in addition to its long-standing, loyal customers. The commitment to consistency, loyalty, and the finest designers will continue, Bashford says, as the business moves ahead and more children and grandchildren of his original customers venture into the Sutter Street shop.

"For 55 years, I've been in this [Union Square] triangle, and there's a history here," he reminisces. "Everything that happens today has an added interest because it's an extension of that history. It's very fulfilling." He seems invigorated by the grind.

Successful entrepreneurship in retail can seem like an elusive golden egg that only few are able to discover. But this natty trendsetter has proven it's possible. And if Bashford has anything to do with it, he will be donning the work of his favorite designers, Brioni and Kiton, supporting San Francisco causes, and outfitting his customers in the finest apparel well into the next chapter of the business he began a half century ago.

Appendix A

FEATURED PLACES BY CATEGORY

Bakeries

Boudin Bakery, 138
Dianda's Italian American
   Pastry Co., 39
Liguria Bakery, 92
Stella Pastry & Café, 42

Bar + Restaurant

Buena Vista Cafe, 19
Java House, 144
Lefty O'Doul's, 88
Mario's Bohemian Cigar Store
   Cafe, 104
Pied Piper Bar and Grill, 132
Pier 23 Cafe, 137
Red's Java House, 142
Sam Jordan's Bar, 150
Schroeder's, 157
Tonga Room & Hurricane
   Bar, 184
Tosca Cafe, 192

Bars

Aub Zam Zam, 10
Bourbon and Branch, 76
Buena Vista Cafe, 19
Caffe Trieste, 194
Gold Dust Lounge, 91
House of Shields, 73
Lefty O'Doul's, 88
Li Po Cocktail Lounge, 96
Specs' Twelve Adler Museum
   Cafe, 195
Tonga Room & Hurricane
   Bar, 184
Top of the Mark, 189
Tosca Cafe, 192
Trad'r Sam, 186
Twin Peaks Tavern, 197
Vesuvio, 202

Books, Periodicals

City Lights Booksellers &
   Publishers, 27
The Magazine, 101

Brewery

Anchor Brewing Company, 5

Chess

Mechanics' Institute Library &
  Chess Room, 112

Chinese Food, Dim Sum

Far East Café, 98

Hang Ah Tea Room, 98

Clothing

Cable Car Clothiers, 23

Gump's, 65

Piedmont Boutique, 127

Wilkes Bashford, 207

Coffee Shops, Diners, Cafes

Benkyodo Company, 14
Buena Vista Cafe, 19
Caffe Trieste, 194
Grubstake, 61
It's Tops Coffee Shop, 78
Java House, 144

Mario's Bohemian Cigar Store
  Cafe, 104
Pier 23 Cafe, 137
Red's Java House, 142
Sears Fine Food, 164
St. Francis Fountain, 82

Cultural Institutions

Mechanics' Institute Library &
  Chess Room, 112
Palace of Fine Arts, 17

War Memorial Opera House
  and Veterans Building, 210

Hardware

Cliff's Variety, 35

Hats, Menswear

Cable Car Clothiers, 23

Wilkes Bashford, 207

Herbal Medicine

Great China Herb Company, 59

Hofbraus

Lefty O'Doul's, 88

The Original Tommy's
   Joynt, 123

Home Goods

Cliff's Variety, 35

Gump's, 65

Ice Cream

St. Francis Fountain, 82

Italian Food

Alioto's Restaurant, 48
Dianda's Italian American
   Pastry Co., 39
Liguria Bakery, 92
Mario's Bohemian Cigar Store
   Cafe, 104

Molinari Delicatessen, 22
Original Joe's, 120
Stella Pastry & Café, 42
Tommaso's Italian
   Restaurant, 181

Jewelry

Gump's, 65
Lang Antiques and Estate
   Jewelry, 170

Shreve & Co., 167

Library

Mechanics' Institute Library &
   Chess Room, 112

Mattresses

McRoskey Mattress
   Company, 108

Membership Club

Mechanics' Institute Library &
   Chess Room, 112

Prime Rib

House of Prime Rib, 69

Records

Aquarius Records, 106

Restaurants

Alfred's Steakhouse, 1
Alioto's Restaurant, 48
Cliff House, 31
Far East Café, 98
Fior d'Italia, 43
Fishermen's Grotto No. 9, 47
Garden Court, 52
Grubstake, 61
Hang Ah Tea Room, 98
House of Prime Rib, 69
Java House, 144
John's Grill, 84
The Old Clam House, 116
Original Joe's, 120

The Original Tommy's
   Joynt, 123
Pier 23 Cafe, 137
Red's Java House, 142
The Roosevelt Tamale
   Parlor, 146
Sam's Grill, 153
Scoma's, 160
Sears Fine Food, 164
St. Francis Fountain, 82
Swan Oyster Depot, 172
Tadich Grill, 176
Tommaso's Italian
   Restaurant, 181

Retailers

Cable Car Clothiers, 23
Cliff's Variety, 35
Gump's, 65
McRoskey Mattress
   Company, 108

Piedmont Boutique, 127
Shreve & Co., 167
Wilkes Bashford, 207

Seafood

Alioto's Restaurant, 48
Cliff House, 31
Fishermen's Grotto No. 9, 47
John's Grill, 84
The Old Clam House, 116

Sam's Grill, 153
Scoma's, 160
Swan Oyster Depot, 172
Tadich Grill, 176

Sex Shops

Good Vibrations, 129
The Magazine, 101
Mr. S Leather, 130

Specialty Foods

Benkyodo Company, 14
Ferry Building Marketplace, 55
Ghirardelli Chocolate
  Company, 179

Golden Gate Fortune Cookie
  Factory, 57

Steakhouses

Alfred's Steakhouse, 1
House of Prime Rib, 69

John's Grill, 84

Tiki Bars

Tonga Room & Hurricane
  Bar, 184
Trad'r Sam, 186

Appendix B

FEATURED PLACES BY NEIGHBORHOOD

Bayshore/Bayview/Hunters Point

The Old Clam House, 116

Sam Jordan's Bar, 150

The Castro

Cliff's Variety, 35

Twin Peaks Tavern, 197

Chinatown

Far East Café, 98
Golden Gate Fortune Cookie
   Factory, 57

Great China Herb Company, 59
Hang Ah Tea Room, 98
Li Po Cocktail Lounge, 96

Civic Center

War Memorial Opera House
   and Veterans Building, 210

The Embarcadero

Ferry Building Marketplace, 55
Java House, 144

Pier 23 Cafe, 137
Red's Java House, 142

Financial District

Alfred's Steakhouse, 1
Cable Car Clothiers, 23
Garden Court, 52
House of Shields, 73
Mechanics' Institute Library &
   Chess Room, 112

Pied Piper Bar and Grill, 132
Sam's Grill, 153
Schroeder's, 157
Tadich Grill, 176

Fisherman's Wharf

Alioto's Restaurant, 48
Boudin Bakery, 138
Buena Vista Cafe, 19
Fishermen's Grotto No. 9, 47

Ghirardelli Chocolate
  Company, 179
Gold Dust Lounge, 91
Scoma's, 160

The Haight

Aub Zam Zam, 10

Piedmont Boutique, 127

Hayes Valley/Market

It's Tops Coffee Shop, 78

McRoskey Mattress
  Company, 108

Japantown

Benkyodo Company, 14

The Marina

Palace of Fine Arts, 17

The Mission

Aquarius Records, 106
Dianda's Italian American
  Pastry Co., 39
Good Vibrations, 129

The Roosevelt Tamale
  Parlor, 146
St. Francis Fountain, 82

Nob Hill

Grubstake, 61
Swan Oyster Depot, 172

Tonga Room & Hurricane
  Bar, 184
Top of the Mark, 189

North Beach

Caffe Trieste, 194
City Lights Booksellers &
  Publishers, 27
Fior d'Italia, 43
Liguria Bakery, 92

Mario's Bohemian Cigar Store
  Cafe, 104
Molinari Delicatessen, 22
Original Joe's, 120
Stella Pastry & Café, 42

Tommaso's Italian
    Restaurant, 181

Potrero Hill

Anchor Brewing Company, 5

The Richmond

Trad'r Sam, 186

South of Market

Mr. S Leather, 130

Sutro Heights

Cliff House, 31

The Tenderloin

Bourbon and Branch, 76

Union Square

Gump's, 65
John's Grill, 84
Lang Antiques and Estate
    Jewelry, 170

Van Ness/Cathedral Hill

House of Prime Rib, 69

Tosca Cafe, 192
Vesuvio, 202

The Magazine, 101

Lefty O'Doul's, 88
Sears Fine Food, 164
Shreve & Co., 167
Wilkes Bashford, 207

The Original Tommy's
    Joynt, 123

Appendix C

FEATURED PLACES BY YEAR OF ORIGIN

1849:   Boudin Bakery, 138

1849:   Tadich Grill, 176

1852:   Ghirardelli Chocolate Company, 179

1852:   Shreve & Co., 167

1854:   Mechanics' Institute Library & Chess Room, 112

1861:   Gump's, 65

1861:   The Old Clam House, 116

1863:   Cliff House, 31

1867:   Sam's Grill, 153

1886:   Fior d'Italia, 43

1893:   Schroeder's, 157

1896:   Anchor Brewing Company, 5

1896:   Molinari Delicatessen, 22

1898/2003:   Ferry Building Marketplace, 55

1899:   McRoskey Mattress Company, 108

1906:   Benkyodo Company, 14

1908/1944:   House of Shields, 73

1908:   John's Grill, 84

1909:   Garden Court, 52

1909:   Pied Piper Bar and Grill, 132

1911:   Liguria Bakery, 92

1912:   Java House, 144

1912:   Swan Oyster Depot, 172

1915:   Palace of Fine Arts, 17

1916:   Buena Vista Cafe, 19

1918:   St. Francis Fountain, 82

1919:   Tosca Cafe, 192

1920s: The Roosevelt Tamale Parlor, 146

1920:   Far East Café, 98

1920:   Hang Ah Tea Room, 98

1921/2006:   Bourbon and Branch, 76

1922:   Great China Herb Company, 59

1925:   Alioto's Restaurant, 48

1927:   Grubstake, 61

1928:   Alfred's Steakhouse, 1

1930s: Red's Java House, 142

1932:   War Memorial Opera House and Veterans Building, 210

1935:   Fishermen's Grotto No. 9, 47

1935:   It's Tops Coffee Shop, 78

1935:   Tommaso's Italian Restaurant, 181

1935:   Twin Peaks Tavern, 197

1936:   Cliff's Variety, 35

1937:   Li Po Cocktail Lounge, 96

1937:   Original Joe's, 120

1937:   Pier 23 Cafe, 137

1938:   Sears Fine Food, 164

1938:   Trad'r Sam, 186

1939:   Cable Car Clothiers, 23

1939:   Top of the Mark, 189

1941:   Aub Zam Zam, 10

1942:   Stella Pastry & Café, 42

1945:   Tonga Room & Hurricane Bar, 184

1947:   The Original Tommy's Joynt, 123

1948:   Vesuvio, 202

1949:   House of Prime Rib, 69

1953:   City Lights Booksellers & Publishers, 27
1956:   Caffe Trieste, 194
1958:   Lefty O'Doul's, 88
1959:   Sam Jordan's Bar, 150
1962:   Dianda's Italian American Pastry Co., 39
1962:   Golden Gate Fortune Cookie Factory, 57
1965:   Scoma's, 160
1966:   Gold Dust Lounge, 91
1966:   Wilkes Bashford, 207
1968:   Specs' Twelve Adler Museum Cafe, 195
1969:   Lang Antiques and Estate Jewelry, 170
1970:   Aquarius Records, 106
1971:   Mario's Bohemian Cigar Store Cafe, 104
1972:   The Magazine, 101
1972:   Piedmont Boutique, 127
1977:   Good Vibrations, 129
1979:   Mr. S Leather, 130

Index

A

Alfred's Steakhouse, 1
Alioto's Restaurant, 48
Anchor Brewing Company, 5
Aquarius Records, 106
Aub Zam Zam, 10

B

Benkyodo Company, 14
Boudin Bakery, 138
Bourbon and Branch, 76
Buckaroo Luncheon Club, 3
Buena Vista Cafe, 19

C

Cable Car Clothiers, 23
Caffe Trieste, 194
Chinese medicine,
    traditional, 59
City Lights Booksellers &
    Publishers, 27, 202
Cliff House, 31
Cliff's Variety, 35

D

Dianda's Italian American
    Pastry Co., 39

E

earthquake of 1906, 43, 84, 138,
    167, 183

F

Fairmont Hotel, 184
Far East Café, 98
fedoretti, 39
Ferlinghetti, Lawrence, 27
Ferry Building Marketplace, 55
Fior d'Italia, 43
Fishermen's Grotto No. 9, 47
focaccia, 92
fortune cookies, 57

G

Garden Court, 52
gay history, 197
gay rights, 197
Ghirardelli Chocolate
    Company, 179
Ghirardelli Square, 179
Ginsberg, Allen, 28
Gold Dust Lounge, 91
Golden Gate Fortune Cookie
    Factory, 57
Gold Rush, 7, 61, 65, 112, 138
Good Vibrations, 129
Great China Herb Company, 59
green goddess dressing, 53
Grubstake, 61
Gump's, 65

H

Hammett, Dashiell, 85

Hang Ah Tea Room, 98
herbs, Chinese, 59
Herbst Theatre, 210
Horseshoe Tavern, 200
House of Prime Rib, 69
House of Shields, 73
Howl, 28

I
InterContinental Mark Hopkins
    San Francisco, 189
Irish coffee, 20
It's Tops Coffee Shop, 78

J
Java House, 144
John's Grill, 84

K
Kelham, George, 74
Kerouac, Jack, 28, 204

L
Lang Antiques and Estate
    Jewelry, 170
Lefty O'Doul's, 88
Liguria Bakery, 92
Li Po Cocktail Lounge, 96

M
Magazine, The, 101
Mario's Bohemian Cigar Store
    Cafe, 104
Maytag, Fritz, 7
McRoskey Mattress
    Company, 108
Mechanics' Institute Library &
    Chess Room, 112

mochi, 14
Molinari Delicatessen, 22
Mr. S Leather, 130

N
National Park Service, 31
National Register of Historic
    Places, 179

O
Old Clam House, The, 116
Original Joe's, 120
Original Tommy's Joynt,
    The, 123

P
Palace Hotel, 52, 74, 132
Palace of Fine Arts, 17
Panama-Pacific International
    Exposition (1915), 17
Parrish, Maxfield, 132
Piedmont Boutique, 127
Pied Piper Bar and Grill, 132
Pier 23 Cafe, 137
Portuguese food, 61
Prohibition, 5, 7

R
Red's Java House, 142
Roosevelt Tamale Parlor,
    The, 146

S
Sacripantina cake, 42
Sam Jordan's Bar, 150
Sam's Grill, 153
San Francisco Ballet, 210
San Francisco Heritage, 134

San Francisco Opera, 210
Schroeder's, 157
Scoma's, 160
Sears Fine Food, 164
Shreve & Co., 167
sourdough bread, 138
Specs' Twelve Adler Museum
    Cafe, 195
steam beer, 7
Stella Pastry & Café, 42
St. Francis Fountain, 82
Sutro Baths, 31
Swan Oyster Depot, 172

T
Tadich Grill, 176
Tommaso's Italian
    Restaurant, 181

Tonga Room & Hurricane
    Bar, 184
Top of the Mark, 189
Tosca Cafe, 192
traditional Chinese
    medicine, 59
Trad'r Sam, 186
Twin Peaks Tavern, 197

V
Vesuvio, 202

W
War Memorial Opera
    House, 210
War Memorial Veterans
    Building, 210
Wilkes Bashford, 207

10/9/15